FROM MAYOR TO FOOL

The Psyography of a Middle Class Man

By Tim Mayeur

authorHOUSE

AuthorHouse™
1663 Liberty Drive, Suite 200
Bloomington, IN 47403
www.authorhouse.com
Phone: 1-800-839-8640

First published by AuthorHouse 5/4/2009

ISBN: 978-1-4389-3891-2 (sc)
ISBN: 978-1-4389-3892-9 (e)

Library of Congress Control Number: 2009900589

Printed in the United States of America
Bloomington, Indiana

This book is printed on acid-free paper.

Table of Contents

Prologue

ENTER TIM THE MAYOR

MAYOR

When reflecting on my life, it seems like a poorly composed play. Neither a tragedy nor a comedy, but just that, life. I remember the words more than the actions or rather, the inactions. Restless and discontented, I look for a major life change. How does one change one's life? First, by understanding all the influencing factors: family, friends, career, finance, possessions, what's important to everyone and yourself, what's helped shape you into the person you are today. By involving those important people in the process of change and touching on the spiritual aspects of it. By taking a step back and watching your life for a short period of time. Late one Spring, I took on this challenge. Who am I? An endangered species. I'm a middle class man and this is my mind. Come with me as I take a risk.

EXIT TIM THE MAYOR

ACT I

SCENE I

05/04/2008

ENTER THE CARDS AND TIM THE MAYOR

CARDS

So what are we doing today? What is on your mind? Did you have something you had mentioned?

MAYOR

Ah ya… this is really… well, I think it is a period of change over the next couple of years. Been leading up for it and I know that something… something's going to be happening, whether … you know… I'm moving away from here or I'm changing my career.

CARDS

You can feel… you're feeling the changes inside. So your question is "How will this manifest?"

MAYOR

Ya, how will things change?

CARDS

What form will that take? OK, good.

MAYOR

Beautiful cards!!

[5]

CARDS

These are beautiful cards!! They are called the Maat tarot... M... a... a... t... Goddess of
Justice and what the Egyptians believed was that when they passed to the spirit world, the
first deity that they would encounter was Maat, and the Goddess Maat was always depicted
with a set of scales. Lest you develop in the spirit world any further you would... and what's
interesting is the work of Corr Richmond, who is a fascinating woman. She lived, between
1840 to 1923. Entities from the spirit world that spoke directly through her and some of the
ways they are describing the spirit world is there is a sphere of justice... and of course
justice... whatever we've done. So we think about that, and if we can't move forward... in
acceptance and self-forgiveness, and we go to the healing sphere and we just kind of move
forth between the spheres until we reach that level. So I don't think the Egyptians were
actually so far off. What's your favorite pile?

MAYOR

Oh, I don't have one.

CARDS

One favorite...

MAYOR

Oh.

CARDS

Just pick...

MAYOR

Hmm, let's go for the middle.

CARDS

OK... this is the Lovers card. It tells us what needs protection in your life. And so this is the
area, as we look into your future unfolding... where you will face the greatest challenges.
Ah and... maybe... the most of what I would say is your purpose... is in the realm of Lovers.
And Lovers... is of course not just about sexual lovers, it's certainly not but that plays into it.
I don't adhere to the philosophy that we have one soul-mate... I believe we come from...
we're a part of a soul family. But it is in the arena of relationships where you can make
wrong choices and you will be faced with all those choices all the time. And those choices
are about risk versus... whether you choose to take no risk and be secure. And those... that
kind of challenge you will be faced with in relationships in particular. So you want to always
be mindful......... What's your date of birth?

MAYOR

January 26th, 1978.

[6]

CARDS

Who is an Aquarian!!. You would have a tendency to… hmm… you're thirty. You're going through a developmental change as well. Do you know what your Moon is?

MAYOR

No I don't.

CARDS

You might want to go to astro.com. You can enter your birthday… they will give you a Coles notes version of your horoscope. Your full horoscope and then if you want to pursue it. I'd recommend you do it because I'm wondering if your Moon is in… this card would suggest your Moon's in Libra or Gemini. It would be interesting to know whether you're Gemini.

MAYOR

OK, I will.

CARDS

As an Aquarian you have… you're always expanding… and looking for what else is out there. Sort of let's look ahead and see… progress would very much grab you, because you're very expansive. But it's in the arena of relationship in particular… where what more is possible. So…

MAYOR

There's no risk because I'm always waiting for something better to show up.

CARDS

Exactly… exactly……… What needs patience has come up the Ten of Swords. And this is… in your experience you have… is connected to something in your life. I suspect it is… it feels that way… that in your work life, what you were expecting or promised or envisioning actually didn't turn out to be that way. And on some level you feel betrayed by that. That needs patience… meaning that… that… the good side of that, or, the benefit to you of that having happened is that it's really closed the door for you on that. And so that's like a period on a sentence or that's like… OK, I don't need to go through this anymore… I don't need any more of this to know that it is never going to work, will never work and to be able to move on and to see the light coming through in a different place. So you can thank that betrayal for having been very helpful. Now this is a Spring card… meaning that by the 21st of June… which is only two months away… you will be done… that will be it.

MAYOR

Yup, that sounds like work.

CARDS

Ya… it does feel like work.

MAYOR

Well... ya... cause I switched over to a new department to start up a project two years ago and the company never backed the project. So I've just been... felt a little betrayed because I made the move over to that area...

CARDS

For that reason.

MAYOR

For that reason... and I haven't been able to or haven't been allowed to fulfill it. So I've been recently looking for new job opportunities and going to interviews. So...

CARDS

Good!!. Congratulations!! That... the oracle has said that by the 21st of June you will be in fact ready to... by then, at the latest. We're seeing the Ten of Swords, so I'm going to say that we're getting closer... certainly into around the 10th of June... someone in that... and you'll say thanks... thanks for having shot me in the hmm... butt... like that. That will really make this done for me and you'll be clean.

MAYOR

If I had stayed, you know, maybe things would have changed.

CARDS

And no bargaining or no sense of... ya... maybe it's... that will be very clear for you.........
What needs acceptance is the Six of Wands. In other words, this is what you are having resistance in accepting. That is about... the Six of Wands... the sixes are always about victory. Wands is about passion. So you... and she shows the snowy white owl here... because the snowy white owl is very good at... no... you're very good actually at identifying what exactly it is you do want. It's probably your Aquarian side, you know, that's always looking for expansion but you're very good at getting it actually. You know the white snowy owl is a very good predator. So... you're not accepting at some level your predator self... which is yourself that's very victorious. But you're kinda... maybe a kind a sense... nice... or maybe I... I should give... I should make it a bit more fair or level the playing field somehow. But that needs acceptance. You're actually very good at identifying what you want and going for it......... What needs release is the Moon... meaning that what you need to release is... you have a natural well-developed intuition side. And the Moon would also suggest here that you have prophetic dreams. So if you go back in your life... and you think... your dreams often do come true. So you... that side of you is also... let that be your guide. You know what you want... identify it and that you also... self that knows when and how and when this should be released. And I would watch out for full Moons and new Moons. Your cycles are very much in tune with the Moon. Which it is for intuitive people... so water. So watch those Moon cycles... start tracking them a little more carefully. And move with the Moon... you will find that really works for you. So in other words... when it's

a new Moon, it's time to really make this act… go out and do and go after what it is you have in your mind to do. When it's getting to be a full Moon… that's a time of completing stuff. If you start listening to your dreams and moving in tune with that… your timing will get very accurate……… Tower comes up in… in insight…meaning that this is something you really do have… Tower is… stress. It's probably the feeling that you're getting… Towers is… we build towers… twin towers in life that tell us that we're very secure, but the way the universe works is that just when we think that we have it all mapped out and that we're just nice and secure… and we're at the top of the Tower and nothing can hurt us or touch us - that's just when we constellate a kind of energy to knock us out of there. Because it's not healthy… it's not the way we grow, when we cling to some concept of security that really isn't there. So… the security foundation of your life is about to blow-out. That's a kind of shock - it feels like "Holy… I thought I was fine… I thought I was in charge!!" Universe is about to give you a little knock. I suspect because you feel these inner shifts going on… you're right… those inner shifts. I don't really want any security… security will become very quickly a golden cage for me… and I really want out of that……… The Queen of Cups comes up in new perspective. The Queen of Cups… which means that… if you were to see yourself in your life from a distance away and watch… you would be the Queen of Cups… Meaning that your intuitions really ties in with the Moon… the Queen of Cups is the Moon. Ah… you would see that…you… perhaps… what you were thinking……… The Queen of Cups… you know… she is sort of the court card that's the psychic of the deck and you do not… have a. very……… You're psychic… but you know that… don't you?

MAYOR

Ya.

CARDS

This could be why you have trouble accepting the Six of Wands. Because you have a psychic sense which is quite accurate… you feel that gives you some kind of advantage… and so you don't… shouldn't use it or maybe that's being manipulative. It's kind of not fair… you shouldn't have to tie one hand behind your back to play the game. Because it's not fair. But that's just who you are and it's a gift. And that gift…you do know what people think… as long as it's used responsibly… not meaning that you don't use it. As long as you use it responsibly, it can be tremendous healing… seeing truly… in people's shadow sides. You can be very truthful… that can help guide insights in them… place, even though that's your fear… So it's not cold and manipulative… even though that's your fear.

MAYOR

Well, it gets taken as cold and manipulative.

CARDS

Ya… but… when it gets taken that way, question that. You will right away think… well is that OK? And the oracle certainly says yes that is OK. if you are at root… you ARE an ethical person. As long as it's used in a manner to help people, it's quite OK……… What needs healing is the Two of Swords. This card comes up to say that you have been... as you're changing and growing and letting and moving to a state of changing unfoldment. As you move into that, you have been already and will be continuing to cut stuff out of your life. It's like pruning a tree... ah, a bonsai tree. You know you just keep cutting branches back so that the energy that's coming up from this tree will go to just what you want it to go. So the resources and energy that are going into this... you have actually had to trim these suckers out of your life and that has been painful for you to do that. Because it's been a process of... geez there was really something in this for me, but the chhh... that feels... that hurts. So I would think because of where we started... at the Lovers... it's in the particular in the aspects of your personal life. Now, we're in your personal life... where some people... hmm... suckers... you've had to trim them out. Had been to these relationships and nurturing them... so that needs healing. And that... I see that as also as something that needs acceptance in your life. And the pain of it can be......... Also... that's why you were with me... because I was kinda... which can lead to cynicism. And so you have to be forever mindful of that. It's not about hurting you... it's just about... sorry I just need to......... The High Priest comes up in the recommended position. Ah, the High Priest is symbolic of teaching. So it's an important card, because it's what the oracle recommends. The High Priest is about teaching, about moral force... or about being ethical and... being... I would say being a calling... kind of the big picture. Do you teach?

MAYOR

No, I hope not... my parents were both teachers, so I avoided it.

CARDS

You have a lot of teacher energy in your life!! Ha... ha...

MAYOR

Way too much... like ninety percent of my family... their siblings and parents were teachers.

CARDS

They had strong morals and they taught them to you well. That's what I would say. What moral responsibility are you embracing or the oracle wants you to embrace.

MAYOR

I'm not sure... would have to think about it.

CARDS

There is a suggestion in this card too... of conformity. But on the light side... conformity to certain values... moral values can be a good thing. That's really what I think the oracle is saying is... cut out a lot of the junk... that is... suckers on your resources and energy. Just let it go. One... an aspect of that right purpose... would certainly be, in the next decade you'll be fulfilling your purpose......... The outcome comes up the Two of Coin. Which is what we see by this Winter. So what does unfold is two-pronged. You will be doing two things.

You will see your dedication in two things equally. This can be spirit and matter. That's one aspect. But to me because of me... it's Two of Coin and we're really talking about what you're going to do, this is about doing two different things. Making a commitment... equal commitment to making this happen and making this happen. Making a living for example... Coin... making a living... doing two separate jobs, but each one bears an equal commitment.

MAYOR

It'll be fun trying to find a balance.

CARDS

Ya, and time-consuming... that will be another reason why this outcome will be very critical. It's a juggling card as well... juggling these two........ Do you want to find out what your life purpose is?

MAYOR

It's hard to see what your purpose is when you are an Aquarius and you're always thinking about all these different possibilities and avenues you can explore.

CARDS

Well... we're in the age of Pisces, as you probably know right now. And the age of Pisces goes on for another... almost a hundred and fifty years and then we move into the age of Aquarius, so that's why you're always hearing it. So we're actually in sort of an overlap time right now, as Aquarius starts moving in and Pisces moving out. Aquarius is a time we're going to see. that's why we're falling in love with Technology. For Aquarians in particular... they would feel... how come everybody isn't catching up? Because you're already there and you're looking at the world like it's very slow in catching up to your way of thinking. I think that is often an experience for many Aquarians who are on the earth plane right now. Expansion... ya there always... hmm we can do more... we can be bigger... we can... ya know... there's always expansion so... it depends on... what's difficult is knowing your sun is Aquarian. There's still all the other elements... if I knew what those were ,I could help you to kind of frame that up. But I want to explore that for sure... I think you'd find it really helpful. It would be interesting to note... for example where your Moon is... your Moon is your needs... and because your Moon came up in the reading as what needs release. It's telling me that your sun up till now perhaps has been dominating a lot of your decisions but your Moon is your needs. And how you react in emotional... and because the relationship... the Lovers card came up here in the beginning as the places where you will be very challenged. The Moon card coming up here is saying... hmmm... look out for where that Moon is, because that is what will dominate over the next while. And if you know how your Moon acts... and it's going to come out in the arena of relationships. Then you kind of know what to watch out and be mindful of that. Balance your sign... it's just so important... so many people... it's so critical, especially when it comes up in a reading.

MAYOR

When there's a full Moon, I'll go on the prowl.

CARDS

Good!!. Good... so you ARE responding to that. And of course it would call you to do that. But it would be interesting to know which house it belonged to.

MAYOR

I always seem to get along best with in relationships... other Aquarius' obviously... Gemini and Capricorn...for business more of Leos because I can... they're very outgoing and I find it... it's a good match for business sense.

CARDS

Ya... ya... and so when you say you get along in relationships with Capricorns and Gemini's, it tells me your Moon... I thought that... yours is either a Capricorn or Gemini. If it's a Gemini... oh boy!... that one's really tough for an Aquarian because a Gemini Moon means everything has to come in twos. So we always have to come in twos. In relationships... is why making choices... you'd always be in two relationships... like hmm... sometimes I'm this way... and sometimes I'm that way... that way. Gemini's... they have that conundrum. Aquarians always expanding... so relationships... I understand why they would be very challenging for you and yet... uh... very impactful in terms of how you make life decisions......... What are we doing next?

MAYOR

I don't know.

CARDS

Want to look at your life purpose?

MAYOR

Life purpose is a good start.

CARDS

I have this... my feeling is... OK... and see... the Three of Cups is friendship card. This is about you... and see THAT... you and two others. Just as I thought. Friendship. Relationship and friendship. You work very well in a team and your friends are really important to you. So how peace... life purpose has to do with communication... peace because of the Queen of Cups... and the Moon and the Lovers. So right now... in particular... at this moment if you were to look around at your close... your life purpose is quite obvious. Bringing people together... for peace. So it sounds big. Ways that you fulfill that life purpose are bringing people together to speak of love and peace and that's the purpose of your soul family. So when you meet other people... or you think about heroes you resonate with, those people are acting in some kind of way to your life purpose.........

Past… what happened to you… this is about sadness… depression and regret. So your experience with relationships in the past… led you to a lot of sadness and regret, that… but that was your learning at that time to understand that, in relationships we can get very disappointed, but it's in communication about those disappointments… It's not like walking away or withdrawing from those relationships that we resolve… in fact, that can lead to war. What resolves it is actually speaking of it and communicating in this way… very openly and honestly about feelings. They happen. It's not in sad… alone and regret… and looking over at these three spilt milks, but not looking at the potential still behind you……… How others see you in your life purpose… is actually… they do see you as moving on. People in relationships with you feel as though… slash and burn. When it's done for you… it's really done… like… throw it up in flames… Next! You really move on and let that go behind you. So people in relationships with you, they get a sense of…like, when you're done, you're done. So that needs some… for you to fulfill your life purpose you need to revisit that, until it reaches a place of peace and love. Because how you've been in relationship……… So the recommended card in terms of life purpose is interesting… so… what you are… what you are really capable of is actually HEALING relationships… almost at a… I'm going to say psychic energetic level.

MAYOR
I can heal other people's relationships… just not my own.

CARDS
But you COULD heal your own by trick… bringing it to… it's like looking at it like a big picture. And saying ya… I can mend these relationships by not giving up… completely and staying with it until we can… you know… we're all sitting around smoking peace pipe. That can… when you pull completely away… like whoa boy, Tim's really let this slash and burn then. There's no healing that can take place.

MAYOR
Ya, when I was younger I had a tendency when there was an issue with a friend… I would just walk away and never talk to them again. It felt like the thing to do instead of trying to work things out. But there were a few issues going on with family, so I had to prune my own tree back then.

CARDS
Keep that in mind for now. That it is possible for you to prune your tree… without people feeling like… whoop… I'm cut off… or I'm… he's letting me crash and burn. You can prune your tree and heal actually… other people in the process and still prune your tree.

MAYOR
Ya, what I… what I've started doing last few years is prepare people for changes. So I prepared my parents six months before I moved out… so that way it wasn't a big shocker for them. And I… I have this feeling that I'm going to be moving away sometime soon and that

I'm going to have to cut off most of my friends. So I've been preparing them for that.

CARDS

Good… Good that's good. Action that comes up is as a Healer… So psychically you're a Healer, even though you might not fully realize it. Our connection to the spirit world reads we're Healers or we kind of bring in… bring in various levels of Spirit beings. So your role in that with your gifts is that you're quite capable of healing people……… Have you ever read anything about Adam? You ever heard of Adam?

MAYOR

Adam and Eve?

CARDS

He's a modern healer. He just… he… took that name Adam… look him up on the internet - dream healer. He's gifted… he's from Vancouver. He's now in University. Basically people, like his family, used this name Adam to protect his privacy. Imagine as a healer… gifted… they wouldn't leave him alone. But he has a website and reading about him… I have this feeling you will resonate.

MAYOR

OK, I will.

CARDS

The warning card comes up Revolution. Ah so… what happens to YOU is… and what you need to be warned about. When, just as you are about peace and love in your life purpose, when people or when a situation fails to respond to your ministrations.

MAYOR

That's putting it politely.

CARDS

You blow a gasket and all war breaks out. So you want to be careful that you don't get too invested in how your administrations are received. You put them out there and you do your work… without looking for… hmm… necessarily success in… you're just fulfilling your life purpose. How others are able to take it in or not is what you will need to let go of, because otherwise you get really mad and that contributes……… Ah, the near future and the distant future cards now come up the Maiden of Swords and Seven of Cups. So in terms of your life purpose… you are in it now. You are in an opportunity at this moment and I don't mean this necessarily by your work, by the way. Life purpose doesn't necessarily unfold in our work… Hopefully it does, because we need to make it pressing for that happen. Which I believe it will, as you go through your thirties. By the time you're forty, what I predict is that you will be very much married… your life purpose to what you're doing… that will be together. But for now, what the oracle is saying is that… you are unfolding as a… you have

[14]

a message already to convey. The Maiden of Swords is like a writer and writes about and studies... very intellectual... Swords are logos. So you're right now intellectually, ah writing, beginning to write about... and communicate as well, in an intellectual kind of way what you believe in. So it's your belief and your... ah... intellectuality and is in communication, where you're conveying love and relationships......... By Fall... and this looks like... it's a Fall card and I'm going to make a leap to say this Fall... at the latest Fall 2009. Ah you will be... the universe will throw at you a conundrum. One of your primary... self-actualization... or enlightenment or real fulfillment of your life purpose, versus really focusing on making money. Do I want to be enlightened or do I want to be rich? You know... it's kind of... so that will be the first challenges thrown at your feet to see where you go. And depending which way you go will be the speed in which your purpose... your primary purpose is...uhmm... unfolds... ya know... is successful... as Aquarius

MAYOR

Can you buy love?

CARDS

Exactly, can you buy love or can I get rich and have love too? And you know it's kind of the difference between... having the opportunity to do a presentation at the United Nations... Love, versus becoming... ya know... the head of some corporation and making two million dollars a year. That's the kind of split... I'm not saying specifically is what will get mapped out, but in your situation it might be the difference between... ah... if you would want to get your word out there... that's going to require... ah, some kind of mass production of what you've written. In which case... a mass production of what you've written... could bring certain financial rewards... on the other hand, in order for that contract to unfold... give up some of your message or the way your message is done... first test.

MAYOR

Well, I hope I pass. Interesting.

CARDS

You will. So what next?

MAYOR

Get an understanding of things that have occurred in my past.

CARDS

Ah hmmm... you want to get some clarity. OK!

MAYOR

Yes, around a deceased sibling.

                              CARDS
So you would like a message?

                              MAYOR
If that's possible?

                              CARDS
Ya, OK. Take your hand across the deck and pull a card and let's see......... The
MAGICIAN!!. The Magician… the message is… making things happen. Ah… the Magician
makes things manifest. Creates things actually… very good at creating. So was the sibling
creative?

                              MAYOR
Yes, she wanted to be in acting.

                              CARDS
What was the cause of her death?

                              MAYOR
Died of anorexia.

                              CARDS
So she killed herself?

                              MAYOR
Well, no!

                              CARDS
Anorexia. Well, she starved herself. She killed herself.

                              MAYOR
Ya… OK.

                              CARDS
So what she's saying is she couldn't… couldn't make something happen… wasn't able to
communicate her… hmm… what was in her soul. She felt that there was a lot of judgment
or she was just judging herself too much. She couldn't let it out and so she left the earth
plane. Which going on to the spirit world, where she felt she would be able to… her soul
could do more than she could do here. But at the same time she's saying that there's a
FIRE… that burns in the both of you about making what's in your heart and soul manifest…
communicating it… ah dealing with that… like making that come out… And for her… it
was… when she couldn't make it happen, she had to leave. I'm sorry that must have been
tough on your parents……… Do you talk her? You can talk to her. She's around… you

know? The spirit world is all around us all the time.

MAYOR

Ya.

CARDS

You can do that. You could... on a piece of paper before you go to bed at night. Write... come on visit me... I'd love to hear from you... I look forward to us having a visit. The veil is the thinnest, when we're of course sleeping, and she can lower her vibration to communicate with you when you're sleeping......... She'd like to talk with you.

MAYOR

Probably......... She tried. She struggled with it for eight years. Lots of judgmental people... especially in the health care system. Which is not unexpected, but still not what it should be.

CARDS

It was hard for her. So you chose to stay. That's good. Your life purpose is about love and peace.

MAYOR

Well,. I'm not done here yet.

CARDS

Oh ya... I know... I know... I can sense that. You'll be here quite a while......... What's next?

MAYOR

Well, since the Lovers card come up...maybe ah... let's look into who I might be meeting up with.

CARDS

Ya... let's see......... And you have... you remember the Tower. That's a Tower card. Remember we talked about... we build our Towers and that was the insight card and how your life is about to go tumbling down. And the Lovers card. You picked a perfect card actually... so you are meeting someone. Ah the Tower is... meeting someone who is really going to rock your foundation... in the ways you which you believed that you were... knowing yourself and what you want in relationship... this coming relationship will be not at all what you would have expected yourself have... to be in. It will be a complete surprise to you. You will not be worried as much about security.

MAYOR

Maybe she's already secure.

CARDS

Very different from who your family would expect or want you to be with. Ah… is there someone you're involved in from somewhere else?

MAYOR

Not really…well, maybe through work… made some contacts in the industry and down south… in the US.

CARDS

Ya maybe. So it's a relationship that happens on faster pace than you're expecting. See… your intuition was very accurate when you said the Lovers card.

MAYOR

Well, I can't prepare for it… because it will be all of a sudden.

CARDS

It will be.

MAYOR

I'll just accept it and go with it.

CARDS

This relationship will challenge you too.

EXIT THE CARDS AND TIM THE MAYOR

ACT II

SCENE I

05/13/2008

ENTER THE HOLY GHOST, THE KALE, BEN THE FLESH SMITH AND TIM THE MAYOR

HOLY GHOST

Here I try to… go love… money… career… travel… romance… karma. Sometimes Spirit comes through.

KALE

OK.

HOLY GHOST

But I… and sometimes, I tell people crazy things . So sometimes women will come to me… about… Am I gunna get married? Am I gunna marry this guy? Everything will come out… business… business… business… and the guy will go away with the Dodo bird. So I'm just warning you ahead of time that, like they say in "The God Father", don't take it personally… it's not personal, you know. But where would you like to start? Or if… and I always say if you would know the five most important things in your life, what would you like to know tonight?

KALE

OK, number one…Am I going to be happy with myself and with my life?

HOLY GHOST

I'm gunna… actually, I want to go, as you say that, I want to go two years ahead of time. Spirit… and when I say Spirit… I mean our guardian angels. They're going into 2010. Where they're saying you're going to take a giant leap. OK? Or I'll say a quantum leap. You're gunna do it. You're gunna do it. You… I have to say, I get a message for you from Spirit and you're not going to be forgotten.

KALE

OK.

HOLY GHOST

You know, some people, we come on the earth… and you think… well we'll never hear from her again or him again. And Spirit is saying no and you'll make your mark. You'll make your mark. You'll travel a lot. But you'll also… Spirit, thank you… I'll go over the next ten to ten years… from now until 2010. I feel you traveling outside of Canada.

KALE

OK.

HOLY GHOST

OK. But… are you waiting for documents in the mail? Because I get documents… just… just as you sit here honey, I get documents coming in for you.

KALE

I don't think so.

HOLY GHOST

Hang onto that. Hang onto that……… Because I just get… Spirit is saying… confirmation will come. So I'll say, even if you haven't filled out documents… because I get the vibration of… and when I say legal I don't mean court.

KALE

Oh, Good!!.

HOLY GHOST

I'll just say "Hang onto that."

KALE

OK.

HOLY GHOST

But Spirit is saying you'll be pleasantly surprised… I want to go to August. And I know today's May 13th. But I want to go this year August 13th 14th 15th.

KALE

OK.

HOLY GHOST

Where I feel Spirit is saying… I get MY mom here… my mom is saying "Doors are going to open to you. But three doors not just one." OK?

KALE

OK.

HOLY GHOST

I want you to think of… Spirit is saying… thank you, Spirit… "Don't doubt yourself. Don't doubt yourself."

KALE

Ha!!. I do!!

HOLY GHOST

Oh no, they don't want you to. Because Spirit is saying you have more ability and… I'll say untapped potential… untapped talent than you think you do.

KALE

OK.

HOLY GHOST

Than you think you do.

KALE

I know I do! I just don't…

HOLY GHOST

Oh, it's gunna come out. I'll tell you something too… August… and you know what… you'll say it's going to be a long time. And your angels would say "no honey, you're going to collapse time." And that's where… just say… somebody thinks they're gunna be… I don't know… Prime Minister in twenty-five years… and I become Prime Minister in ten years…but just like that…or like Barak Obama… you would say… who would think a black guy with a name like that would ever be running for President but he's doing it. Just like people… say… oh THAT will never happen. But Spirit is saying… by August, you'll see three, and I want to go career wise… someday would you like to have your own business?

KALE

Yes I do. I really would.

HOLY GHOST

You should. I'm not telling you… you should… but I'm telling… I'm saying you WILL. OK?

KALE

OK.

HOLY GHOST

And that's where Spirit, your angels are coming through, and saying do not doubt yourself.
Do NOT doubt yourself. And I'm going to give you a name… a last name. You're going to
meet somebody with the last name Sullivan. Like we all know Ed Sullivan on TV. But I
don't know if this Sullivan… I feel it's a female vibration.

KALE

M-hmm.

HOLY GHOST

That the last name is Sullivan. I feel that this girl… I should call her a woman. This woman
has a business already. And Spirit is saying "Honey, you're going to follow in her footsteps."

KALE

Oh.

HOLY GHOST

Hang onto that. Now I get as we sit here. I get a vision of you. Spirit is showing me… your
feet are going to… and your feet are going to touch down in Tennessee. And you'll say, "oh
my God, I don't know anybody down there." But hang onto that. Because I feel… Spirit is
saying… thank you… it's an open invitation. It's an open invitation. Where you'll fit right
in…it'll be… Spirit is saying… Summer time. I don't feel it right now this Summer. Could
be next 2009… 2010.

KALE

OK.

HOLY GHOST

But I feel you down in the States for business. So you may say I would like to do blah…
blah… blah… and he says… I'm not doing that tonight, but I'd like to. So your angels would
come in and say… well… just be you… you are going to do that. And not only will you do
business, honey, in Canada but also into the United States……… Do you know somebody
that has seven brothers and sisters?

FLESH SMITH

Fern.

HOLY GHOST

If you don't know. You'll know somebody that has seven siblings. There's seven kids in the... in the family.

KALE

Fern. Fern. OK.

HOLY GHOST

OK, for some reason Spirit is going to that person. And I'll say... and not that we don't like you and not that we don't like you guys. But if that person... do they have a question like they just have to know? Like if they sat with us what would they like to know?

KALE

I don't... I don't know because I don't know him that well.

HOLY GHOST

OK, well, I'll tune him out... I'll say... uh... the reason why that came up... the reason is that they'll get their answer soon. [FLESH SMITH] So if you know him better than she does. The message would be... whatever there... there... I just... I just need an answer right now. I need it right now. So Spirit would say they are going to get their answer. Like that's also a sign that when that happens... that the doors are going to start to open for you. First this guy... Fern is going to get his answer... you're next. Like three... three events... three... you know how... when we graduate say from High school or what not. There's a celebration that is an occasion.

KALE

Uh huh.

HOLY GHOST

So Spirit is saying between now and April... there's going to be three occasions for you to mark. But each one you're taking a step up. Each one. I have to step over here [MAYOR]... is there a somebody sitting on my sofa that wants to talk into a microphone? Hang onto that. Or I'll say... who wants to... I'll be the... want... who wants to work in broadcast?

MAYOR

Me, I'm guessing.

HOLY GHOST

Am I with you? Your vibrations... not that we don't like you.

MAYOR

I'm distracting. I can go.

[23]

HOLY GHOST

Oh no… no… this is very common. Yes… the answer's yes. I will… we'll get to you. But the answer's yes. Now I'll come back to my girlfriend. And I'll say pick out any seven cards. Any seven you like. From the top… in the middle… on the bottom… whatever you like……… I'm taking that one because you almost took it. So there's a reason you're supposed to have it.

KALE

Is this six and that's seven?

HOLY GHOST

Well, you pick another seven. I picked this one for you. Almost took this one, so my teachers always say if it falls off… if it sticks together… keep that card. And I'll… I'll tell you the one that you choose. Can… would you be surprised if somebody from a past relationship comes back? Or I get, I'll say… you know… you may not want to see them but they'll be back.

KALE

He is… ya he is back. He is back.

HOLY GHOST

Oh well, there he is. There he is. But not to upset you but does he rather… push your buttons at times?

KALE

He's very devious. He… he…

HOLY GHOST

Oh well, he's not a devil, but this card means that… well, first of all, this is a little boy and a little girl that used to know each other…symbolically, someone from your past is back. Don't let him push your buttons. OK?

KALE

OK.

HOLY GHOST

I'll say he's gone through more of a struggle.

KALE

OK.

HOLY GHOST

Thank you. It'll clear up. But this does not mean hanging yourself. It means change is coming. And I feel more changes for him... I feel you're going to be fine. I get Spirit... thank you Spirit... saying it's gunna be smooth sailing. But you'll be invited to go to Ottawa. So I don't know if you want to go. But I just hear Spirit saying you're going...you're going. Ya know. I also want to say... can you understand a situation? I'll go a personal situation where you think that the door is shut. OK, so I don't know if somebody said... ah I don't have time or whatever. I don't have time or we can't be friends or wha... la... la... or something personal. Spirit is saying that door is going to reopen. And I'll... not this... not just this guy. But somebody that in a personal situation that said... oh you know...

KALE

Ya, he shut me out.

HOLY GHOST

Oh. But this one. There's somebody else.

KALE

Ya... ya... ya.!!.

HOLY GHOST

There's two.

KALE

This one is the one that's coming back and this one has sort of cut me off and...

HOLY GHOST

Oh, he'll be back.

KALE

Ya?

HOLY GHOST

I hear this so strongly. That... I get my mom here... my mom... I always call her the relationship lady. Because all the kids in my neighbourhood would come to my mom. I get my mom saying somebody that shut a door on you is going to reopen that door. And you know how you say somebody is going to eat humble pie? They'll eat humble pie. And they may say... I don't need her... I don't need to talk to her... And I wouldn't talk to her if she was the last girl on earth. They're going to talk to you.

KALE

OK.

HOLY GHOST

And Spirit is saying… and… I'll say it this way… there's something about ah… a Tuesday… Wednesday. Not tonight. But something about a Tuesday with that person. But where Spirit is saying… they should never say never. Like they would say I would never talk to you again. Or don't use my name and your name in a sentence… never do that. And Spirit is saying they should never say never because they're going… they'll see… you'll see the karma come around. And also… are you thinking about moving?

KALE

…

HOLY GHOST

I'll just say… hang onto that. Hang onto that. I'll go towards not… not right now. Towards the end of the year. Because Spirit is saying… first, all these changes are coming for you between… in August… before August… around that August time. But the end of the year. Because I'll go financially. Where I get where… you know how you say… if you wanna say… I'm rolling dough. Or… I got where… I got x amount of dollars. That's my asking price and I'm gunna get it. I'll say career wise, any obstacles they're being removed. They're being removed……… Now, I have to… I don't know who this is. [MAYOR] Does somebody in this room know someone who works for global television? I have to come back to you. OK, so you're the culprit. I shouldn't be pointing fingers… that's not nice. But hang onto that. Just hang onto that. Remember the name Martin. And I do feel like Marty… it's his first name. It's not Martin Scorsese… but I wish it was. But hang onto that. Because that's who I feel is……… [KALE] and you're gunna be reaching your goals. You will be reaching your goals. I hear the name Anne with you. So if you don't know a woman… and I get her a little bit older than you, but Anne is going to help you obtain your goals… Absolutely you will… you'll meet somebody like me… somebody that looks a little bit like me… But what I get from Spirit is… her hair is a little bit shorter…but in a work vibration… in a work vibration. I also want to go into… when you have and I do feel you're going to have your own business. But there's a girl… her name is Patricia, but they call her Patty or some… I get that name Patty.

KALE

OK.

HOLY GHOST

But I get Spirit saying she'll show you the ropes. She'll show you the ropes. And Spirit is saying go sit by water. Not that you have to. I just get…. when you do… first of all I get Spirit saying… you'll feel energized and the answers are going to come to you. The answers are going to come to you……… Can you go into a vibration of your life right now where the situation… and if it were me… I'd go… boy is this taking forever, like, oh my God is this slow. Like… you know when we're waiting in line… like when is this… when is this going to change. See Spirit is going to that vibration. And saying it's going to happen like overnight. You know like in the Winter… like it was OK and the next minute, there's like a foot of snow. And it's like when did that happen. It was like overnight.

KALE

M-hmmm.

HOLY GHOST

And Spirit is going into your career. And they're just saying, it's gunna happen in a flash. It's gunna happen in a flash. I also… I have to say… I know where, in May 2008, but Spirit… thank you, Spirit is going out thirteen months. Thirteen is a good number for you. It's not bad luck. It's nothing bad. But they're going up into… where are we… June of 2009…where Spirit is saying things are going to be lining up just how you want them to… just how you want them to…….. What would you like to ask?

KALE

… OK… I want to know if I'm going to be… if I'm ever going to have kids.

HOLY GHOST

As you sat there, I see two with you. I see a girl and I see a boy. Because I felt that… but did you di… and I'm not trying to be smart, because I'm not a doctor. But do you have a health question?

KALE

Yes, I do.

HOLY GHOST

Because when you sat down, and I know I'm not a doctor… and I know THE HOLY GHOST never gets arrested for practicing medicine without a license. But when you sat down, and I said, I'll try to go love… money… career… travel… romance… Spirit was going to health. Health… health. Can I ask what would be your concern about health?

KALE

… if I'm capable of having… like carrying kids. If I'm like… like if I'm just going to be able to carry the kid to term because of my mental health problems? Or problems with… like… with my… I have diabetes and stuff like that. So it all contributes…

HOLY GHOST

It's all combined.

KALE

Whatever…

HOLY GHOST

Ya, it's all combining. OK. But as you sat there, I get a boy and a girl. I feel the girl stronger.
The vibration of the girl is stronger. Where I feel the girl will be first and the little boy
second. And, think about children. Think about that. I get the diabetes like being under
control naturally… where… I don't know if you're on insulin or anything like that.

KALE

No.

HOLY GHOST

Where… if you would call it… alternative medicine. Ya know… health… I can email you
some stuff about meditation. It's pretty unbelievable……… Have you ever heard of Adam
the Dream Healer?

KALE

Nope.

HOLY GHOST

Well… he's… well… I'll give you his email… or his website. He cured Ronnie Hawkins of
pancreatic cancer in 2002. The doctors gave him like two months to live. And he's still alive
and kicking. And I went to one of his seminars last September 1st. So there are… there's
in… at this time… there's new medical discoveries that have nothing to do with the old
ways. But think about kids or marriage… and pick out any seven cards. I feel as we sit
here… this little girl is going to come to you some sunny day. Something about… she'll be
born in the Summer time……… Thank you……… You have good cards. You have good
cards. First of all, I have to… I have to say… in your… you will be married. There's a
proposal. There's an engagement.

KALE

Oh.

HOLY GHOST

OK… this is… don't be embarrassed. Don't be shy and there's your family home… and I
mean you and your husband… and your children. This card represents the birth of a child.
But I got this card… this card represents… that's the person I'm reading for.

KALE

Uh huh.

HOLY GHOST

Has… it's called a Magician. It represents the person I'm reading that has the ability to focus
on what they want and to achieve… and like I'm just so powerful that… as they say,
whether they call it visualization… the law of attraction… the secret… there's no secret.

That when you see it in your little third eye, you'll get exactly what you want. But you will have a child... I'll go into three years from now...where I feel this girl is coming to you in the Summer time. But I do feel you grounded mentally emotionally because Spirit is saying... thank you... I'll go into the person that you're with...your partner... it's... Spirit is saying... they'll share. They'll share. And by that I mean that... only can... they'll be there... when they say I'm going to be there at seven o'clock... or we're going to the movies... they're there. OK, they're going to wait... they're not going to play games. They're reliable... dependable... OK... there's something about the month of March. So I don't know if the month of March means anything to you right now... or if that represents anything. But I'll say into the future... there's something about March. Hang onto that.

KALE

OK.

HOLY GHOST

I don't know if you get engaged in March or if you get married in March. There's something about March. There definitely is. The person you marry is going to be grounded and... but also in business. OK. And I don't mean, hon, that you're looking at his wallet.

KALE

Aha!!.

HOLY GHOST

You're looking at his heart and his soul. No... but know that you're not going to be living hand to mouth. Where you're going to be financially...Spirit is saying you'll be financially secure. You definitely will...but you will do a lot of International traveling with your partner too. I'll say husband. Use that term. You're not going to be alone. You're not going to be alone.

KALE

OK.

HOLY GHOST

Absolutely you're not......... Who around you raises horses? Can you place somebody like that?

FLESH SMITH

... my mother owns a horse.

KALE

Your mother owns a horse.

FLESH SMITH

My brother owns a horse too.

HOLY GHOST

Your mom is going to get more. You're mom is going to have more… I'll say… and… your mom may not want to hear this but I just get you… there's something about your connection here [FLESH SMITH / KALE]. OK. You know how you say… like we're friends for life. When you meet somebody it's like… you know… that bond will never be broken. That there's something about… ya… I'll say your kids are going to be around horses. They won't be scared. Sometimes kids are afraid of a dog… like I'm afraid of that dog. No he's OK. But kids can be afraid of horses cause they're so big… and… but I get your children very calm. Very… very… your little girl is going to be very artistic. Very artistic. The little boy is going to be a handful, but I get my mom saying…

KALE

Ha… ha… ha!!…

HOLY GHOST

You'll be able to handle him.

KALE

OK.

HOLY GHOST

They say boys are easier than girls… I don't know if that's… girls are so fussy…

KALE

Ya.

HOLY GHOST

But you definitely will. There's something about the month of March……… Was there something… I don't know… I'll go back to this past March. Was there something that you wanted that it didn't come through? Something that…

KALE

… not in March but it came in April. My disability didn't come through so…

HOLY GHOST

I want to say… I want to go back… So was it supposed to come in March?

KALE

Ya… well it was supposed to come in-between the time of…

HOLY GHOST

March... April.

KALE

Yes.

HOLY GHOST

So Spirit will... will go... that... that... disappointment... you know that anxiety... you know sometimes we can get anxiety? You go, oh my God why is this taking so long? And Spirit is saying that... that's over with. That's over with and it's not going to happen again. Because I just feel things coming in for you are going to be... when I say I'm on a different vibration... OK... stuff on earth... people, yes people let us down. That's human nature. But I just get a lot of blue light around you for healing. And Spirit is going to August... September... August... September you're busy. But happy busy.

KALE

OK.

HOLY GHOST

Happy busy......... Who do you know that just changed their telephone? Or something with their phone? I don't know if it was a cell phone or some... their number.

KALE

... not that I know of.

HOLY GHOST

Hang onto that.

KALE

OK.

HOLY GHOST

Because I'll... I'll... you'll hear of... and I'll say... you'll hear of... where somebody's... package of whatever changes. But Spirit is saying that's a sign of affirmation... when you see... or hear of this... from your friend... that the phone changed or something. That ya... you are going to be settled down and you'll be... and Spirit is saying you'll be very happy. You know how you say I know... you know that's like too good to be true. It can never happen, but I get with you is it's too good to be fiction. It's not fiction. It's reality. It's the truth.

KALE

OK.

HOLY GHOST

It definitely is. What else would you like to tune into?

KALE

… I don't know… that's my two main things.

HOLY GHOST

Well I'll tell you something… Spirit is saying… your… I'll go into your vibration… they're saying… you know how we were just talking about this… and the hurdles. You're going to jump the hurdles. What was challenging in the past… in the future… and this may sound very flippant, but it will seem like a cake walk. So I just get strength coming to you and I do get a lot of blue in your aura. And blue is healing. Green is healing. And you're also going to know… and I don't know… I mean I don't know who this is. But you'll know somebody that… I feel the music industry around you. Hang onto that. Hang onto that. Like somebody that produces videos or music videos. But I feel where you're hands are in it… you know… that Spirit is saying you're multi-talented. OK, and I feel as though your light was under a basket… OK, now it's time for the light to shine. And… I'll say it this way… it's going to be you stepping into the spotlight. And I'm not saying that to puff out your ego or… you know… stroke your ego.

KALE

I don't have an ego… ha… ha…

HOLY GHOST

Oh no… I mean, we all have an ego. But Spirit is saying it's your turn to shine. And you'll be able to handle it. You definitely will. You're also going to know… if you don't know… you're going to know somebody… a woman… that has a company that's a natural company. That has to do with… natural… not make-up… but… essential… essential oils… natural soaps… natural like maybe massage oils and stuff like. Hang onto that.

KALE

OK.

HOLY GHOST

Because I feel where… you know how you say… I just met this friend but it seems like I've know her… it seems like I know her from somewhere before. And Spirit is saying that's no accident. That's definitely no accident.

KALE

OK.

HOLY GHOST

Absolutely not. I still get you in Ottawa. Are you planning on going to Ottawa? I get that so strongly…

KALE

… I have a trip to Montreal.

HOLY GHOST

Where somewhere along… I feel… I feel this is separate though… with Ottawa… hang onto that. Hang onto that… because… I get Spirit going like this… with your money. You know sometimes it's like… it seems like… it's here one day it's gone the next day or whatever. Spirit is going from now till August… it's well… it's increasing. Spirit, hon. is talking about income streams. You're not going to have just one source of income. Or say… like you say… there's other things to do or other things for you to do. And you'll accomplish them. Ya……… Have you ever written anything? Because I see… that in front of you… and I feel that when you write, Spirit is saying you'll write from the heart. But when you write it's not… that I need to research anything. It's just where I'm inspired. And I get it. Because I do get a Spirit guide with you. She was… thanks Spirit… I hear the name Rita. She's standing a back of you… I see her… dark-haired woman, about five seven. She was an author… she was a single woman back in… in… the forties. And she's saying… and she was published and you'll be published also. And I don't know if you wanna be…

KALE

Ya… I do. I do.

HOLY GHOST

Well, she's your guide and I already have… thank you Spirit… and I'll tell you something I… because Spirit is saying to me… she sits beside you on your bed at night time. Don't be scared. I don't know if you feel the bed… I don't know if you ever feel…

KALE

I have!! So…

HOLY GHOST

And I'm not trying to scare you.

KALE

No… no… no… no… no… ! I… it freaked me out, but yes, I'm so interested in the spirit world… but ya… I felt the presence of someone sitting on my bed. You know… and like whatever.

HOLY GHOST

Because and it's… and I'll tell you something. Mark Twain wrote in bed and so did Benjamin Franklin. And I get like around eight o'clock and that's not too late. seven… eight o'clock… nine o'clock at night where this woman around you to inspire you. And sometimes… oh my God! I had such a great idea. And not to hurt your feelings and it would hurt my feelings too… it wasn't my idea… it was like Spirit… well nothing like… it was Spirit or your angel giving you this idea. And I just get this woman Rita saying… you know it's where… I can just see you writing like three pages all of a sudden, it's like well… it's like five o'clock and now it's six thirty, and… how did I write all this? It doesn't seem possible. But she's saying, I'm giving you… I'm giving you the ideas. I'm… and it's gunna flow. And I do feel you're going to meet a woman on earth… in phy… physical form. By the name of Catherine. That's a magazine publisher or something to do. Where I do get a cheque?. money… you're not going to do it for free, honey. You're actually going to make… and it's not… I'm not a starving artist. You know you're not a starving artist. Where you're actually paid to do what you love. You'll actually… you'll get… you know how you say… hey, look there's my name… there's my name. There's my name… there's my bi-line. And Spirit is saying you'll keep a scrapbook. You'll have your little port… not little… your portfolio.

KALE

I actually have one… ya!.

HOLY GHOST

Well Spirit… this is where Spirit is saying, your name isn't going to be forgotten. Because it's going to be out there.

KALE

OK.

HOLY GHOST

More than you think. You may think that… ya… here's my portfolio…

KALE

Ya.

HOLY GHOST

It's not this big right now, but Spirit is saying you're going… you have doors opening that… Spirit, thank you…. thank you… don't be afraid to dream. Don't be afraid to dream. Because I just get where you start with one magazine and it's just going to mushroom. Absolutely……… You'll also visit Alberta for some reason. Hang onto that.

KALE

I know somebody in Alberta. Well I know somebody who lives… around Alberta.

HOLY GHOST

Well, it may not be because of them. I… I honestly get where it's going to be because of you. Because of who you are and what you do. And I'm not trying to make you conceited, but because of your name recognition. That the doors are going to open.

KALE

OK.

HOLY GHOST

Because Spirit is saying you'll surprise yourself. But don't be surprised… it's no accident. And some people say… oh that was just luck… well no it wasn't luck it was tal… your talent. It was your talent. Spirit is saying it's going to arrive right on time.

KALE

OK.

HOLY GHOST

You know. I just get Spirit saying you're going to have… and I'll say… I'll say an idea notebook. You know and you may just carry it with you. Or like your recorder. When you get an idea… I'm just going to like… you know… like shout it into my recorder. I'm just going to jot it down. Because I do feel you're gunna… Spirit is saying… you're gunna roll with it. You're gunna roll with it. Because I feel… and I'll give you an example… like Sex and the City started as… the girl Candice… wrote a book. Something about four blondes. And it evolved into Sex and the City da… da… da… I feel with your writing… I don't know if you ever thought of scripts, but I feel you'll evolve into that. Or a play. Or you know… where you're not just in magazines but different areas of the arts.

KALE

OK.

HOLY GHOST

What else would you like to ask?

KALE

OK, well, what about my family? … I have an adoptive family and my real family. And I've cut my real family out of my life because they don't accept me for who I am.

HOLY GHOST

OK, think about your… you want to go into both families?

KALE

Just my real family.

HOLY GHOST

OK, think about them and pick out any seven cards......... Well, I'll tell you something now I'll say this... in that... in that... particular family there's obstacles. Can you understand how... they don't work as a team. Like they don't work...

KALE

Yes.

HOLY GHOST

I feel as if they're splintered. Like I'll just say... if there's ten people in that family... I feel like ten people off doing their own thing.

KALE

Yup!

HOLY GHOST

It's not where I'm sitting down for turkey dinner or I'm not sitting down... for you know... birthday parties or what not together. It's like... it's not the vibration of a family that I get. It's like everybody's an individual.

KALE

Ya.

HOLY GHOST

It's not where my family is... or like team... I don't know... John Smith or team Jane Doe. We're not united. We're all very scattered. Which is sad. Which is sad. I have to say something... although you ask about your family, your child comes up again. Your husband comes up again. This person from the past comes up again. And this is what I mean when... when like you ask about the family, but it's where what's happening... not... we can go back to them. But what's happening for you is going to be so powerful. It's going to overshadow them... or... and I'll say it this way... this is what I feel with this... when you name... when you get name recognition and it will be your name and you'll stand on it. They are just gunna like... they'll know... they'll know about it. They'll know about your success. They'll see your little name. They'll hear about your works and I'll say works... plural. Whether... and I do feel that you're going to write a play. I don't know if you ever think up characters or... oh my God, could I write a story!!

KALE

Ya.

HOLY GHOST

But I do get where the biological family is going to say... holy. God... I can't believe it. That's our girl. Ya know. And it's just that... who can I give you as an example. Gosh, so many people in Hollywood that this has happened to. That... you know... it's where... when... when you do the work. Then they want to come back and they want to be with you. You know... hope that your success rubs off on them. And I honest to God feel that it'll be... Spirit is saying... over the next two years. Cause Spirit is saying you're going to be an author. You're going to be an author. They're going to know about it. They're going to know about it. You definitely........ Who knows a person by the name of Jim?

FLESH SMITH

Jim?

HOLY GHOST

Ya... I feel I'm over on this side [FLESH SMITH].

FLESH SMITH

I know a few Jims.

HOLY GHOST

I feel I'm with you. Hang onto that.

KALE

I know a Jim but I don't have... no connections with him whatsoever.

HOLY GHOST

[FLESH SMITH] I feel I'm with you. Oh, you may hear from that person. But I just get... as you talk... I get that very strongly........ But I'll tell you something. There's going to be communication down the line. It might not be you contacting your biological family. Just... I'll say... be prepared. Because I feel that there will be a phone call... it's going to be like eight o'clock at night. You'll see that on the clock. Where somebody in your biological family. You may say... eh... good luck... or goodbye... good luck or whatever. They're going to try to worm their way back into your life. And Spirit is saying that's when you'll have the power. And you may have felt powerless with them in the past. Where they have the control... they have the last word. But Spirit is saying you'll see like there's a circle. So you... you'll seem like... sometimes we're on the bottom but it will be you in the authority position. And then you can either... it'll be your choice. You can either say... you know... do you want to go for coffee?. this is what I do. Or you can rub it in their face... you know like... you know... I would be tempted to do that I must admit. I would be. But ya know... you can go to a higher spirit vibration or you can say... you know what, where were you when I needed you? You know when I was a struggling. writer. When did you ever call me to... urge me on or give me encouragement? It's your decision........ And they definitely. They're... Spirit is saying... dysfunctional. But you can go... you'll go to a higher vibration.

KALE

OK.

HOLY GHOST

And... their attitude... their vibration won't affect your success. OK?

KALE

OK.

HOLY GHOST

Because Spirit is saying, honey, you're not limited. You're not time-limited. Sometimes actors... they say... oh you know once I hit fifty or forty or whatever... Hollywood... they're not going to want me. But Spirit is saying you have... you have no limit at all. Because your talent. Your potential is untapped. Limitless. OK?

KALE

OK.

HOLY GHOST

But your marriage is there. And I'll just... and the vibration I get with that is your own success. Your own life will out-shadow any pain that was inflicted on you by that family. By those...by those people. And... you know... every dog has their day. You know... someday... it will happen. Well, I just get you now and over the next two years... I just get you writing... and you can either type it out or you can write long-hand and type it in the computer later. But Spirit is saying success is on the way. And everything now... it may seem like, oh my God... you know... twisting... winding but Spirit is saying... "the road is going to straighten out." It's going to be... Spirit thank you... easy as pie. Easy as pie. It will. Now I want to... I'll just say... your biological mother does she have like certain... does she judge the world by certain definitions?......... Because Spirit is saying... definitions... definitions... definitions. Like if she would say... I'll just say... a successful psychic should I don't know... be on Montel Williams. To be made Silvia Brown. Or whatever... and this is the criteria... and that would be... if that was my daughter... she's got to do blah... blah... blah... Spirit is saying you can throw the definition books out the window. There are... God doesn't have definitions. He's beyond definition. We're all beyond that. No words... Spirit thank you... no words, honey, can define your talent.

KALE

OK.

HOLY GHOST

And that's... she'll be caught speechless with her mouth open. Because you will prove her wrong. You prove her wrong. Whatever her standards were. Like some people think... I can think of people that... oh my kids... they're going to have to go an Ivy league school. Well maybe somebody wants to be an electrician. Maybe I don't wanna go to an Ivy league... maybe I don't want to go to college... maybe I want to be a plumber. There's nothing wrong with that......... Because Spirit is saying things are going to turn around.

You'll feel… how we say… a hundred and eighty-degree turn and the ball is going to be in your court. Absolutely……… Who around you likes basketball? I get you… I get somebody either giving you tickets or inviting you to a ball game. Well, basketball is over, but hang onto that. So maybe into the Fall, when it starts up again. I guess it's over now. But hang onto that.

KALE

OK.

HOLY GHOST

Hang onto that……… You're also going to know a girl that designs clothing. Hang onto that. I don't know if you know anybody right now that does that, but I get Spirit saying she's a free soul, no, a good person. Knows what she's doing. A free spirit. And she's actually going to make a living out of it. And Spirit is saying… and you're going to be like that too. You're going… and I'll say… you're going to do your own thing. You're going to be a free spirit. Very creative. And you'll be fine. And you… you can just… you can do your thing and you don't have… and Spirit thank you… you don't have to… I get my mom here saying, you don't have to explain yourself to anybody. As long as you know what you're doing and why you're doing it. Who cares what everybody else thinks.

KALE

OK.

HOLY GHOST

You know… what everybody else thinks… it's not what they think it's what you think of yourself. And that wasn't me, that was Abraham Lincoln that said that. It doesn't matter anybody else thinks of me… you know… Because people thought he was nuts too. But he was an OK guy. Spirit is saying… Spirit is saying… you'll get your chance to laugh. You know. You're not going to be laughed at… you're not going… you'll be laughing with people but you're going to be celebrating. So as we sit here symbolically… I don't know if you drink but Spirit is showing like a champagne glass. A flute. And just saying many events to celebrate.

KALE

Hmm… ha… ha… OK.

HOLY GHOST

And whether you put 7-up in the glass or whether you have it alcoholic… that's up to you. But Spirit is saying it's not just a dream. Because when you dream it you'll do… Spirit is saying… thank you Spirit… you can dream it, you'll do it. You're also going to know… thank you, Spirit… a girl… oh, a woman… named Sheila. Sheila.

KALE

OK.

HOLY GHOST

And I also get Spirit… somebody… I get you invited out to Oakville. And I don't know anybody in Oakville. You'll get there before I will.

KALE

OK.

HOLY GHOST

I don't know if you…

KALE

I do.

HOLY GHOST

Well, I just get you drawn in that direction.

KALE

OK.

HOLY GHOST

And Spirit is saying… thank you… when that happens, that's just a little sign that everything else is falling into place. You're going in the right direction.

KALE

OK.

HOLY GHOST

Don't doubt yourself. You can… you can be good at… don't doubt yourself. Because then I'll come after you. Don't doubt yourself. Don't because… you're not wrong… I get my mom here and she's saying you're not wrong.

KALE

OK.

HOLY GHOST

Where I'll say in the past… Spirit thank you… I get my mom saying… in the past nobody listened to you. In the future they will. Your words that you write they're going to be heard. And they're going to be heeded… But ya… and we'll… and I'll say who gives advice… Ann Landers… Dear Abbey or Dr. Phil but Spirit… but you'll give advice. When you do… you're not going to beat it into somebody's head, like Dr. Phil. I don't mean it that way.

But through your writing… through your examples and your stories. Through… Spirit is saying… a whole new world will open for you. Absolutely……… What else would you like to tune into?

KALE

Well… OK, well my brother… my biological brother always told me that I might… I may have some psychic ability, but they don't know whether or not. If… if it's true or not, because he could see Spirits… and I can feel them every once and a while. I mean it's my… you know childish… I get scared, so you know like I just…

HOLY GHOST

Oh, you're like my sister. You're like my sister is. Now that she's older, now she's not afraid. But when we were younger, God she used to freak out. But she took after my mom. I took after my dad. But that's a different story. But I think you are. I have a gut… I feel you especially sense things before they happen. Where you'll get a feeling like… and I'll just say like… oh, I shouldn't go down that street or I shouldn't take the subway. And the next thing you know like you find out, you took the bus instead of the subway. And the subway had an accident and it's stuck at St. Clair. And you'll see it. Spirit is saying they come around you a lot. There's something in the night time.

KALE

Ya, they always come to me at night.

HOLY GHOST

Something at night-time. Ya, but not to scare you.

KALE

OK.

HOLY GHOST

Is it because you're calm and quiet at night time?

KALE

No, I usually am hyper but sometimes when I have… I don't want to watch TV. I don't want to play on the computer. I don't want to listen to music. I just sit in my room and just listen…

HOLY GHOST

You know what. I'll tell you something. I did that Friday night. And I forget what I'm supposed to be doing Friday night but I said… I'm turning off the computer… I'm not putting on TV… I'm not watching anything on TV. Usually I watch Jeopardy, you know, like what the hell. And… and I'm thinking… I just want to sit here and you gotta come over some night. We'll have… we'll do this…, we'll just see who comes in. Because I really do feel you're gunna develop. You know. That... strange... at night, and I don't believe in coincidences. I did that on Friday night, and I thought I'm not gunna answer the phone unless it's God. Unless it's His number. Then I'll answer but I'm not going to do anything. Just going to tune into Spirit. I said I have more friends that are dead... I count something like forty-seven relatives and friends in spirit. I don't have forty-seven friends on earth and I know it. But I do feel that they come around you at night time. Like seven... eight... nine o'clock at night, especially that writer Rita. But you will see them. You may see a shadow come by... you may see a shadow...

KALE

Can... will I be able to communicate with Rita?

HOLY GHOST

Well ya... absolutely.

KALE

Ya?

HOLY GHOST

Absolutely.

KALE

OK.

HOLY GHOST

Ah, I'll tell you what to do. Some people think... all you do is light a candle. Oh, you don't need these lessons that so... you know I get so upset... like two-thousand dollars to learn how to whatever... you... just... not. Get a candle. You put your candle on. Just look at it. That's it. Ya and surround yourself, honey, from your head to your feet with white light for protection. And you just look at the candle. You will sense... now if you get really brave... you... when I first started to do this, I did leave the lights on... I was like twenty I think. But anyway, as I got older and more... more brave, I turned the lights out and that's when you'll see a sparkle. Just a little spark. And then she'll form from the head down. Not to scare you. And you may see a flash go by. Like... oh my God... I just saw somebody walk by. And it's not your imagination.

KALE

OK.

HOLY GHOST

But she does get... I get... she does get... I get very strongly that she sits with you and helps you write. She sits with you. I feel... she was in Canada, but her family came from England.

So you know how like,… you think about tea and you know and biscuits. I get her family was very proper and she's… she never married and just…

KALE

Wait!! Tea?!!

HOLY GHOST

Ya.

KALE

The other… just the other day I was sitting in front of the TV, and I just… I rarely drink tea. I mean, there's only a few times that I drink tea. But I actually got up and made myself a cup of tea.

HOLY GHOST

That's because she used to drink it when she was on…

KALE

Ha… Ha… uh… ha…

HOLY GHOST

See that connection is so strong.

KALE

Ya.

HOLY GHOST

And you may do something and say… why am I doing this, because this isn't me. Why am I doing this?… or you may put on TV and… I don't know… say Sherlock Holmes or you see something… something on TVO that's a British film or… uh… like people with a British accent. Like… why am I watching this? Like this is isn't the movie… this isn't the kind of movie I usually watch. That's because your Spirit is coming so close to you that you're… you're not… you're not taking on her characteristics, but you're feeling what she felt… and what she did when she was on earth. But she won't hurt you. She won't hurt you.

KALE

OK.

HOLY GHOST

But I feel that you have a lot of psychic ability. I feel very strongly. Think about that and pick out any seven… just think about that. Pick out any seven cards……… I have to come to Tim [MAYOR]. Tim has… not to be a downer… but Tim… did someone invite you to go to a cemetery? Hang onto that. Hang onto… because I get where… you know… like… I'm not… saying that someone's going to ask you out on a date and say let's go to a cemetery, but there's…

MAYOR

It's in the past. The one down the street.

HOLY GHOST

Sitting in a cemetery or something? You're going back. And you're not going to be planted in there, but I just get that so strongly with you. You're going back. Not anything bad with that… [KALE] I just… as we're talking… I just get that… Spirit will… will bounce… bounce around him……… [KALE] I'll tell you something. You have… you have super changes coming but that doesn't mean disaster. It doesn't mean a disaster. It means… like… out with the old and in with the new.

KALE

OK.

HOLY GHOST

Out with the old. In with the new. You're gunna be in the right relationship. But the person you're with is going to understand your psychic ability. They're gunna understand. They're not gunna be freaking out about it.

KALE

Ya… he already does.

HOLY GHOST

Ya.

KALE

Ya.

HOLY GHOST

They're not gunna get upset. He'll be very calm, but you're gunna have a great marriage. And… I have to say… this person from the past. You'll put him in his place. I shouldn't say that… that doesn't sound nice.

KALE

Ha… ha… ya… !!!

HOLY GHOST

But you'll know exactly how to handle him. But ya… you'll have… and… in your psychic… and I'll say… Spirit is saying… I wasn't going to say psychic adventures, but something made me say that. But there's something… I'll say… in your journey… it's oh… and I'll say over

[44   ]

the next seven years. Where Spirit is saying "take notes and write down" because I feel someday you'll write a book about my experience. Not just my... my plays are something personal... I feel the plays and magazine articles... personal, and... but your book will be about your psychic awakening, I'll say it that way. This is... uh... you back on the path... like I've come this far and going that far. And it'll come... Spirit is saying... it'll come right on time. But I want to go personally over the next few years. I just get the marriage, but and... I'm not saying you have to be married in order to make you happy. But where you're going to have... Spirit is saying... thank you... you'll have the best of both worlds. Sometimes we say, oh I can't do that... I can have either or...a career OR a family. But no... you'll have... you'll have exactly what you wanted. And it's... it's meant to be, but I do get Spirit saying don't be afraid. They will appear to you. Do you also hear somebody call your name?

KALE

Yes.

HOLY GHOST

Ya... because I feel that they're... they come to you, because they know you can hear them. They come to you. Like say... if somebody that don't believe... they wouldn't bother.

KALE

Ya.

HOLY GHOST

But they know that you have the ability and that's, honey, why they come to you. And it's not that they're after attention. But they'll give you... and they'll guide you. And they will guide you with... and I'm telling you guide you... career... love... money... they'll guide you every step of the way. When you don't know what to do. If you're mom's not around, talk to your angels and your spirit guide. Because they will guide you and they will help you. And give you the right answers. And when I was younger... oh my God, I didn't want to make a mistake. I made so many mistakes, but anyway... Nobody wants to make a mistake. And you go OK, well now it's time for Plan B because A didn't work. And then once I started to meditate and tune in. I learned that... help is all around. It's... sometimes it's through people on earth. But then there's our invisible friends who are always with us. And you'll go... oh how did that happen? How did you?... I didn't find this apartment. I had to move... and I searched... and I searched. And I couldn't find anything and I had one more day. And I just called a girlfriend and I found this wonderful one-bedroom and I said... I can't believe this. And somebody said, man, you let this go to the last minute. I said I looked everywhere and I just couldn't find it... the area I wanted. And you'll find that but Spirit... your Spirit... I know Spirit helped me... Spirit... they come to you know because they know you can hear them and you... you will see them. But they won't scare you.

KALE

OK

HOLY GHOST

They won't scare you.......... What else would you like to ask about?

KALE

... I don't... I'm happy now, and I'm... I'm...

HOLY GHOST

Well, I want you to be happy every day. And you know what... Spirit wants us to be happy every day too. They really do. My teacher said "God never put us on this planet to suffer." And I went "man, that's not what the church taught me you know... I'm supposed to be...doing penance and said... da... da... da... da... da... da... da... da... da." I like her attitude better. God did not put me here to suffer.

KALE

Ya.

HOLY GHOST

So try to remember that. Ya. You're going to know a Caroleena or a Carolina. I feel you're going to know people from South America... and I'll say... Spirit thank you... people on earth from South America, that are spiritual. They meditate and can see Spirit. Because besides me, I feel you're going to make this other connection here on earth. Absolutely you will. Well, it was a pleasure... I want to say... thank you for letting me work with your Spirit.

KALE

Ya... Thank you.

HOLY GHOST

But I want to invite you over... any night you want... any day... or any time... and see... because when I hear, at night-time, tap... tap... tap and it's not the neighbors... and it's not the dog... but... somebody I don't know if somebody died in this apartment... but things move around... do you ever have that happen, where things move around?

KALE

Not often... I do hear little creaks, and I know...I think I know the house well enough... to know that... sometimes I just... have to think about it think about it... was it actually the furnace or...

HOLY GHOST

When I lived at the old house... the house was about a hundred years old... Charlie Chaplin was big at the box office when this house was built... and at night-time, the house would

[46]

settle… but then, at night-time, I could hear people upstairs having a party, and I was the only one in the house and I'm a night owl… and I really wanted to go to sleep, and I couldn't sleep. And this party went on and on and on. I went to the top of the stairs and I said… WOULD YOU PLEASE BE QUIET!! I'M TRYING TO GET SOME SLEEP. And I was really irritated. And I'm never ever irritated… all of a sudden silence and the rest of the night… I went back to bed and that was it. And I just thought… there must have been some parties going here like the nineteen twenties or the nineteen thirties or whatever… but it was something……… Well, who would like to be next? Which brave soul?

KALE

Benny.

FLESH SMITH

I don't know.

HOLY GHOST

Which person wants to move?

EXIT THE HOLY GHOST, THE KALE, BEN THE FLESH SMITH AND TIM THE MAYOR

ACT II

SCENE II

05/13/2008

ENTER THE HOLY GHOST, THE KALE, BEN THE FLESH SMITH AND TIM THE MAYOR

HOLY GHOST

… so the US army and the government outlawed the ghost dance. Because it's so powerful.
So whenever I need anything. Whenever I need anything ,I just say chief do a ghost dance
for me. My prayer is answered.

KALE

Ya.

HOLY GHOST

So if you ever need anything, just say Sitting Bull do the ghost dance and spirit… actually
there's the book that I want you to see. So I said to Spirit… Spirit this ghost dance… I wish I
could know more about it but where in hell am I ever going to get a book on the ghost
dance. So… I'll say that and I go down… downtown and there you go… the ghost dance.

KALE

Oh wow.

HOLY GHOST

The ghost dance is in it. And then I said Spirit… if I can find the other book… I said Spirit I
can't believe I got that ghost dance. So I have it now and I asked Spirit… sorry bible… I said
Spirit you know what I would like. I would now like a book on history. But I don't want it

from the white man's perspective. I want it from the Native American's perspective. Native history.

KALE

Wow.

HOLY GHOST

There ya go. So what you ask for be very specific what you want. I told Spirit I gotta get the other side of the story and it gave it to me and so, anyway now that you know that. [FLESH SMITH] Where shall we start? Where would you like to tune into?

FLESH SMITH

I don't know.

HOLY GHOST

Oh, never say don't know. Whenever anybody do... I go, oh man... don't say that, because I'll tell you crazy stuff... I don't know. Cause it just goes... one girl came in... and I said... and she said I don't know what to ask. And so I said pick any seven cards. I said are you waiting for... it was a Saturday... and I said are you waiting for a proposal? "I am". I said well he's going to propose very soon. That's it... goodbye. Ya know, I don't... I'm not joking around. And he proposed on Tuesday. So Saturday... Sunday...Monday... Tuesday... four days later it happened. So be careful when you say I don't have anything to ask, because anything can happen. Where would you like to start? Don't be afraid. I'm harmless. I'm harmless.

FLESH SMITH

... I guess financially. Everything.

HOLY GHOST

OK, think about everything. Think about your life. Pick out any seven cards. Seven is a spiritual number. Pick out seven......... So when I'm feeling adventurous I say to go... I don't know if I say it the right way. I try. OK, first of all the thing that came up... do you have a question about a relationship? Ah... like... male-female relationship. OK, well I'll tell you something you're going to hear of one. OK. And not to upset anybody... you're gunna..., not necessarily, you... hear of somebody splitting up. Not... not to be negative or anything. But I'll say that when that happens... I know you asked about money... when you hear about this, and it's not a marriage, it's a relationship. When you hear about the relationship going... that's where you are going to hit your stride with money. OK. Because I'll say... I want to go into the next year, and I want to go into right now and I'll say you don't have to tell me what you make or how much you make. But I want to go into this time next year... where you're doing something totally different. I feel as if you, I feel like you doubled your income. And you can say THE HOLY GHOST... how the heck is that gunna happen. But I just get where Spirit is saying... ah they're showing me a stage and you're standing on it alone. And… and I'll say it this way… when I see somebody like a standup comedian on the stage. They're doing their own thing. OK and whatever you do now, I just feel you're gunna branch out. You're gunna to be fearless. You're gunna be fearless……… I hear Spirit… and I'm gunna give you a last name. And I get the last name Carling with you… C… a… r… l… i… n… g. And if you don't know anybody with that last name… I just get Spirit saying… I get an infusion of cash coming for you…OK… hang onto that. There's something about when you meet this person that Carling… where I feel financially. And I don't mean this in a crazy way. Your mind is going to flip. But I'll say it this way, I'll go into prosperity thinking. Where… and I'll say it this way where… where… some people may say I have a job… you know nine to five… ten to six… I have this job. Spirit is saying between now and August-September time you… it's where you're gunna do a mind flip. Your… your way of thinking about money is gunna change. Where I feel your old concept is gunna dissolve. Where say… I'll just say… I'll say… here's my… I won't have a budget. Because a budget limits me, but here's my cash flow. And I just get Spirit saying you're going to let go of your old attitude and concepts of thinking. And I'll just give an example. So say… and I've never taken any of his workshops… but let's say like Tony Robbins or whoever… fill in the blank. Whoever about prosperity thinking. Because I just get Spirit saying you're going to do a mind flip and have a whole new set… I won't even call them rules… I'll say ideas… concepts of… this is what I really want to do. You know what I mean… where… I feel you're going to step… and I'm not saying… you're not jumping off the ledge but you're going to step out onto a ledge. And take a chance… and Spirit is saying the chance is going to pay off big time……… Cause I feel… I'll say it this way… an opportunity is going to come to you later this year. And it will be offered to you. Whether it's a partnership… it's a stake in a different company. Where Spirit is saying, I feel like you don't… you won't even think twice to make up your mind. I don't want to scare you but I just feel that, because Spirit is talking about a whole new concept. A whole new way of life. And I'll say… I know there's a lot of scams out there. And there's multi-marketing and I'm not talk about that… where people you see on infomercials and stuff like real estate… have this and have that. The millionaire lifestyle you know… on a champagne budget… you know… champagne life on a beer budget. But Spirit is saying it's going to become a reality……… This represents you… and I want to say… can you understand where you would have two occupations at the same time? I don't want to scare you but this is going to be you. Except Spirit… not except… but Spirit is saying it's balancing… that the bankbook is going to… exceed your dreams. Where you would say have x amount and that's my goal. And Spirit is saying you'll get that plus more. And it's not just a dream… it's a reality. It's all a reality. Where the concepts… Spirit is… can you understand someone around you talking about different concepts? About work and money and the whole thing about cash flow.

FLESH SMITH

Ya… a little.

HOLY GHOST

Well, it's going to increase and I'll say, oh in the next three months, so I wanna go... May to June... June to July... July to August where over the next three months, your mind is going to be saturated. It's just... I have all these books on psychic stuff... and all... affirmation... and all sorts of stuff. Or the magic of believing. That you're... it's going to be like breathing to you. Where it's not going to be impossible. You're going to know somebody by... and I don't know if it's a first or last name... I get the name Vincent with you. And Spirit is saying... Spirit, thank you... you're going to step into a new set of shoes. And... you're not... and there's no fear. There's absolutely no fear.

FLESH SMITH

OK.

HOLY GHOST

I also want to say I get property with you. I don't know if you want property, but I get it coming to you. And I know it's crazy real estate blah... blah... blah... but I get where... I'll go into 2009. And I'm not trying to make you feel good. Do feel you signing for property, but it's solid. I'm not losing it... I'm not stressed out... I'm not... my budget's not stretched...or stretched... I mean, it's not stretched out, but I'll go into..., and this is a different time of year. January of 2009. Where I feel that real estate vibration. OK... I also get you, Spirit is saying... over the next... in 2008 into 2009, you're going to meet a lot of Americans. Not necessarily with the company you're with right now. But in like... like... another... when I say another vibration... in another opportunity. OK. Nothing wrong with Canada, but I feel you drawn to the USA. But business-wise. Business-wise. And I... I get New Jersey with you. Remember that. Cause I'm getting the Atlantic Ocean but I'm not in Canada... feel like I'm down in New Jersey. Spirit's saying you'll be fine......... Oh, you know how they say sink or swim. And Spirit is saying... and... you'll swim. You'll swim. You'll definitely go into business... Spirit is saying two... two... two. And I feel with that not just two incomes, but... with this prosperity... Spirit, thank you... they're saying you have... you'll be a generous soul. You know how some people can have money and they get very uptight... and think, you know, now I gotta keep it and I can't share it. But that the Spirit is saying you'll be... not just generous... and I don't mean you're gunna just blow money. But you'll be... thank you Spirit... you'll know people in... and what's the word I want... in certain organizations... certain charities... certain... foundations. That... not that you're not a respectable guy now... but this... you know what I mean... like this will put you out there. This will put you out there, cause if you don't know... and you don't have to know them... but I feel even in Toronto you'll know people in politics. I feel... where it's I get the vibration... and I'm not trying to scare you. I don't mean parking tickets or anything like that... but like City Hall and this Honor or Councilman... I feel this is because of... Spirit is saying... the nature of your work. The nature of your work......... And this again has to do with the balance in your home, where... Spirit is saying... your home will be your saving space. I'm not saying it has to be like a Church or Synagogue or Mosque but that it's gunna be... thank you, Spirit, your relaxation zone. But I get Spirit also saying ... October... there's someth… I feel that… I'll go into October, where in this year, there's a special event that you're involved… Spirit is saying… that's the key. That's the key. Hang onto that. Because I'll go into… I don't know if you do marketing but I feel somebody is going to ask for your advice. Can you understand that?

FLESH SMITH

Marketing?

HOLY GHOST

There's some kind of special event. Hang onto that.

FLESH SMITH

OK.

HOLY GHOST

Or they may ask… I'll say this… your two cents worth. Or what do you see… what would you do if you were me or what would you do about this? And Spirit is saying… they'll listen. They'll listen. You may think… I don't know… Spirit is saying you'll come up with the answer. But hang onto that. I hear… I hear this name Vincent with you. I do feel it's their first name. So Spirit would say… Spirit is saying… when the person Vincent… when this happens know… I want to go financially… solid as a rock. I know the economy is goofy right now, where the stock market's doing this… real estate's doing that… or Spirit is saying and you'll be grounded… it's just where a lot of businesses like the subprime mortgages… it's like quicksand. Spirit is saying it's where your feet… you're going to be in cement. And I don't mean that you're going into any trouble. That you're… you're not going in with the… with the fish… to swim with the fish or anything. That there's any danger or that you're going to be on solid ground. But somebody is going to ask your marketing advice. Hang onto that. And you may not care for that or you may not be interested, but there's something… some idea that you come up with… where that… you'll feel like… oh that's just a shot in the dark, like this is taking a chance. And Spirit is saying that's exactly what they need. That's exactly what they need……… What else would you like to tune into?

FLESH SMITH

M-hmmm… m-hmmm… give me hints.

HOLY GHOST

Oh God… me… when I go… when somebody said to me, I don't have any questions… I go oh my God… I always have at least two or three things I want to know about.

FLESH SMITH

You see I didn't… I didn't think of things before-hand.

HOLY GHOST

Well, what about… what about your life? Like… what mysteries in your life would you like solved… not that I can do that… I'm just saying like boy, man… did I have questions when I was younger… I mean I still have questions… but…

FLESH SMITH

I guess uh… I've been halfway through college… close to finishing college and I just don't know if I'm going in that direction or something different.

HOLY GHOST

Hang onto that. Hang onto that. What are you studying right now?

FLESH SMITH

Transportation engineering.

HOLY GHOST

Pick out any seven cards. Somebody's going to ask you something about Marketing. You may not know… know anything about… you may know how to get them to the event but hang onto that.

FLESH SMITH

Six… seven.

HOLY GHOST

I have to say you're gunna go through changes. So I still feel there's something besides transportation engineering. There's going to be another opportunity coming at the door. Spirit is saying… it's going to find you. I feel… it's like… you're not going to have to go looking for it. OK? I'm not trying to scare you. There's somebody around you that is breaking up. Hang onto that. This is not you. This is not you, but when this happens it's a little sign that this other opportunity is coming to you. OK? Again this comes again,, where it represents two… and I don't want to say two jobs… I'll say two opportunities. Cause a job sounds like… oh I hate my job… I hate my job… but I'll say two opportunities. The one that you're studying for, but there's still going to be something over… Spirit is saying over the next three months. It's where it's gunna drop… I get my mom saying… she's saying it's going to drop in your lap. It's gunna drop in your lap……… Do you have a laptop?

FLESH SMITH

Ya… and I dropped it!

HOLY GHOST

Ya… ha… ha… and I'll tell you something, my mother never used a computer, but she's saying there's going to come an opportunity that drops in your lap… and honest to God… you may be at a coffee shop on a laptop and something just catches your eye or some… and it's not... I wasn't really thinking about it. I'll say it this way... I'm going to go into the vibration of what you study. Do you understand where you'll... and you may... and I'll describe it as what I do and what I study... I'm very logical... I'm very analytical... can you get... like do you know what I mean? Something is coming to you that... and I'll say something like you'll end up on American Idol. You know what I mean like... that would never happen in a million years. How will I end up, you know what I mean?

FLESH SMITH

Ya.

HOLY GHOST

Where... where... my day job or I'll say it this way... kids... the kids... the young kids go on American Idol or... or... Canadian Idol. One was a post office clerk or whatever and then they went on American Idol and then that other one, the one that Simon said "My God, well you don't have any talent and you look like... whatever... you can't dress nice"... And she won an Oscar for Dream Girls. Jennifer Hudson. I feel... and I'm not trying to make you feel happy tonight. That besides your real job, there's going to come something out... I get my mom here so strongly something out of the clear blue sky. That it's... just something you just can't pass up. It's like the opportunity of a lifetime... you say, oh my God. I'll do it... I... you know... but it's going to pay off financially. It's where I... where I just... and I get my mom saying it's going to land in your lap. You're not looking for it. It's going to find you. It's going to find you. And I get Spirit saying between now and August... between that time. You'll have the strength like... you may debate back and forth... like should I... should I not... Spirit is saying not you should, you WILL... And they're not... they don't tell you what to do but it's where it's something and I get gold around... to... me... gold is a higher spiritual vibration. Also represents money, like there's silver... there's copper... that's pennies and small change and silver's a little bit more, but this is a golden financial opportunity......... That it will get you the financial security that you want. And you're not being greedy. You're not being selfish. You know. But you also have someone from the past around and I don't know if... they're... and I'll say the same card came up for her. Someone from the past is gunna reappear. But... you will... you'll be... you won't be shocked. Think you'll be very calm about it. Very calm. You'll be very calm. And I have to say... I get, I know. I'll say... into 2010, I get you on a vacation in the Mediterranean. Over in Greece... Cypress or Italy. So I don't know if you ever... ever thought of going there. But there's some reason why you go there. And... and it's not that... I love to give trips away, but as you sit there, I see it so strongly. And. I just get Spirit saying transportation is one area of your life. Then there is another opportunity. For some reason, this other opportunity... I feel... and I'm not trying to make you feel good... there's going to be a phenomenal amount of money that... you know I could pick up and go to Italy. I can pick up and go to Europe. And I'm not worried about the money... The money's there. I didn't rob a bank... I'm not dealing crack... I have the money. But I have the money because I'm really smart. Not only... not only do I have a degree, and I have that job... but I'm also a creative individual.

And I'm smart... when an opportunity comes I won't pass it up. And do you have a question about marriage at all?

FLESH SMITH

Ya... sort of.

HOLY GHOST

What would you like to know? Cause there it is. See it will get... you picked the card somewhere you're supposed to know the answers to that question.

FLESH SMITH

Ya.

HOLY GHOST

That's why I said... you pick out any seven cards. See [KALE] she's calm, cause she had her reading. Now you're in the hot seat.

FLESH SMITH

Ya, well, I don't know if it's so much a question about marriage but...is it necessary to get married?

HOLY GHOST

Oh, I get Spirit saying the choice will be yours. I also get my mom... and my mom is saying don't let anybody pressure you. Where somebody might say... it could be an ultimatum. You know. Like I was Joe Torre of the Yankees and saying and you better get in the World Series or I'm leaving... I'm out of here. Spirit is saying don't let anybody give you an ultimatum. Where... a... a person would say... I'll... I'll... I'll just say if we don't get married by my birthday or by Christmas time or what not... and Spirit is saying... don't let somebody push your buttons. So I don't know if I...

FLESH SMITH

I mean I'm going out with her [KALE]. And marriage is... how would... it's one of those things where it's like... you know... whether we get married or not... There's not... it makes no difference to us. So is it really... is it important to get married?

HOLY GHOST

I think that you're together and your soul, now this is my take on it, that the soul is... the soul vibration, like go through soul, I mean you know... I know people have a piece of paper and stuff like that but I'll still say... I still get the two children. And I'll say and I believe that kids pick their parents... That... and... and I believe this. That only you and she can... the boy and girl I spoke of. Only you two could teach those two kids what they need to know this time around. And... and [KALE] I'll tell you something... and I believe this... you'll see it... you'll see it. You'll see it eventually. A year and a half before the mother becomes pregnant and you can tell me if you've seen this... I'm not trying to scare you... I don't wanna scare ya. You will see lights on the floor... this high off the ground. Little sparkly lights. Just like twinkle lights on a tree. Alright... and a child will come to you... just to get used to your soul vibration. But you'll also... you know how you were saying about you feel... the Spirits at night time. Well, the kids will come through too. Not to scare you. But the little sparkly lights.

KALE

Ya.

HOLY GHOST

So I mean... whether you get married or whether you don't get married, I really do feel these two... the boy and the girl... I feel the girl first. They'll come through just to... to... to... get you ready. Ready... emotionally. You know. But I... and I also believe that every baby brings a loaf of bread... and that's symbolic, that they always bring money. So the money will be there. The money will be there......... But you can think about marriage. Now that we said that... I'm curious if the cards will come up similar to hers. First pick out any seven cards. Then you can think... should I... or shouldn't I?

FLESH SMITH

OK... ready.

HOLY GHOST

And this one came out.

FLESH SMITH

Ya,... I don't know what's the matter with that card.

HOLY GHOST

Well, sorrows in the past. So that's over with. There ya go. You have great money, I'll tell you that. I'm not trying to make you feel good. I'm not trying to make you feel good. I will say... same card came up... regards engagement and marriage. So that's that. But I'll tell you something... this... card represents the birth of a child. OK? But it also represents the prosperity like... like you're not going to be in the homeless shelter with your kids. You know... because this card...

KALE

Ha... ha... ha...

HOLY GHOST

Because this card is about children but money together. And I... you know... I used to tell my dad the French have a saying... a father is a man that keeps pictures of his children in his wallet where his money used to be. But... that's a joke... anyhow I'll tell you something, and I'm not trying to be smart. Are you two [FLESH SMITH / KALE] thinking about moving in together?……… OK.

FLESH SMITH

We do live together.

HOLY GHOST

Well I know… I… mentioned this before about a move. But it comes up again. You're not being evicted. You're not being evicted.

FLESH SMITH

We already were.

HOLY GHOST

Well, there's a diff… I'll say there's a different place for you… This… represents a move. But business is gunna be great. Phenomenal money. Phenomenal money. This card is this little angel, and what he's doing… he's mixing the male and female energies… if you want to say, the ying… the yang… and what this card represents is, as you see things in your mind's eye… it'll happen… where, whether it's your perfect relationship… your perfect family… perfect career… you picture it… and daydream… you know… teacher would say… don't stop daydreaming but this card says keep daydreaming. Because as you dream about it, you create the perfect job over in spirit or the perfect relationship. Whatever it is. But when it's in spirit, it's just a matter of time and it comes through the veil and it will land in your lap. It will appear on earth. And this… and I'll say over the next three years… it does look like a marriage. And I'm not just saying that because I'm going to be a wedding planner… no, I'm only kidding… I'm only kidding. No but really, it does show up in your cards. And it's not that you have to… go… and I'll say it this way… you may think I'm not gunna get married, but the cards that have come up point in that direction. And you may think of it as a formality and that's OK, because I said a lot of things… and never say never. Ah, never say never, because as soon as you think… oh, I'll never do that, then it happens… and I did it. Or just things that you may think you're never going to get married, not that you have to get married or the pressure's gunna be on you to get married, but it will evolve naturally. Where it won't be… it won't feel like pressure. Like right… like tonight and I don't know if I feel like, I don't know if I should… like shouldn't I?… but when it's the right time… they say timing is everything. You know in your heart it's the right time. I feel very strongly you're with the right person. You know. And I'm not saying that to make you feel good.

FLESH SMITH

OK.

HOLY GHOST

I get a Steven around you. Do you… know a Steven?

FLESH SMITH

Ya.

HOLY GHOST

What would he wanna… or what is his life like or…

FLESH SMITH

I don't know right now. The only Steven I know is my uncle.

HOLY GHOST

Is he married?

FLESH SMITH

I don't know anymore. Cause I know he had this common-law thing. It's off and on and… all weird.

HOLY GHOST

Well I'll say, cause I feel where he's got his act together. But Spirit…

FLESH SMITH

I think he does now. Because I know he had all these problems before. But I don't know if they're resolved, and he might have that together now.

HOLY GHOST

For the reason… and I'll tell you the reason… Spirit… why Spirit would go to Steven. OK and say… well OK, he was confused too at one time. But now he's got his act together. And you may feel as confused as uncle Steve, but don't worry about it because everything's going to be fine. Like it's gunna work out. But naturally. Naturally. Not… she's not going to get a frying pan and hit you over the head you know. Or coming after you like that. It will happen naturally.

FLESH SMITH

OK.

HOLY GHOST

And I'll say. I wanna go work wise and Spirit is saying… this may not make sense… but you'll work less hours and make more money. I don't know if that makes any sense, but hang onto that. Because I feel where what you do now through your school… your transportation is one but Spirit is saying your second opportunity is less hours. I get to make my schedule and I'm happier. I got more freedom and that's where I feel… with the two of you [FLESH SMITH / KALE] it's gunna be the time to… like some people that… and I don't mean you… some girls feel… and I hate to say this… like they have to be with a guy all the time. They're very needy. But no, Spirit is saying you're going to have your schedule…

you're going to do your thing. [KALE] You're going to do your writing and you're going to do your thing. You're going to blend. Your energies are gunna blend… your energies are gunna blend… that's what that little angel card was about… where he's mixing the female and male energies. That it's a blending and a balance of that… of that energy. Where it's body… mind and spirit. Where the relationship is balanced. Sometimes it's lop-sided… you know… or like somebody saying, How can I miss my girlfriend when she won't go away?

FLESH SMITH / KALE

Ha… ha… ha!!!…

HOLY GHOST

I don't feel you having that problem, where… where it's… it's balanced out.

FLESH SMITH

Ya.

HOLY GHOST

Ya know… it's like… it's like too much together. My aunt… she goes, ya did I ever think about divorce? No, murder yes, not divorce.

FLESH SMITH / KALE

Ha… ha… ha…

HOLY GHOST

It's gunna work. It's gunna work, but I still get two kids with you. So… and I get my mom saying…thank you Spirit… it's not gunna be Murphy's law. Murphy's law is like… oh my God, if something can go kurflooey! It will go kurflooey!

FLESH SMITH

Ya.

HOLY GHOST

And my mom is saying that your relationship…. your marriage… your togetherness… it's not going to be… it'll be the opposite of Murphy's law, like it was meant to be. It's no accident that you guys met.

FLESH SMITH

Ya.

HOLY GHOST

How did you… I'm curious how did you meet?

                                KALE

We met through Tim.

                            FLESH SMITH

Tim met her online, and for some reason I ended up driving him to meet her. And…

                                KALE

Things just never worked out.

                            FLESH SMITH

Never worked out and we never actually started dating…

                             HOLY GHOST

[MAYOR] And I do get the vibe that the gentleman that you are you stepped aside.

                            FLESH SMITH

Well no. We never actually started dating until five years after.

                                KALE

Ya.

                            FLESH SMITH

Pittsburgh and my ex-girlfriend.

                                KALE

That ride there.

                             HOLY GHOST

Oh Pittsburgh, I was from the other side. Ya… ya… but that was no accident. Because
there is… you know what… we're all connected. We're all connected. The more that I
read for people I know we're all conn… we're all connected. And even people that we
don't like… like… uh… I wouldn't even want to have rat poison with that person. There's a
reason why you met then, you know… we learn something from everybody… you know. I
get again with you a connect… someday you two are going to visit London, England. Hang
onto that. And not… not to make you feel like a hot shot, but it's going to be because
[KALE] of your writing. You know how I said about that lady Rita was of a British
background. I feel that you'll… you'll… maybe your play will play in London. What's that
something over there… that theatre or whatever… but there's some reason why the two of
you guy to London. I feel that very strongly. Absolute……… What else would you like to
tune into?

                            FLESH SMITH

…

HOLY GHOST

Did somebody's refrigerator just go on the blink? Hang onto that. It's just a little... I'll say it's just a little sign... not that you have to buy a new fridge but I just get that. You'll... you'll... it's a little sign that Spirit's watching... your angels are watching over... you know beside you.

KALE

Your health?

FLESH SMITH

[KALE] My health? Ya... we can do that.

KALE

Cancer. Your dad?

FLESH SMITH

OK, let's do health. I'll do health because I actually had someone... not a psychic but a numerologist talk about that.

HOLY GHOST

And what did they... I have my numerology done years ago and it was freaky.

FLESH SMITH

Ya, that one was pretty freaky.

HOLY GHOST

Because it was... my year... I moved from one State to another, and my year went from like a number nine to a number one. Now what are the odds? And then I said to this psychic... I know... that I'm going to move to the big city. She said you'll never move there. I'm moving! And I moved and I stayed for three weeks with my girlfriend. I couldn't get a job... I couldn't find an apartment. Spirit was telling me no, but I was trying to make it happen. Didn't happen. She said you'll never move to the big city. And... I... came here my number... my name is a number nine. Toronto is number nine. Toronto and I have a great love affair. Nothing goes... I mean... it's just like the best things and so your numerology. What did the number... and that's why it's pretty accurate I think. But what did they say about your health?

FLESH SMITH

They said that I'd be on and off with sickness until about now. And that from now and beyond everything will get better.

HOLY GHOST

And I'm just curious, have you been sick off and on?

FLESH SMITH

Ya, it's actually been getting a little better lately. But ya, like I used to get pneumonia every year.

HOLY GHOST

Oh my God.

FLESH SMITH

Ya.

HOLY GHOST

You're too young for that.

FLESH SMITH

Pneumonia every year. I got it eight years in a row.

HOLY GHOST

Wow! Wow. I'll look... I'll look at your palm then, see what your lifeline is like. Just think of your health and pick out any seven cards.

FLESH SMITH

OK.

HOLY GHOST

Well, I'll tell you something. I have great news I have to say. First of all, your dreams are gunna come true. OK... and that... and I will say when you... when you do focus on what you want to reach and achieve your goals... this little hand coming through... it's from Spirit... so that represents your angels on the other side. Spirit guide. When you do say... when you hit the crossroads or you have a big question mark... and you say now where... now. where do I go? down... down this road... that road... where do I go? You'll always... Spirit is saying... intuitively you'll know. Intuitively you'll know. And I'll say in the future, you'll have a female doctor. But I don't get you dying... I don't get you ill, but I just get you... I feel where...and it's a light haired doctor. Like dirty blonde hair. But she'll have... Spirit again... you know how I was saying about you and your mind flipping... your attitude towards money and your whole attitude towards careers and stuff. It's going... it's gunna go in any direction... I feel that doctor is there already with medicine. Where she would never take... impossible... like for her, there's no incurable disease. There's only incurable people. And she would tell you... she will tell you... attitude is everything......... But I get... I get Spirit saying that... in your lung area. You'll get clearing coming there. But I don't feel it... a pill or a prescription but... Spirit thank you... actually I feel more natural foods with you. And I'm not saying, you'll have to run out and buy everything at the Health Foods store. But I just get Spirit saying there's gunna be clearing... clearing... clearing. Like some people do a toxic detox, but I feel more I'm drawn to the lung area. Can... can you place a man in spirit?… I don't know if it's grandfather who was a smoker. Because I get this man coming here… I feel like I can't breathe. Because I… he smoked a lot. Hang onto that. I don't know…

FLESH SMITH

My family, my family never really smoked.

HOLY GHOST

Hang onto this. I'll say… I feel like… that a guide or something that would come through here and he's saying… I learned my lesson. I feel that he works with you at night time… not to scare you. When you sleep… to do healing on you. And he's saying when you do… I don't know if you wake up in the middle of the night but… not to…

FLESH SMITH

I work all night.

HOLY GHOST

Well… well I feel he's with you at night.

FLESH SMITH

Because I work at night.

HOLY GHOST

Hang onto that. Or I don't know if you have trouble sleeping. I get him around you… a lot. But I feel like he smoked a lot. Hang onto that……… I hear the name Winston around you. If you don't know a Winston… and to me that's a very British name. If you don't know a Winston… you're gunna know a Winston. And again I feel that's in a work vibration. But something else besides what you do now… there's going to be this other person coming in. OK… Uh… health wise… uh… changes, but positive. This means changes…it doesn't mean you're going to hang yourself. But it means a series of changes which affect a long term advantage. So I will say… uh… I'm drawn to your knee area. We'll just say…watch the knees. OK. And I don't mean just bumping them into a table. I don't know if you… I don't know what it is but… Spirit is showing me… I'm drawn to that area. Just watch your knees area. You know… like some people, when they're older they… you're too young for this… fall and break a hip. But I'm drawn to your knees area. And that's the only… part I'm… I'm concerned with. The next two years… I'll say… you'll… you'll, again Spirit is saying you'll exceed your dreams. You'll exceed your goals. But I get where… symbolically I get where you're making a list… you know… you're making a list of what you want… how I want my life to be and I just get you like for the next two years… we're in 2008 now. You're going like this and checking them off……… I also hear the name Jason with you. If you don't… and I know that's a very common name but Spirit is saying they'll be with you a long time. Hang onto that. You don't know them. You haven't met them yet. Again, you have the same card as she did. About making the right choices in life. And again Spirit is saying… thank you, Spirit…she doesn't doubt yourself and they don't want you to doubt yourself……… Who do you know that wants to open up a restaurant? Hang onto that.

FLESH SMITH

Guy I used to work with.

HOLY GHOST

Hang on… well I'll say… just get that very strongly. You'll hear from him. I don't know if he invites you to… I'll say… to the grand opening. Oh… Spirit is saying that again is a little sign where he went off to do his own thing. You're not gunna shun your job. You're not gunna turn your back on it. But again… you're going to do this flip, where… I know that opening a restaurant is a risk, but Spirit is saying you'll see from your friend that he took the risk. He did just fine. Just fine and I can do it too. And I don't mean you have to follow exactly in his footsteps. But Spirit is saying you too will be… you know… doing your own thing. Outside of what you would normally do… Outside of what you would normally do……… So this card represents the determination and I was saying about… not second-guessing yourself. But… it also represents progress being made, as we were saying, about a shorter time span. Where you may think… oh my gosh…, that's going to take me five years to do. And Spirit is saying no, because when you focus…Spirit is saying… thank you… focus on what you want, not on what you don't want. Focus and see what you do want, and it'll arrive. It will be attracted to you. Because I get Spirit saying you have a very powerful mind… like a magnet… you'll draw exactly who and what you need to get you where you want to be. And Spirit… you know… I'll say this… even if you said, oh I just want to be happy. I just want to be happy. I just want a simple life. You're going to have more than just a simple life……… There was an old TV show with Paris Hilton called a Simple Life. And I know it was a joke. Spirit is saying… you'll see things and… thank you Spirit… they're saying about the 22nd of the month will always be significant to you. Like how some people have lucky numbers or time of the year they look forward to. But Spirit is showing me the number twenty-two. And I know we were just… I don't know… check in your… do you still have your numerology chart?

FLESH SMITH

Ah… it's somewhere.

HOLY GHOST

When you find it, look and check to see if the number twenty-two shows up. Because that's actually a very spiritual number. But Spirit is saying… twenty-two… hang on… there is significance. And you'll see in your life. And I'll say it this way… in your address whether it shows that you live at twenty-two something… something… or have apartment twenty-two or whatever. Whatever. Spirit is saying you'll always know when you turn and see that number twenty-two that you're not alone. And again the same card came up about the angel. Mixing the energies of a male… female. But I feel good with your health. My mom… she's saying just watch your knees. Just watch your knees. I don't get anything bad.

I don't get any… operations or any emergency room visits or anything like that……… [KALE]
But who do you know that has allergies? Can you place somebody…

FLESH SMITH

I… I have allergies.

HOLY GHOST

OK so… see the connection… OK, so I'll come into your vibration about the allergies…
where Spirit would say you're going to get some answers through natural cures. What are…
do you know what you're allergic to?

FLESH SMITH

Ya, cats.

HOLY GHOST

Oh brother. I could say two words. Dim Sum. I'm only kidding… I'm only kidding.

KALE

[FLESH SMITH] You love Dim Sum.

FLESH SMITH

I love Dim Sum.

HOLY GHOST

I got in trouble. The other day I was at… at a coffee shop. And well, they won't allow dogs
in anymore cause the owner feeds the dogs. And somebody was upset…and I had my
coffee and the owner said "Ah. I feel terrible. You know, in some countries like France…
and England, you can take your pets right to the restaurant." And I said "ya, they may end
up on the table." Ahh, did she get mad at me. God, did she get mad!! I was joking. She
said you never say that to a dog lover. I said I would not eat a dog or a cat. I would never
do that. Although there are some countries that do.

FLESH SMITH

That's like saying to someone who's Hindu. "Hey, let's go out for a big nice beef steak."

HOLY GHOST

Ya… the cows are… sacred cows… you're not kidding……… Ya… I get a Roger with you.
So I have to say, as we sit here, I get Spirit saying you're gunna own property. And you may
say God, I don't know how that's gunna happen. But… remember… I'll just say… or play
the tape back… It'll happen… It'll happen naturally.

FLESH SMITH

OK.

HOLY GHOST

Because I feel where…and I'll go…I do feel down the road you're gunna… Spirit is saying… you'll have your home, but you'll have an income property. So whether you have… I don't know… a townhouse or a house and rent out the basement. A house and have the double, where you have an income coming from a piece of your home… it's your property but it's an investment property. But you'll get what you need. Also hear the name Darlene [MAYOR]… I think I'm with you. Hang onto the name Darlene…I feel that very strongly……… I also… I just… I just want to go to… to… I just get Spirit saying… watch your eyes. You're not going blind, but I just get eye drops with you. So I don't know… if they get… I don't know… tired sometimes, or if it's the pollution. Spirit… and Spirit is saying, but you'll… you'll… your allergies I feel, are gunna be… Spirit thank you… they're gunna be going, but Spirit is saying naturally. Naturally. I also get… I also get… the two of you being invited to Arizona. So I don't know anybody down there. Ya but…but I'll say an area called… I think it's called the Four Corners. And I just get where Spirit is saying you may not know anybody there tonight. but the invi… invitation is coming. The invitation is coming……… Now I'm going to ask a question… Does anybody know… and I don't mean to upset you… does anybody know somebody with leukemia?

FLESH SMITH

Not…not really.

KALE / MAYOR

No

HOLY GHOST

Is it something like leukemia?

FLESH SMITH

No, well I've known a lot of people that have had cancer. Not leukemia.

HOLY GHOST

Well, I'll say,, I'm picking up… you'll hear that they are going to go into remission. So whether it's gosh…I don't know if I'll get…like a name… lymphoma…Hodgkin's lymphoma… it's an adult leukemia. Where Spirit would go ahead of time and say they'll… they'll survive. They'll get through it and they'll go into remission. And they'll be fine. They'll be fine. Just so… and you may hear this down the road. That I… and I feel a male vibration… a male friend. And…uhmm…Spirit is saying you'll know that they'll come through with flying colors. So… when you can… and you don't have to say you heard it from me… but you can just… oh you know… I just… I just have a gut feeling you're gunna pull through. You'll be OK… Spirit is saying you'll give them the advice and you'll… you'll listen to them and you'll… you'll ease their worry. And help them……… What else would you like to ask? That you can think of.

FLESH SMITH

I don't know.

HOLY GHOST

Ah... me... I had so many questions.

FLESH SMITH

I don't really have questions. I don't know why but I don't really have questions to ask.

HOLY GHOST

Ah, I'll tell you something as you say that, one thing I hear from you, is going to be in a receiving mode. And what I mean by that is... you're not a greedy... I know you're not a greedy person but Spirit is saying you... you know how we were saying about concepts about money and stuff. Spirit is saying 2008 is number one, one year of new beginnings... number one where you're going to be in a receiving mode. And you'll have the mindset of... I feel worthy... I am worthy and Spirit is saying that's when things are going to show up on your doorstep. I know I was saying about when opportunity is falling... about opportunity falling in your lap. But Spirit is saying you're going to have this attitude of you deserve the best and I do deserve the best. But I'm... I'm not better than everybody else and I'm not arrogant but I understand. I wasn't put here to suffer. I'm here to enjoy all the abundance on earth......... And Spirit is saying this year 2008, you're gunna see this spark of prosperity in abundance arrive on your doorstep. I will look at your hand but... just go like that and... bend it up a little bit. Because... cause your life... your lifeline is long. Your lifeline is long. Your career line goes all the way up... here... it goes through your headline. This is your head... This is your heart line. You have love for a long time... goes all the way around here but your career goes right up into your heart line. And what that represents is not only do you have work... you have work that you love. You would be bored out of your mind, you know, if you weren't doing it. So in your hand, in your palm, it shows that your career... it'll be your passion. So and then I'll say, you don't feel that transportation engineering is... I don't know how passionate you feel about it.

FLESH SMITH

Not really.

HOLY GHOST

So... I'll say something is on the way. I'm not trying to scare you. But your... your success line... your career line goes right up to the heart line. So I honest to God don't feel that transportation engineering... and I don't wanna... I don't even wanna hear what you spent on college... my... your mother will kill me. But I honest to God don't think that that's your passion in life. It's gunna... Spirit is saying it will be replaced. That don't... don't... it'll happen naturally. I don't feel where... you're not gunna have to go looking. You're gunna find. You know what synergy is like... certain people meet or certain things happen. Or certain souls get together. And it's like ka-boom. All of a sudden... this happens... that

happens. He gets this job… she gets this contract… he gets this… he gets that. I just get
Spirit saying stars are lining… and I'll say… I don't mean this in a joking way. Stars are lining
up for you. Ya. Some people are star-crossed lovers like Romeo and Juliet but you… your
passion it's not gunna be the transportation. It's something else…What would you, if you
could do anything and not fail, what would you like to do?

FLESH SMITH

And not fail?

HOLY GHOST

Oh, you're not gunna fail. If you knew that you weren't gunna fail, what would you… what
would you dare to do?……… Oh my God, I could… I could talk for the next five hours.

FLESH SMITH

Well just… there's too many things that I'd rather do.

HOLY GHOST

Well, name some.

FLESH SMITH

Well, I can't sit here and say that I'd want to do one thing for the rest of my life.

HOLY GHOST

But what would… what would… what would make you… what is… what is your passion?
Is it painting or car racing?

FLESH SMITH

I lost all my passion.

HOLY GHOST

Well, I don't think so.

FLESH SMITH

Can't think of anything that I… enjoy passionately.

HOLY GHOST

That's gunna change.

FLESH SMITH

Because I don't know. I prefer different things… different times. Like I… even in a job I get
bored doing the same thing every day… every day.

HOLY GHOST

Ya.

FLESH SMITH

You know I'd rather I have somewhere where I can do something different today and tomorrow it's going to be different again. I don't really have… anything that I've tried to get into… you know whether it be anything simple like sitting and playing video games. I don't… I can't get into playing video games for a long time because it… goes away. You know I don't really have anything that I'm overly passionate about.

HOLY GHOST

That'll change. Just… you know what… I… you'll see it change in you. I just feel that emptiness… the energy is gunna… you know how you say being the end. It's gunna change. Where you won't be bored with a job. It'll be… Spirit is saying… it'll be more than a job… it won't be just a job. It'll be that… this is what I absolutely love to do. OK. Because I feel that you're very creative. You may say "oh, my God I can't draw a line. You know I can't draw anything." But I feel you creative. But I also feel that when… when… and I feel there's something about this Summer. That when it comes along, you're not gunna let go of it. That you're gunna say… oh… you know, I can do this, but I'm damn good at it.

FLESH SMITH

Ya, I always thought I was creative mentally. Like I would come up with great ideas. Great visions…, and…,

HOLY GHOST

Concepts.

FLESH SMITH

Concepts and everything. But getting it from inside my head out to there. I lack those kinds of skills. Those kinds of aptitudes. Right? It's almost like I can come up with the idea, but I'd have to hire an artist to do it or hire the right kind of person to bring it to life.

HOLY GHOST

I'll tell you who did exactly that. It was Henry Ford. He was in a big court case back in 1910 or 1912 and blah… blah… blah… and the question was… the Judge asked him what would you do if blah… blah… blah… blah… blah…? And he didn't know how to do something. And Henry Ford just said I would find the best people and hire them. Oh, and he won his court case or whatever but it… cause I'm telling you… I get Spirit… I get my mom here really strong, saying you'll do more than you ever dreamed of. What you… what you think of… as a concept… you will… you will get it out there. You know. Cause I just get Spirit saying you're an idea person. You're an idea person. But I also get where… OK Thomas Edison was an idea person… Nicolai Tessla… but you'll have your list. I just get you going… chh… chuck 'em and it's not that… they're not going in the waste paper can. You're checking them off and you're actually accomplishing it. And you'll say… oh my… I don't know how. I… I can't see how… I can see you here now but I can see the end result. And it's the middle part that it will just happen… serendipity. Serendipity is where things just line up and you meet the right people or you're at the right time or you're. in that zone… whatever you want to call it. And it will happen naturally. It will happen naturally……… Do you know somebody who works in sort of a… pet… industry. Something to do with animals?

FLESH SMITH

Used to. It wasn't really in the industry; it was just a pet shop.

HOLY GHOST

Hang onto that. Because I mean that's… that's creative too. Spirit is going and saying… it's going to change gears. You're gunna change gears. Hang onto that… you may not feel like it tonight but where you are today in… in career wise. I don't feel you… or in school wise… I don't feel you staying there… I just get where your mind… Spirit is saying… it's not going to be racing like… a bad… like sometimes we can't sleep… I wake up in the middle of the night to make coffee or something. No, Spirit is saying your ideas are… thank you Spirit. your ideas are gunna change your life. But you're gunna connect with the right people to make the changes. Like I'll just… give you the example… the Beatles… damn they were good. They're playing in a basement cave… a cavern and they didn't really get anywhere until they got Brian Epstein as their manager. So Spirit is coming and saying you're going to be like… them. And you've got these ideas. You've got them. Now you can put them down on paper. That you will connect with other creative minds. Or how they say… what do you call it… a think tank is what they call it now. An idea… a group of… uh… meet up or a group get-together of like-minded people to make something happen. Cause I just get Spirit saying, you're not gunna stay at this level. You may feel here's my status quo. And this is what I'm doing tonight on May 13th 2000… 2008. But Spirit is saying no. Your ideas are going to take you to places you never dreamed of. It's just like Bill Gates. He… applied for some job at some analytics software company and Bill Gates promised him he'll make the software in two weeks. He didn't have the software. He ran… he quit college. He went home and in two weeks… he had promised the guy something he didn't have. He went home and he created it and two weeks later he started his Microsoft company. That's… the rest is history……… And I feel the same vibration with you. Not that you have to go into computer software. But your ideas… they're in there. Spirit is saying they're going to come out. They're… in your mind but they're going to come out here and hit reality. And it's not just a pipe dream. It isn't. Anything else you can think of?……… Or want to ask?

FLESH SMITH

Nope.

HOLY GHOST

Well, I hope I didn't confuse you……… I had one girl say, "I'm going to go home and commit suicide." I said "before you do that, call me". But she didn't commit suicide. Anybody else want to ask anything?

FLESH SMITH

You, Tim?

MAYOR

Nope I'm going to be back here tomorrow.

EXIT THE HOLY GHOST, THE KALE, BEN THE FLESH SMITH AND TIM THE MAYOR

ACT III

SCENE I

05/14/2008

ENTER CAROLYN THE UNIVERSAL MOM, SERGE THE SHEPHERD, THE HOLY GHOST AND TIM THE MAYOR

UNIVERSAL MOM

You want to go first, Serge?

SHEPHERD

Sure.

HOLY GHOST

I feel you should be first. I feel… I just feel… have a seat. And my name is THE HOLY GHOST and it's very nice to meet you. And I think it's wonderful that your son is treating you.

UNIVERSAL MOM

Isn't this neat!!

HOLY GHOST

You know my mom… my mom's family… they could see Spirit walk through the house but it always meant somebody was going to die. My dad's family … to them, it's like breathing… my father loved what I do… my mom said put those cards down and go to church! But anyway, what would you like to tune into? I try to go love… money… career… travel… finances… and I have to say… before you came over… I wanna go for both of you. That I just get… that you are entering a new… a new time in your life but it's going to be better than you can imagine. I just get… how you would say… we say out with the old in with the new on New Years. But I get for the two of you… in the same…

UNIVERSAL MOM

That would be wonderful!!

HOLY GHOST

Oh not would be… it will… it is going to be. Because I'll say not it would be nice, but it's going to be great. Cause it's not just a pipedream. But I feel you're… ah… you're going into a new phase of your life and it's actually… and if you thought the first half of your life is good, this is going to even…. get better. Cause sometimes… you know I'm getting older… and you think you know… the best memories and the best stuff is behind you, but I'll say no it's in front of you. And so I'll say where would you like to start? I get a lot of travel with you and this I'll say Spirit… I'll say… guardian angel, this was just a little trip today… this one up to… to Toronto. Because I feel your bags packed… 2008 to 2009 but I'll say International travel but not just to the United States. So I do feel you'll visit over… over to Europe. But what would you like to ask about or tune into?

SHEPHERD

Oh, I don't know… health? Health.

HOLY GHOST

Think about that… Focus on that… and pick out any seven cards.

SHEPHERD

Seven? Oh…

HOLY GHOST

Seven is a good number… shows up in the Bible a lot and, if I say nine, there's nine choirs of angels. Did you see the news yesterday - where the Vatican says it's OK to believe in extraterrestrial life?

UNIVERSAL MOM

No… you're kidding?

HOLY GHOST

No, I swear to God. My friend is a priest and my phone rings… and this man said I'd like a reading and we're talking. And I started to go into his personal life… and he said I have to tell you I'm a Roman Catholic priest. He goes to Rome twice a year.

SHEPHERD

OK, I got seven.

UNIVERSAL MOM

Extraterrestrial?

HOLY GHOST

That's good… so I said father when you can take me to the Vatican… So I can go downstairs and take me to the library. They own the biggest telescope in the world in Arizona. They're looking for something. Or they know… they know something strange is going to happen. Well, I'll tell you something… no health problems. Knock on wood. Good money and I'm going to go over the next seven years. When I say prosperity it's where… I'll say it this way… I hear a little… when you share you have more spare but because you're such a generous soul, it's going to come back to you. I hear somebody… I get an… Anthony… around you on earth. So if you don't know Anthony… you'll know an Anthony. So that's… it could be… a first or last name… but I get very strongly that's his first name… that's his first name……… I also get… I have to say… symbolically I see you as a Shepherd. You know how they say the Shepherd takes care of everybody. And I'll say… even as you go… further ahead… like the next ten to fifteen years… you're not slowing down… you're not slowing down. You'll get to put your feet up… symbolically… you'll get to put your feet up, but you're still on the go. And you'll just say… your energy… it's not going to be depleted. Sometimes when we get… and I'm… I'm getting older and I know I don't have the pep that I used to have. I get with you… your… nothing's going to stop you from doing what you really want to do. OK……… You're going to know somebody else like me, whose got lighter hair, but and I'll say it may around where you live now, that you meet them at party. Cause I feel like you're going to know somebody else who does what I do… and I feel… and I hear the name of Vicky…or Victoria. Victoria's her name and I don't mean of long weekend… Queen Victoria. A Vicky and either she has a party or is invited through a friend and somebody else at this party is going to confirm about what we talk about… today. Also… this also has to do with making plans… solid plans where… some people say… have an idea. And they'll talk the talk, but they don't walk the walk, but I say over the next… I get three years… 2008 to 2011, it's like what you say… you don't even need to write it down, because you remember, this is exactly what I want. And for some reason… I know I just mentioned the month of July but this month of July is very important to you. I'll say that… I don't know if you have a doctor's appointment. I know you asked about health but I want to say… I feel good news. Like relief. Like I'm not worried… like if I had a blood test done… or if I have this kind of test… a cardio… test I feel where I'm getting good news. I'm getting good news……… Do you have a question about a property?

SHEPHERD

Ha… ha!!

HOLY GHOST

It's good news… it's not… it's not going to be a mudslide. But do you have a question about it? Because there it is.

SHEPHERD

Well… well ya… I guess I take care of my… my neighbors grass and lawn mowing… and so on. He's ninety-two years old so I…

HOLY GHOST

Oh wow… no, he'll be around for awhile. I don't feel him going anywhere. I don't… feel him going anywhere but… I just get with him… the month of August with him. So I don't know if that's when he has to get his check, but I feel you're both getting good news. You know how you like talk… you're like neighbors… and in my neighbourhood, we used to talk… over the fence and everything, but I get you comparing notes and it's going to be good news. Good news… very good news and I'll… I'll say this represents for you balance in your life. And by that I mean mental… mental health. Financial health and physical health. I also hear the name of… Le… Leonard or Leonardo with you. So if you don't know a Leonard or Leo remember that name. And I get where… you'll… you'll listen, because I feel as though this person, whoever this Leo is, he needs to vent. But I don't mean that in a bad way, but I'll say… I'll just say, as an example, say the property tax or something goes up, he's gotta have somebody to talk to and I feel that you're going to be that someone. You definitely will. Are you thinking of?… I'll say that this means a second property for you. So remember that. I don't know how… I don't even know if you're looking for one, so I'll say you'll… you'll have it where it may be given to you. OK? And I don't know if… it's like when you're neighbor passes over, he bequeaths property to you or whatever but this represents a second home……… Now do you also know… know somebody that's trying to start a business? If you don't, I'll say this is only May now but I'll go between now… and again I'm seeing August the 8th on the calendar, where somebody is going to be asking you for your advice. Not just your opinion, not just your two cents but asking… well what would you do if I… if you were in my position, what would you do? What would you do? But… I'm not sure if I'm with you or with you [UNIVERSAL MOM] but I'm hearing telecommunications. Now I don't know if you have stock if like… I'll just say… mobile or something like that but hang onto that. Because I feel like… I'm not going to say… like invest your like trading… like insider trading or anything illegal but I feel over the next six months where somebody is going to give you a little tip ahead of time. Whether… whatever it is I do feel it has to do with telecommunications. And again I see this name Victoria… but I feel it more with you [UNIVERSAL MOM] but if you don't know a Vickie… where this invitation is coming to you. I just want to… come to you [SHEPHERD]… am I where… energy. watch where you put your energy. Like don't… don't try to do too much for everybody but save it for yourself. Like… where… instead… like what I was saying about like being a Shepherd and helping everybody and helping everybody… I get from your guardian angel to put your name at the top of the list. And to treat… to treat… sometimes you can give, but they're saying it's time to pamper yourself. Absolutely.

SHEPHERD

Hmmm.

HOLY GHOST

What else would you like to tune into? Who do you... do you know somebody that... that's concerned about Alzheimer's disease? Because I get this... as you sat down... am I with you? [UNIVERSAL MOM] or with him? [SHEPHERD]. I don't mean that you have it... but when he said about... health that's... I heard it but I'm not sure... who... which one I'm with.

UNIVERSAL MOM

Could be one or the other.

HOLY GHOST

Well, I'll tell you something [SHEPHERD]. I don't feel it developing... I'll say you'll keep your... literally and figuratively... you'll keep your eye on it and this is where your energy... and... I just happened to read something about tin cans... you know like years ago. That is... that's an urban legend. It doesn't... you know... you can eat all the baked beans you want. Because it was just... it was just something I saw but I... I just get where. Ah, my mom used to work in medicine and I just get my mother coming to say... your mind. your mind is going to be put to rest. That... you may forget... where you put your keys or something, but it doesn't mean that it's going to be a major problem with Alzheimer's because I... honest to God... don't get you... I don't... I don't get it... escalating. So your angels say, let your mind be at rest and... and put your mind at ease. You know?

SHEPHERD

M-hmmm.

HOLY GHOST

Cause I feel... you could... I get... you could give your doctors a few tips. Let's say it that way.

UNIVERSAL MOM

Aha.!!.

HOLY GHOST

You could tell the doctor a few things to live longer. I feel you should tell your doctor to have a glass of wine. I don't know if you have a doctor that doesn't drink. I just get that... where you say... a little bit... a glass of wine isn't gunna hurt. Where you could give out...

MAYOR

That sounds like something you [SHEPHERD] would say.

UNIVERSAL MOM

Yes.

HOLY GHOST

You know what… I'm with yo… doctor… I'm telling you I'm with you because… I feel you'll outlive your doctors… I really do. And it's going to be your attitude… where… you can just… stuff rolls off like water off a duck's back. That's the attitude to have… where… it's just like the old book… Don't sweat the small stuff. And it's your attitude that… is… you're going to be around… you're both going to be around a long time [UNIVERSAL MOM / SHEPHERD]. Who do you know that does scuba diving?

UNIVERSAL MOM

Ross… Ross Kyler.

SHEPHERD

Ya… Jerry.

UNIVERSAL MOM

Bruissard.

SHEPHERD

Jerry Bruissard… ya…

HOLY GHOST

Cause I get somebody inviting you to go… on a boat. And… and… hang onto that. Like I'm not going to jump off the boat. But I get where… but I do feel this Summer where the invitations are coming. See someone in scuba gear… gear… with scuba diving gear. But it doesn't mean that you have to follow off… into their footsteps. But it's going to… you're going to more… you're going to be busy… you know how they say the social season… the season. I just really… you're going to be… you're going to be booked. Your calendar is just going to be jam-packed with things to do. Definitely you will. Who has… ins… a question [UNIVERSAL MOM / SHEPHERD / MAYOR] a question about insurance? I don't know if it's life insurance. A home… a home policy. I just… I just get that as we sit. You know… that… it's a renewal. Uh nothing bad. Nothing bad. But I'll just say around that time… you're going to be extremely busy. Whenever that policy is going to be renewed, I feel like… you're on the go because you're out and about and really… doing quite a bit of traveling. Absolutely……… Now… this isn't you, but do you know somebody who either… I get this and I know it's not you. That either wants to take a second mortgage out… lien on a property. I keep seeing lien… l… i… e… on a property. But I don't feel it… it's not you but somebody. I feel that somebody is going to ask your advice. And I know I said before about somebody coming around you asking for your advice… but there's somebody. I feel that they're somebody younger, that is in a situation. Well, it's like that… they overextended themselves and maybe they missed a payment or something… something. They're going to ask… well what would you do if you were in my shoes? And I'll say… you'll… you don't have to give them any money to pull them out of that situation, but they'll listen and they'll take your messages to heart. Like you'll guide them where I don't feel that there's going to be any legal entanglement. They might be worried that there will be. But I get that you'll show them the ropes and things will settle down......... What else would you like to know? Or ask about. You're so calm. Your son takes after you. I was telling him yesterday you're so calm. At least here I don't know what he's like at home.

UNIVERSAL MOM

Ha... ha!!... No, he is.

HOLY GHOST

He's very calm.

SHEPHERD

No... he's very calm.

HOLY GHOST

Ya.

SHEPHERD

That's about it really.

HOLY GHOST

OK? You don't have anything else to add? Want to switch seats?

SHEPHERD

Well, what about wealth?

HOLY GHOST

Well, OK. I'll teach you how to make money while you sleep. I'll be like Tony... Tony Roberts. Think about that. Think about that. Think about money. Pick out any seven cards......... Do you have a question about grand-kids? [UNIVERSAL MOM] Ya, well... you don't have any now but I feel very strongly just as I sit here. Don't be nervous... ya know.

UNIVERSAL MOM

Ha... ha... ha...

HOLY GHOST

But I get that with you.

UNIVERSAL MOM

How exciting would that be!!. Well, I told Tim that only if... if that's something that... that's what really what he wants.

HOLY GHOST

What he wants.

UNIVERSAL MOM

Interesting.

HOLY GHOST

But I feel it will happen. In all due time……… [SHEPHERD] Well, I'll tell you something…
somebody is going to come around to ask you for help with this. Somebody's got a situation
with property. It's not you but somebody around you. And I will say… you have excellent
cards again. You will have a second property. Don't… I don't know it's going to come but I
will say it's going to come with no struggle. Any financial concerns are in the past and I'll tell
you your card. You're going to travel extensively over the next three years. Three to four
years. Between now and 2012. Cause I feel like this…

UNIVERSAL MOM

Hey, we're going to win the lottery!!.

HOLY GHOST

I feel as if every four months packing up and… not living out of a suitcase but the money is
there… that you'll have it. You'll have it. I'll tell you something… and you will have a
daughter-in-law. Here she is. But anyway…

UNIVERSAL MOM

What's… she like?

HOLY GHOST

A good… a good person. A good solid person. Now do you know somebody that wants to
get into law school? Hang onto that. Hang onto that. It may come as a surprise… it may
even be somebody who has a career and says you know what I'm tired of blah… blah…
blah. I always wanted to be a lawyer… I never really did it and I'm going to do it……… I
have to say this is my favorite card. This is called the Wish card. It's the Nine of Cups. You
don't have to tell me what you're wishing for. So I want to say financially, that was your
question. you'll get what you're keeping your fingers crossed for. OK. I don't feel… stress
around that. But I do get… I get where, over the next four years things are… you know how
they say some people are flush… Flush on payday and broke on Saturday or Friday night
and broke on Saturday. I get that every four months you're going to go on a trip. And I
don't know if you're hoping to go on a cruise but I get one with you. You may not like
water but I do see a cruise.

UNIVERSAL MOM

Ha… ha… ha…

HOLY GHOST

I don't know if you ever thought of that but I do get one coming around. But... and I also hear the name Patricia around you. But again I feel it more with you [UNIVERSAL MOM]... remember that. [SHEPHERD] But I get where that... I actually do... this may sound very strange to tell you this. But I get you actually in Toronto more often that you thought. You didn't want to come here. Somebody I feel, that they're either going to give you tickets to a show... like My Fair Lady. Tickets down to the Princess of Wales Theatre. But you may not like the hustle and bustle of Toronto, but I feel you will be flush... and I get my mom saying the cash is going to be there, so you may as well spend it. You can't take it with you. Ya, you'll have it. You definitely will. I also see three business men. OK and I do feel you know them now but I... I. feel that... where... sometimes we look at other people and we say...OK they... some people have more than me... some people have less than me. But the Spirit is saying financially over the next four years, your bank accounts are going up. Hang onto that. And... I just get where... Spirit... I feel as if...... how can I say this? You think I didn't think that could happen in a thousand years or a million years. How can that be? But I do feel... I hear the word benefactor. But I feel somebody... you're going to be remembered. And I just feel that... it's not just necessarily your neighbors will. But I do feel... somebody leaving you... maybe somebody does actually win the lottery and says, oh you know what? Well, you helped me now here's some for you. But I get money coming... I. see a cheque handed to you and it's from an unexpected source......... I don't know if you remember years ago there was a show called millionaire. Michael Anth... Michael Anthony and he'd go around giving money out. Some kind of a mysterious... you know... men's... God's ways are mysterious. And I just get where you're going to be blessed. It's because you earned it. Don't need to be looking for it but it's going to show up. I'll say like a super... like a supernatural transfer. I can't believe it but......... Can you also place somebody on oxygen right now? With a little... with a portable oxygen tank.

SHEPHERD

Hmmm?

HOLY GHOST

And I feel it's a female. Hang onto that... or I'll say when somebody around you... they're not going to cross over. They're not going to leave the earth but when that happens somebody says... you know... I had oxygen. I was ready to pass out at the mall. You'll know that... it's a sign... that this unexpected windfall is going to arrive right on time......... I also get the name Robertson with you. So if you don't know any... and that's their last name. So if you don't know anybody by that last name... then remember that because that's also a sign that this money is going to arrive on time. You're not expecting it... you don't really need it. It has something to do with the Summer. July or August. Because I'm seeing the sign of Leo not just... just the name of Leo.

SHEPHERD

Hmmm?

HOLY GHOST

I get you down in New York a lot. So you don't know anybody in New York. Try to remember that. That New York thru-way… it won't… you'll be fine. Some people don't… like that particular… you know around Buffalo… the toll zone. I get you going south of there. There's some… I get an event down there that you're invited to. So I don't know if it's like… I'll just say it's like a Chautauqua Institute, but there's some kind of event and you got the tickets. Ah, I feel as if the tickets are a gift… that… you know that you have stocking stuffers and stuff at Christmas time. Well, what I am going to put in the stocking? I'll put these tickets, but I don't feel that it's Christmas time. It's before that… that you're given these… but I have to say… [MAYOR] I have to come and say are you planning to visit Los Angeles. Because when you do, they're going to visit you. I'm telling you and I have to tell you something… I get airline tickets for your mom and dad going out to Los Angeles. OK. So I know that… I know there has… I just get this so strongly. [SHEPHERD / UNIVERSAL MOM] When I was saying about there being tickets to New York. I also feel that you're out in Los Angeles. I would say… doing the same thing. Going to a special event but I feel it moved to your son. And we may not know tonight exactly how that happens or why that happens. But I get… I get your airline tickets and I get your passports being stamped. I feel that very… very strongly……… Don't you want to switch?

EXIT CAROLYN THE UNIVERSAL MOM, SERGE THE SHEPHERD, THE HOLY GHOST AND TIM THE MAYOR

ACT III

SCENE II

05/14/2008

ENTER CAROLYN THE UNIVERSAL MOM, SERGE THE SHEPHERD, THE HOLY GHOST
AND TIM THE MAYOR

HOLY GHOST

But what would you like to tune into?

UNIVERSAL MOM

Oh dear!! M-mm, purpose?!

HOLY GHOST

That's sweet. That's sweet. We all need a purpose. I'm like the pope. Am I still here? Am I
still here? What am I doing here? I have days like that... I'm still here... I know somebody
that wrote a book about... if you're here, there's a reason why you're here. OK? Think
about why and your purpose. Pick up any seven cards.

UNIVERSAL MOM

OK. Got seven.

HOLY GHOST

You have... phenomenal cards... I'm impressed. And the reason I said... you pick them out
is because there's a saying that your subconscious minds knows the answers already before
you came in the door. You'll be guided to pick the right cards. OK the very first thing is... it
looks like change is coming up for you and your husband, but positive. It's like, oh my God,

we're falling off a tower but that's actually very positive. Where... I will say a change of energy but I have to say I get with the two of you a change of lifestyle. Nothing wrong with your lifestyle that you have now...

UNIVERSAL MOM

Oh, I don't know about that... ha... ha... ha...

HOLY GHOST

But I'll say it's going to be different... different but I got my mom here saying you'll take to it like a fish takes to water. Like... I just get... a lot of travel... a lot of I can't believe we're doing this but look we're doing this.

UNIVERSAL MOM

Ha... ha... ha...

HOLY GHOST

And the purpose for this... I get where... OK... you're done. I don't want to say, the hard part in your life, but now's the time to enjoy it. But the purpose is... you set an example for others... people. And I'm not saying that just to stroke your ego and make you feel good. But... you set the example... where your action... people will know you by your actions.

UNIVERSAL MOM

I have...

HOLY GHOST

And you know... and I'll say wha... if you were to say your life path... you followed it. You did and I just get your angels saying well done. Well done.

UNIVERSAL MOM

Ya, I guess I've had such a strong sense of purpose through teaching.

HOLY GHOST

You know what... I was going to ask you if you were teacher, because your purpose, you came to this earth as a teacher.

UNIVERSAL MOM

Ya, I still functioned in that role with Danielle's Place. I founded it... so... but I no longer have any of those...

HOLY GHOST

Why does that sound familiar to me? Why does Danielle's Place seem familiar?

[83]

UNIVERSAL MOM

Eating disorder support centre.

HOLY GHOST

That's where… that's where I know it from… I saw… this is strange… gives me Goosebumps. I found it on the internet about two weeks ago… before I met you. Forget what I was doing… I have a little radio show… a. pod cast. And I was going to invite somebody from there to be on the radio show but I found… and that's why when you said that… I'm like I know that name. I know that.

UNIVERSAL MOM

Well, I'm not involved with it anymore. I've just really been struggling to find something other than being a maid for a purpose in my life.

HOLY GHOST

There's something new coming for you.

UNIVERSAL MOM

Oh, good!!.

HOLY GHOST

And I'll say… it's going to come along sooner than you think. But it's going to have to do… and I'll say it again… I'll say it this way. The vibration I get with that is with younger people. But again giving them… I get my mom saying giving them hope and a reason for them… because I feel that you'll be around kids who are surviving. Or I don't know if they survived sexual abuse… or… whatever.

UNIVERSAL MOM

I had that at the centre for two and half years and I miss that.

HOLY GHOST

There's something to do with… abused children that… you know how they say… that you're the mother hen. And you'll have your pecking order and you'll keep them in line. And I'm not… you won't just volunteer… there is money involved… I'm not just trying to put money… a price on everything. But you'll be given what you deserve. It won't be…. I have my hours to donate… because I do feel that you will be reimbursed properly. Sometimes we're not… ya… sometimes we're not appreciated or told it. I'll say I don't want a title. Put it in my pay cheque. And I feel you'll have the title and the pay cheque. Not trying to be a smart alec but that too is reality.

UNIVERSAL MOM

Even at my age?

HOLY GHOST

Oh, your age has nothing to do with it. Ya… and I'll tell you something. That your age will be an advantage. I'll tell you… it'll actually be an advantage. It will be.

UNIVERSAL MOM

Oh good!!.

HOLY GHOST

I know that's true because I know that. If I've learned anything over the last couple of years is that age isn't a deterrent. It's actually… it's a plus… it's not a minus. Unbelievable and I'll say now… it used to be that they wouldn't hire anyone over forty… now it's like… you have… over… over forty… that you have the experience and you know how to run… a… a centre. That you don't have to be trained… Because you'll pick up in like a week…

UNIVERSAL MOM

Well, that's interesting.

HOLY GHOST

No I feel that very… that your age does not limit you whatsoever. Because I feel you will be around people that have struggled. And you'll… you'll show them how to dissolve the burdens in your life. You know… and I'll tell you something, I feel also that you'll speak in front of people. You won't be nervous about it. You won't be nervous.

UNIVERSAL MOM

Sounds like you're talking about my last two years… three years. Ha… ha… ha…

HOLY GHOST

Well, I'll say… I got my mom here saying transition. You'll be able to do but I get you as a you know… key note speaker.

UNIVERSAL MOM

Ya, I've done a lot of that.

HOLY GHOST

And you'll do a lot more.

UNIVERSAL MOM

Oh, very interesting!!.

HOLY GHOST

Ya and you know… I just get my mom… and she's saying you know you're not going to be shy. You know… you're not… you're not… some people get stage fright but you're right in your element. You're right where you belong. And you know… I. get…

UNIVERSAL MOM

I was... he... he...

HOLY GHOST

And you will be. You are going to be. I get my mom saying there's so many kids that still need you and I'll say... you're like everybody's mom. The universal mother. You know. And you'll be doing two... you'll have your house life but you'll have the balance of this... if you want to call it second career. Third career or I forget... there's an organization in Toronto. Second... I don't know... Second Mile or something like that.

UNIVERSAL MOM

Ya.

HOLY GHOST

And... and I just get Spirit saying you'll take the opportunity. You'll have a development role and to develop the program the way you would like to see it. Because I get where the ideas... you'll not just express them, they'll actually... the powers that be, or the board of directors will actually listen to you. And put your plans into action. You won't be... it won't fall on deaf ears.

UNIVERSAL MOM

Oh... now that's very interesting.

HOLY GHOST

Am I talking...

UNIVERSAL MOM

No, that's exactly what happened ha... ha... ha... and that's very interesting ha... ha I'm going to need a completely new Board.

HOLY GHOST

Well, you know what, it's going to happen. I get my mother saying it's going to happen sooner than you think. And like your husband, you got the Wish card... so you know what...

UNIVERSAL MOM

Oh, really?!

HOLY GHOST

Ya... they say... Oscar Wilde said there's only two tragedies in life. Not getting what you want and getting what you want. But you'll know how to handle it. Because... and I get... my mom saying you'll be treated fairly. You'll be treated fairly. And I know... I know... my mom...

UNIVERSAL MOM

That could make me cry !!.

HOLY GHOST

Well, we got Kleenex over here.

UNIVERSAL MOM

How... now that's very important... to me.

HOLY GHOST

Absolutely. Absolutely. Well absolutely. Well not just that, but my mom's saying you're a role model. Your self esteem... you'll instill the young kids... kids that don't have self esteem. That were told you're stupid... you'll never be anything... you know... you're flunking out of school... you'll never amount to anything. Where you're going to give them that beam full of... hope.

UNIVERSAL MOM

That's wonderful!!. That's always been something... something that's really important to me throughout... the career. That's an exciting prospect.

HOLY GHOST

I'll say you've always been on the right path and you're not done yet. Not in a long time.

UNIVERSAL MOM

Oh great!!. Well, that was probably the first question I had coming in. ha... ha...

HOLY GHOST

I get my mom saying you're going to throw your hat in the ring. I don't know if you find it... find it on the internet or the local newspaper where there's a notice. People are needed for such and such an organization.

UNIVERSAL MOM

Right.

HOLY GHOST

I get my mother saying it'll be short-listed. Because I feel there will be two or three candidates that they may... they may want two and you'll be one of them.

UNIVERSAL MOM

But will I get my energy back? Since I've had the relapse of fibromyalgia... really been unable to do that much for eight months now.

HOLY GHOST

I feel you will. I feel that you will.

UNIVERSAL MOM

That would be a blessed relief.

HOLY GHOST

I'm going to tell you something and you may think I'm nuts, but I have a friend whose a Native American healer. He told me years ago when… THE HOLY GHOST… when you need energy go sit and put your spine up against a tree. Just sit back on a tree and keep your feet on the roots. And imagine roots coming out of your feet and down into the earth and you're sucking up all the energy in the earth. One night I had to work like four to midnight. So that afternoon I did what this Indian guy told… Indian medicine man told me to do. That night… man… now maybe it was mind over matter. I was so full of energy. I worked four to midnight. Came home… it was like… I was wide awake and I'm going… I can't bel… and that… I didn't have any coffee. I didn't need any. And it was like… he didn't tell me how to stop it and that the whole is that when you're done your work, then you come home and you have a meal to ground yourself. But any time… now, anytime I walk by a tree… I'll actually step on the roots…

UNIVERSAL MOM

Ha… ha… ha…

HOLY GHOST

People watching may think I'm nuts but… step on a tree… oh and he said tell thank you to the tree. So there's a tree down the street. When I go for coffee in the morning, I step on this tree's roots and I go… I need energy today. And I'll say… thank… I'll say thank you Mr. Tree. It's not just a tree… it's Mr. Tree. If anybody… people must think who is this idiot standing on a tree!?.

UNIVERSAL MOM

No, some of the Native healing practices are so wonderful.

HOLY GHOST

No question. Absolutely. But I'll never forget that one and I did… a seminar with a healer… Adam Dream healer. And he does these meditations where whatever illness it is, you meditate and you picture yourself being healthy etc… etc. and then at the end of the meditation like… so… if you want energy you do this with the tree and thank the tree. And then you picture yourself under a blue waterfall so… I… years ago actually went down to Table Rock at Niagara where you're right next to the water… this is thirty years ago. So I imagined in this meditation being under Niagara Falls. And I felt wonderful. So two weeks later… and… I thought in that seminar I wish I could… I really should get down to Niagara

Falls. Two weeks later I won a trip to Niagara Falls. What are the odds? That's not an accident.

UNIVERSAL MOM

Ha... ha... ha... I don't believe in coincidences.

HOLY GHOST

Oh me neither. I don't. And... oh... there's a book called When God Winks. All the coincidences in your life, it's God saying hello and you're on the right path. But I went to Niagara Oh before I took this seminar I could walk ten minutes... and... then... and then I would look like I was drunk. I had MS or something was wrong with me, but after I did this seminar and I went down to Niagara Falls, I walked around... I couldn't believe it... I walked around Niagara Falls for four hours. And I came... and I... I... in my particular... this is bizarre but in my particular meditation, you're supposed to imagine lightning striking you to reboot and restart your nervous system.

UNIVERSAL MOM

... well...

HOLY GHOST

So I meditated on that and so... when I got back, I emailed this healer in Vancouver. His parents they protect him so... he cured Ronnie Hawkins of pancreatic cancer in 2002 so I... I meditated and in... on... January 17th, there was a big storm here in Toronto. It's snowing... it's thunder... it's lightning. Lightning struck my railing and I thought... I got to watch it cause I... I'm attracting lightning and I don't want to be struck by lightning.

UNIVERSAL MOM

Ha... ha...

HOLY GHOST

And it hit in... In five seconds, it hit my railing twice and I'm going, that's not accident... that's a sign. God is talking to me, cause I'm meditating that I want this lightning, and I emailed this healer in Vancouver... saying "and you're going to think I'm nuts" but you showed me this meditation to visualize my nervous system getting restarted and I said my railing was just hit by lightning but not once... twice. A month later a girlfriend. She'll come once a week. She's sitting here. I swear to God, right in front of my computer screen, there was a horizontal lightning... like this... about seventeen inches and I'm going... did you just see that? She goes... see what? The lightning that just... OK, God... OK... just I gotta... I gotta change my meditation cause... I'm going to get hit by lightning bolt.

UNIVERSAL MOM

Ha... ha... ha... ha...

HOLY GHOST

We're getting... we're getting a little too close here.

UNIVERSAL MOM

Now I want to ask you about... my book. Should I go ahead with it or not?

HOLY GHOST

Absolutely. Please do. Please do. And I'll help you with it. I'll help you... may I ask what your book is about?

UNIVERSAL MOM

It's about my daughter's experience. The years that she was ill and the lack of support for her within the health care system. And her dad.

HOLY GHOST

Think about your book. And you'll get an offer... you'll get an offer. Think about that and pick out any seven cards.

UNIVERSAL MOM

I'm not a... a writer who makes up dialo... you know dialogue and setting and that. It's really... it's a stark account of a... what happened. Interspersed with some of her poetry and mine.

HOLY GHOST

Also... you know... and I... to me... that's a story that has to be told. That's a story that has to be told. You'll have spiritual guidance to write that book.

UNIVERSAL MOM

I... Danielle has been spiritually present to me at times since her death.

HOLY GHOST

I believe you. I believe you.

UNIVERSAL MOM

And I... I just haven't been as aware of that in the last little while. And I do... I do wonder if she'll be there for me.

HOLY GHOST

She will be... I'll tell you something. If you have her picture... I'm sure you do. This is how to get her to visit more often. Light a candle. Put some flowers. They don't have to be expensive. Little flowers and her picture and light a candle and that will draw spirit loved ones to you. I know that... a and I'll tell you... and it's painful for me to do this. I have uh photo albums over there... but... my teachers would say when you sit with the photo album. I know… I'm like the waterworks. I'm like Niagara Falls… I'm… I'm just… I'm very emotional. And they said that your… they don't want us to cry, but when we look through the photo albums, they'll come and sit beside us. And I believe that. Or…

UNIVERSAL MOM

Well, I'm not one to cry.

HOLY GHOST

Well I am… oh my God. My mother, when she was in the hospital, she said… "and if they put me on life support don't let THE HOLY GHOST". she said… "you know how our HOLY GHOST." I said "Mom… if you were gunna go into heaven, I'm not going to keep you here to suffer."

UNIVERSAL MOM

Oh, I was trained not to cry. Nothing…, that I don't wish I could do, but I don't.

HOLY GHOST

Well, hang around me and you will…

UNIVERSAL MOM

That… spiritual is interesting. I had a few wedding dreams lately…that have sort of concerned me. Where dad and Danielle were there… I just didn't know who… it was for.

HOLY GHOST

Like a happy… happy wedding?

UNIVERSAL MOM

No, oh… well. No… I think it was a symbolic death dream. But anyway…

HOLY GHOST

No, I've heard that. Because years ago I had a wedding dream. And my neighbor… my next door neighbor said that means somebody's going to pass away. I never… but… that's in some dream books. That's where…

UNIVERSAL MOM

Ya. Well, and you don't pick anything… pick anything up on that?

HOLY GHOST

No I don't feel it's anybody… right now.

UNIVERSAL MOM

M-hmmm.

HOLY GHOST

Right now. But I will say… when you write your book. Not if… but when… You'll look back at the sorrow that was, but this card also means that the sorrow… you can look in the past but look to the future with hope and happiness.

UNIVERSAL MOM

Ya.

HOLY GHOST

And I'll tell you something. When you look for an agent, you'll hear back from one. So I don't know if you know anybody, but I can help you with that.

UNIVERSAL MOM

No. I haven't had much success.

HOLY GHOST

Well, I'm going… I'll give you my email and I'll… I'll tell you something strange. Back in December, I know how hard it is to get an agent. So I went to a website called agentinquiry.com. And it… they list all agents, if you can email them with your proposal. You can email them. You don't have to send the whole book, you don't have to send your proposal. You just… it will say… and they accept lett… emails. And they'll put their email address there. I'll give you my email address and I'll send you… But I will help you because you're definitely gunna hear back. Definitely will. And again the balance will come in. With your writing… with your new organization, and your writing. I get my mom saying you're going to do this… I should do this… I should take my mom's advice. She said you're going to settle into a writing routine……… So say if you have an outline already. Or say if you… say… I'll write ninety minutes a day from eleven o'clock in the morning till twelve thirty and then I'll break from like…

UNIVERSAL MOM

I have an original draft but it's a… needs to go back…

HOLY GHOST

How long is it?

UNIVERSAL MOM

Oh, it's not that long. You know, in my pages… a couple of hundred with… with poetry.

HOLY GHOST

Well, that's good. That's good.

UNIVERSAL MOM

You know… but… there's a lot that I need to… fill in upon reflection. And also in terms of information I've got that could be useful to families going through it.

HOLY GHOST

And you will. Now I'm not trying to make you feel better but you will make money from that book. But it's not about the money. I know that…

UNIVERSAL MOM

M-hmmm.

HOLY GHOST

And you know that too. You know that too.

UNIVERSAL MOM

Ya, I was going to originally donate it to the centre, but…

HOLY GHOST

Give it to yourself… put it in… hey you know what…

UNIVERSAL MOM

Ha… ha… ha that's what my son…

HOLY GHOST

Give it to yourself.

MAYOR

Just travel a lot.

UNIVERSAL MOM

We could use it to pay off our debt?

HOLY GHOST

Give it to your husband and that can be his windfall. Surprise money.

UNIVERSAL MOM

Oh well… that could be it… you could… Hey [SHEPHERD] you'll vacuum and I'll write.

HOLY GHOST

That's… that's doable. That's doable but you know… you will have a happy marriage. You definitely will. And once more… your Wish card… you will write that book…

UNIVERSAL MOM

My goodness!!.

HOLY GHOST

And that's the last of it… you know what… there's seventy-eight cards in this deck. And for you to even get that once… and for him [SHEPHERD] to get the same card and for you to get it twice. That's no accident. That's no coincidence.

UNIVERSAL MOM

Oh that's neat!! ha… ha

HOLY GHOST

But I do get… and I'll tell you something. And I'll tell you when… I get my mom saying that in view… but when you start there's something about January 2009, where I feel… where… what do they call it… when they have Summer books which is too late for you and I right now. The book can't come out now for the Summer. Or there's September… like… for Christmas and then there's January publishing and I feel January for you.

UNIVERSAL MOM

My…

HOLY GHOST

Can you place an Agnes? Hang onto that. That's an old fashion name but I…

UNIVERSAL MOM

I have an aunt Agnes. You know… hmm… just trying to think if I know any other Agnes.

HOLY GHOST

Well you may hear of… hear from her. I don't know if she's on earth or if she's… she's…

UNIVERSAL MOM

Ya.

HOLY GHOST

You may hear from her out of the clear blue sky. I just hear her name.

UNIVERSAL MOM

We went to stay with them in Newf… in a… Nova Scotia.

SHEPHERD

Nova Scotia I think.

UNIVERSAL MOM

Ya and… she has a… she has a son. Married. In this area. I think so. Anyway… Agnes, that sort of covers a lot of ground……… [SHEPHERD] Can you think of anything that?. oh… ha… ha… ha… [MAYOR] should I ask her what's going to happen to the centre? What's going to happen to Danielle's Place?

HOLY GHOST

Think about that. You'll hear more. You'll hear more. Or I'll say… I get my mom saying activity and action. Activity and action. Where is it… it's not… in… Tor…

UNIVERSAL MOM

Burlington

HOLY GHOST

Oh, OK.

UNIVERSAL MOM

There were six-hundred… people… used our resources in the first two and a half years.

HOLY GHOST

Wow!!.

UNIVERSAL MOM

Teens. The average young woman is fighting an eating disorder for eight to ten years. The delusions of the mind are very hard to get out… It takes a long time to get them out of there.

HOLY GHOST

And one friend with bulimia said to me something… she… whatever about it… it was about control or something… I don't know. But… in a million years… and she looked like… who's the girl?. Geena… Geena Davis or something

UNIVERSAL MOM

Oh ya, the red head.

HOLY GHOST

… in "A League of their Own".

UNIVERSAL MOM

Oh yes!.

HOLY GHOST

A League of their Own. Well… look… she's… gorgeous. And I've gone… I can't… I just…

[95]

UNIVERSAL MOM

You wouldn't know.

HOLY GHOST

I wouldn't know. I didn't know.

UNIVERSAL MOM

Ya.

HOLY GHOST

And people say. People when they see me they go… is THE HOLY GHOST anorexic? she's so thin. No, I'm not… And they say oh no… not if you saw THE HOLY GHOST eat. Because I was at Mandarin for lunch and I sat for ninety minutes. I just shoveled it in. And I try to gain weight but I can't… obvious I can't gain it… I wish I could.

UNIVERSAL MOM

Ya… ya… some people just are wired.

HOLY GHOST

Ya and…

UNIVERSAL MOM

There's a lot… there's a real genetic quality.

HOLY GHOST

It is. I believe… I believe that.

UNIVERSAL MOM

So you don't get a real sense that the centre's going to fold this year or not?

HOLY GHOST

Think about that. Pick out any seven cards.

UNIVERSAL MOM

Because I sort of get the feeling that they're not going to be able to raise enough monies to keep going forward.

HOLY GHOST

I'm going to take that one because you almost took it.

UNIVERSAL MOM

OK.

HOLY GHOST

My teacher say if it falls off the table… or if it almost sticks together or if it sticks together… take it.

UNIVERSAL MOM

How are we doing for time for you, sonny? [MAYOR]

MAYOR

We're good.

HOLY GHOST

And I'll tell you when you said about that… that's the balance and you know how you say justice is blind. But and I will say… I don't know… I'll say… that represents also the stress between… if you want to say the politics or the powers at be or whatever… the… the… a little petty jealousies…

UNIVERSAL MOM

Ha.! ha.!

HOLY GHOST

And…

UNIVERSAL MOM

That hits it on the head…

HOLY GHOST

You know… and… and…

UNIVERSAL MOM

Politics wasn't ever my thing. You have to be willing first to confront and you have to be willing to be ruthless.

HOLY GHOST

I can't be ruthless… I can't be ruthless… I can't. Do you know when I first saw Survivor, I thought it was about surviving like a first… like a Boy scout. When I saw it was about… I wouldn't last two seconds… I'd be the first person thrown out… I would never last. And that's cause… I can't work… I had to work in Medicine. I could not work for a Corporation… ever… ever…. ever.

UNIVERSAL MOM

You have to… you have to have a different mindset… you know…

HOLY GHOST

But I'll tell you something. You're going to do fine. You're gunna have… and I'll tell you… you're gunna have two careers. Again, your writing but there's another organization. This… Danielle's Place will survive if everybody works as a team.

UNIVERSAL MOM

Ha… ha… ha…

HOLY GHOST

If you can, you know, like the lion tamer… crack the whip.

UNIVERSAL MOM

I'm not involved with them anymore.

HOLY GHOST

Well, they need somebody to really get them working as a team.

UNIVERSAL MOM

Well, I have somebody on the board who I think might be able to do that.

HOLY GHOST

It's not… it's not hopeless. It isn't hopeless. And this… I don't know if it's your son but there's a dark-haired man. Who will I'll say… I won't… well I'll say… you know how you say we got rescued right in the nick of time. And I do feel money is going to come in there just like… and I get my mom saying… you know when… when you have a cash float or whatever when you open up a cash… snack bar or something. You open up your float. And I do feel that it will happen. This strength… you'll have emotional strength… you know what you were saying about your fibromyalgia. You'll have emotional strength and financial strength. I feel there possibly could be two sponsors of Danielle's Place.

UNIVERSAL MOM

Yes, we need a couple of big sponsors.

HOLY GHOST

I feel that there's gunna be two.

UNIVERSAL MOM

Oh good!!.

HOLY GHOST

There's gunna be two.

UNIVERSAL MOM

That's... that's... that would be good.

HOLY GHOST

I can help you out with that too. And... I'll say... and you know what I make Mother Teresa look like an amateur. I could... I'll just say I could be a Corporate beggar. Like what you said about what you were put here to do. I was put here to help other people and money doesn't really fascinate me. But I believe in using it for good causes. And it can work out... ya know?... I get my mom saying it'll start slowly but the money will trickle in. I feel there's going to be a benefit. Like a benefit night or a special event night for the... for the centre. Again you'll hear good news about it. I don't feel it's gone forever. I don't feel that going yet. Because I feel... you know how they say... in the 11th hour... the sun broke through the clouds. And I do feel that you're gunna...

UNIVERSAL MOM

OK.

HOLY GHOST

Gunna hear something... you're gunna also know somebody by the name of Gail... G... a... i... l. A female Gail that is going to be very beneficial.

UNIVERSAL MOM

Oh, good!!.

HOLY GHOST

So if you don't know anybody by that name...

UNIVERSAL MOM

I do. I am not too involved.

HOLY GHOST

I feel that there's gunna be some... you know how you say some fresh air...

UNIVERSAL MOM

Uh huh.

HOLY GHOST

Breathed in or you know how we were talking about oxygen... somebody with oxygen. Where there's gunna be fresh air breathed in to the centre. There will be.

UNIVERSAL MOM

Oh Good!!! Mm...

HOLY GHOST

Ya I don't feel… and I'll tell you something too… I do feel that your daughter will come through to perk things… to percolate like coffee…

UNIVERSAL MOM

She did when I was there. Ya.

HOLY GHOST

Well she can… she can see what's going on.

UNIVERSAL MOM

Ya, I know that.

HOLY GHOST

Definitely.

UNIVERSAL MOM

Ya… I… I wouldn't mind having some justice. Ha… ha…

HOLY GHOST

Oh I believe in… there is a God… I'm telling you I know there is…

UNIVERSAL MOM

It's Timmie's turn now. Tim?!.

MAYOR

I think dad wants to leave.

SHEPHERD

Are we done?

MAYOR

You're done.

UNIVERSAL MOM

Ha… ha… ha…

EXIT CAROLYN THE UNIVERSAL MOM, SERGE THE SHEPHERD, THE HOLY GHOST AND TIM THE MAYOR

ACT III

SCENE III

05/14/2008

ENTER CAROLYN THE UNIVERSAL MOM, SERGE THE SHEPHERD, THE HOLY GHOST AND TIM THE MAYOR

HOLY GHOST

And I'll say… where would you like to… finally you're here. Can you believe it? What would you like to tune into?

MAYOR

Ah, let's start with career. It's the biggest thing on my mind.

HOLY GHOST

OK… well I get my mom saying you're going places. You're going places. And so think about that and pick up any seven cards……… Do they look good?

MAYOR

They look good.

HOLY GHOST

He's going to read his own cards.

UNIVERSAL MOM

Ha… ha… ha… ha… ha… ha…

HOLY GHOST

The Spirits are about to see… hey I can't believe it.

UNIVERSAL MOM

Another Wish card?

HOLY GHOST

Ah I can't believe it… it runs in the family.

UNIVERSAL MOM

There ya go…

HOLY GHOST

Well I'll tell you what… this card came up for your mom too. Change is coming but it's not disastrous… it's actually positive change. This represents a new beginning. So I'll say… whatever your career has been… it's like well… that was like the first 3rd of my life. 1st quarter of my life. And that's that, but now a whole new ballgame. It's a whole new ballgame. And again like your mother, you'll have that spiritual influence. Where when you put it out… and sometimes you think… oh am I alone? No you're not alone. Like… your sister will come along to your mom. But your angels are very… you have three angels around you. You have three… and I'll tell you something I get my mom saying. When you walk and I don't mean that you have to walk for exercise but when you walk, you're going to get some of your answers. You may start out the door and not have a clue… now what the heck…, I did this…step one… step two…, step three… now what am I going to do? And I just get your angels saying walk and we'll walk with you. And as you go out and walk the answers are going to come down right on time.

MAYOR

That makes sense.

HOLY GHOST

Well I'll tell you something. You'll have a new location. I don't know if you want one but I do feel a move for you OK. Later on in the year. Again I was just telling your mom about team work. You'll have that team work. OK, where sometimes where you wanna…, you wanna make an impression. But, and I'll say it this way…, I'll say for example Steven Spielberg. He went… I think to Universal or whatever but he had his team and so will you. So again you'll balance it out. And I just get Spirit saying it's a fresh start. It's a whole new ballgame. We're talking about a League of their Own. And I get my mom saying you'll be in a league of your own. But you're going to put a lot of hours in. And I'll tell you something…

MAYOR

That's a given.

HOLY GHOST

I get like... an... a twelve to fourteen hour days. You know? It's as if you were a plastic surgeon. Doing your thing. Where you'll put in extremely long hours but you will get what you're wishing for. Again you picked out that Wish card. So I'd say don't... you know it's like blowing out your candles on birthday... OK... don't tell us. But you're going in the right direction. You really are. And I know you want to go into a creative field. And I'll tell you a company I hear with you... and I don't know anybody there. But I hear... and I'll say this into the microphone. You'll know people... and I think their called Miramar... Miramar not IMAX but Miramar. Well there's something at Miramar. You know somebody at Miramar? Do I have the name right.

MAYOR

No but you have the industry right. I just went for a job interview with Cineplex. Same thing as an IMAX. Actually I think they operate IMAX.

HOLY GHOST

Well I'll tell you Garth Dabrinsky interviewed THE HOLY GHOST to write... this is years ago... so they call me to interview me as a writer... Blah... blah... blah... blah... blah... blah Years later in Toronto. They were going to do this show ... blah and then they didn't hire me. And I... I can remember standing and thinking I could just... I could die right now. So upset. I'll never write again... you know being that discouraged. Because oh... I went all through the interview and his assistant goes... well, you know. We don't really need a writer and I said well why did you call me down there... and she said... well, I liked your resume, so I wanted to meet you but there's no novel to adapt this... there's no adaptation, so we don't really need you......... So you call me in... got me really hyped up and now I'm crashing down. But you will not have the same experience. My mother's saying you'll come out much better than my HOLY GHOST did. Where... but I did pick up to write again. But it hit me... the rejection was just devastating. But I learned something... never to take it to heart. Never take it personally. But I get where... you'll get chosen... you know how you say there's a handful. Like the inner circle. The inner circle. That I feel very strongly... that... like when they open door and say come on in. Or if you go to New York... and... come on in... come on in. You'll be there. You'll be there. Definitely......... You're going to know a Louis. And I don't know if he's at that company now, but hang onto that name. I do feel Louis... Louey is his first name. That... OK... have they asked for a script from you?

MAYOR

Not for... not for writing.

HOLY GHOST

Someday... I get where you're gunna... you're gunna have a script. Your script. And even though... whatever... whatever... department you enter in. Somewhere down the road over the next two years. Like from now until 2010 where... I feel that... it's your script. It's your film. And you're the boss. And I'm not saying that to make you feel good, but you're the director... you're into producing... into the... I'm not... I'm not where I started. There's a lot of people who started on Wall street as a mail clerk and they own this company. And I feel the same vibration with you. Where you start at... is going to be a very quick rise to the top. But I do get where... I get you signing. I get you signing the contract and the offer being made. Absolutely. Absolutely. I feel that very strongly......... Do you know somebody that owns... owns a chain of grocery... of coffee shops. Hang onto that. You're going to know somebody. You don't know... I'll say you don't know them yet but that's a little sign that you're on your way. And I'll say that the person that has that... whether they own Starbucks or a couple of Second Cups. That... what that... they call the shots. I get my mom saying and you'll be... give yourself time... don't put yourself down. Like pace yourself... give yourself credit. That in time you'll be calling the shots. You'll get to do what you really want to do. You definitely will. You'll also know an Andrew. I feel that's his first name......... But I'll tell you something. I feel you're going to know Andrew Alexander from Second City. He's the man that owns Second City. He... I think he lives in Chicago now. Speaking of Bob Fosse in Chicago. We weren't talking about Chicago. He has the Second City here, but now he lives in Chicago but I feel your paths will cross. You'll know people in the theatre... in film but also in the theatre. It's different divisions......... What else would you like to tune into?

MAYOR
Well supposedly. I'm going to get married. So...

UNIVERSAL MOM / HOLY GHOST
Ha... ha... ha...

MAYOR
Let's focus on that.

HOLY GHOST
Think about this wonderful person and pick out any seven cards. You may meet her at work. You never know.

MAYOR
How many is that... five...?

HOLY GHOST
Two more......... Oh my God...

UNIVERSAL MOM
The Wish card again?

HOLY GHOST
I can't... I can't believe it.

UNIVERSAL MOM

Ha… ha… ha…

HOLY GHOST

You'll meet her. You'll meet her. I'll tell you something. She out… I'll say it this way…
she'll be an extremely smart woman. Extreme… and I'll tell you something else… she may
work… and I was just thinking about law… she may work in the legal depart… she may be
an entertainment lawyer. Remember I said that… Mark my words. That… I feel she… I feel
somehow you'll connect with her through your career. I won't just say job. But… either
entertainment lawyer or Spirit… my guardian angel is saying acquisitions. Like certain
lawyers get… they acquire a script or they have to options a script or option it. Definitely a
love match. But not just… you know sometimes we just look at the physical but I'll say
you'll be body… mind… spirit… emotionally… that Spirit says…

UNIVERSAL MOM

Hurrah!

HOLY GHOST

It's not just… you know… it's not just infatuation. But I'll say one thing that you'll like is that
she also has a career path. She's not out to use you. Some people think… a ha… you
know… I'll live off of him. Ya know he'll work and I'll stay home or what not. But no…
she'll have… she'll already have a career. She absolutely will. And I will say there's property
for you coming up. And I'll say… I'll go into 2010.

UNIVERSAL MOM

Poverty?

HOLY GHOST

Property……… Ya… what did you think I said?

UNIVERSAL MOM

Poverty.

HOLY GHOST

No… no… no… that's in the past… this card… is the card that represents wealth…
prosperity and investing not just time but your money too. Like… ya know… sometimes it
goes through your hands like water. Here today and gone tomorrow but you'll hang onto it.
You'll hang onto it……… Again I get this female around you. Who works in acquisitions.
Hold onto that. Hold onto that. Again your mom had the same card… it's about looking
back what I came through… what I've gone through. The trials… the tests… I passed them
all. And… and the path ahead of you is filled with hope and optimism……… You'll also…
I'll say… when you… when you are at Cineplex. You will… feel very at ease. I get… you
know how we were talking about the Board Room. I get the stock… the share holders

around you. So they may give you in time... I don't know if they've given you stock options but I feel that's coming. Hold onto that. Hold onto that. But I do feel... that... a female is coming in... first the career... first, let the job offer... I'm signing it. Then when you have that... question is settled and answered... then the growth... then the girl... then the other person... the other half... your better half comes in. And you will get what you're wishing for. And I'll tell you something. She'll shop... but she's not a shopaholic. Like my sister. She's like... ya... like the total opposite of me. But I do get where you're going to be... you're going to be... like when you get there and your ground... and you will be grounded. But you'll be noticed too......... You'll know somebody with the last name of Clark. C... I... a... r... k. I feel they've been there for awhile. And I just get where... you know when they say... a brother... we're like brothers. You know and we'll be tight and it's somebody is a real friend. Not just a fair weather friend but somebody you can trust. Absolutely.

MAYOR

OK. I'll check their employee list.

HOLY GHOST

Do that... do that. And you know if somebody comes in for an interview and their name is Clark... keep an eye... keep an eye on him.

MAYOR

OK.

HOLY GHOST

Because I feel that... but I do get you'll also travel with the company. So hold onto that. Remember that. What else would you like to know?

UNIVERSAL MOM

Australia...

MAYOR

I'm being fed something. [UNIVERSAL MOM]

UNIVERSAL MOM

Ask about Australia?

MAYOR

Ya sure why not... what's the deal with Australia?

HOLY GHOST

Does it come up a lot? Or is it... ?

MAYOR

I'm just always thinking about it.

HOLY GHOST

I think there's a reason for that. My grandpa used to have a dish... a little candy dish with pink candies... Winter green and they were stamped Canada. And like, when I was three years old... I used to take it and say I'm going to Canada. And I had my mind made up at three. I knew as a kid I was coming to Canada. So maybe it's the same with you and Australia. For some... spiritual connection. It's a very spiritual place I think. And it's a very healing spot too... there's a lot of...

UNIVERSAL MOM

Free air?

HOLY GHOST

Aboriginal healers. Ya... think about Australia and pick any seven cards......... You didn't sneak a peek... ha... ha! You'll travel... there it is. Travel card and you know what... your wife will be with you. She... and I'll say dark... darker hair... darker hair and there you go. Again I'll say the struggle... or dissatisfaction is in the past. In the past. In the past. But you're going... you're going to meet this girl. That is in the legal profession. Ya... so... you may meet this girl through a blonde. But I feel the one that you marry will have dark hair. You'll get to Australia. But this card... doesn't mean death... it means a transition that you're going through into a different phase of your life. Just like I was telling your mom and dad that they're going through a different phase. But I do feel between now and 2010 you'll get to... and I'll tell you what else I hear. You're going to get to Ireland too. And even if you don't know anybody in Ireland... hang onto that.

MAYOR

Ireland... I already been.

HOLY GHOST

Well, you're going back. What..., they didn't deport you? I'm only kidding. I'm only kidding. You're going back. What part of Ireland were you?

MAYOR

... near Shannon Airport. So west.

HOLY GHOST

And I'll say you'll spend more time there. You'll spend more time. Australia and Ireland. Oh, you'll make and I'll say..., it'll be, Australia first and Ireland on the way home. But... and I'll tell you something... I get..., I want to go into the vibration of Cineplex. And I hear that they're going to bend the rules for you. Remember that. Where..., they won't break them but they'll bend them. So maybe let's say they have for a particular program and it'll be there you have to be an employee for five years but… they'll bend the rules that you'll qualify for this particular program or a benefit. Like a bene… like some… companies have… we'll pay for your education… if you want to do this class or that class we'll pay for it. There's something about Cineplex… where they'll go that extra mile for you. But I get… you'll get to Sydney. You'll get to Sydney. It won't be just Sydney but… you'll get there. You definitely will.

MAYOR

Great.

HOLY GHOST

Can you place a Diana on earth?

MAYOR

No.

HOLY GHOST

Hang onto that. I feel she's coming in soon. She's not here yet but she'll be here soon. And I feel that good… I don't know if that's the lawyer. But maybe you meet the lawyer through this girl Diana. Absolutely……… Somebody you know… I don't know if you know… but somebody around you is going to deal… and when I say antiques… I get silver… like, say silver from old rail road cars or old hotels. Antiques and silver. Hang onto that. You'll know somebody around you… not necessarily you… doing a documentary about that. So… but somehow… but… it will link with you and I just get where… when that happens, it's that a busy time in your life. But you're definitely on the right track. Well… I'm like… and Spirit has a sense of humor too. Where a train goes on a track and they're saying you're going to be on the right track. Absolutely.

MAYOR

OK… great.

HOLY GHOST

What else would you like to tune in? You're so calm. God… we should clone you. There's so many people stressed out. What would you like to tune into?

MAYOR

… no, I'm good. [UNIVERSAL MOM] Unless you want to feed me anything else.

UNIVERSAL MOM / SHEPHERD

Ha… ha… ha… ha… ha…

HOLY GHOST

Oh I feel… I feel where there's going to be somewhere that you're at that where there's a fireplace. I don't know if this is… a location… like a shoot… like say like a film… TV shoot. But I do get a fireplace but it's… a red brick fireplace. But next to it… off to the side there's like a green… like a sea foam green kitchen where tiles… instead of being white or anything else but Spirit is saying you're on location. You're on location. Hang onto that.

MAYOR

OK.

HOLY GHOST

Oh, you're so calm.

UNIVERSAL MOM

OK.

MAYOR

I'm good.

HOLY GHOST

[UNIVERSAL MOM] You know what I'll give you my email. I wanna… I wanna… send you some… a couple of writers sites. I do feel… I feel… I'm interested in your book. I don't think it's an accident that you and I met… I met your son. I really honest to God feel out of all the people I met I was supposed to meet you. And no offense to your son… I don't… or the two people that were here last night or to your wonderful husband. There's a reason why I met you. There's a reason and I'll tell you something… I work with a lot of corporate sponsors. And I'll be more than happy to get them to write a cheque for your organization. Trust me on this one. I'll find you money. I'm an expert. My mother…

UNIVERSAL MOM

Well, I no longer have all the data because I'm not current.

HOLY GHOST

Well, I'll help you. I'll help you. Because I don't believe in asking for the universe. And don't be afraid to email me……… Here's my email.

UNIVERSAL MOM

Ha… ha…

HOLY GHOST

But you know what. I don't treat people like that……… And uhh… what goes around comes around.

EXIT CAROLYN THE UNIVERSAL MOM, SERGE THE SHEPHERD, THE HOLY GHOST AND TIM THE MAYOR

ACT IV

SCENE I

05/27/2008

ENTER THE INSIGHT AND TIM THE MAYOR

INSIGHT

Are you comfortable like that or would you like to move this out a little bit or…

MAYOR

I'm comfortable.

INSIGHT

Ya? OK……… Now Tim. Timothy. How do you spell your last name?

MAYOR

M… a… y…

INSIGHT

She just said it quickly and I didn't get it. M… a… y…

MAYOR

e… u… r.

INSIGHT

Is it Mayor?

MAYOR

Mayeur.

INSIGHT

Mayeur? Much nicer. Very good. Let me guess. Is it French? Ha… ha… ha… ha… ha…

MAYOR

A little bit ya.

INSIGHT

Just a little French. Mayeur. Much nicer. OK and today is May…

MAYOR

27th.

INSIGHT

Thank you, honey. Now before we move into the reading… what I'd like to do if you don't mind. It doesn't take long at all. I've got water on a pot. If you pick something to drink, because I know my throat will get as dry as you can imagine when I'm talking. I'll write your name here too. Timothy Mayeur. Ya.

MAYOR

Peppermint tea.

INSIGHT

Wow, that's popular today. Ya me too. I've been drinking… OK……… Wonderful. Think I put the day on the back. Oh bad. I'm terrible with dates. In terms of remembering what day it is. Oh my God ,I'm horrible. Last week I'm swearing it was Thur… it was Friday and it was Thursday. Bad… bad. OK. I'll be right back. So you said peppermint tea?

MAYOR

Yup.

INSIGHT

Do you like anything with it? Or anything in it?

MAYOR

Some sugar.

INSIGHT

OK I'll put that on the side because that's a personal thing. OK. So you can do your own sugar.

MAYOR

OK.

INSIGHT

Because I don't want to be responsible for that one. Nope. I'll leave that to you.

MAYOR

OK.

INSIGHT

Hiya! I'll be right back......... OK. Hiya one and hiya two. I'm going to get your sugar too.

MAYOR

Oh it's fine.

INSIGHT

Don't worry it's right here. Don't worry it's not that far......... There's a little bit. I'm a bit of a perfectionist. There we go. I love drinking a tea. Oh it's going to drive me crazy isn't it? There we go. Anyways, it's nice to meet you.

MAYOR

You too.

INSIGHT

And... Timothy...

MAYOR

M-hmm.

INSIGHT

I'm just going to give this to you. I do not read handwriting at all ,but yet I still ask that people who come for readings... if you don't mind... you can just give your signature. Your normal everyday signature.

MAYOR

Alright well...

INSIGHT

Is it funny?

MAYOR

You'll have fun with the way I hold a pen.

INSIGHT

Ha… ha… which way? That's OK. That's kinda cool. I betcha if I did read handwriting there would be a lot to that story. But I don't see. If I did, there would be a story here for sure. I'm sure there would be. Well I just… I used to be one of those people who signed perfectly. And now I just do this… that's why I had to grow up. Ha… ha… ha……… You. Yours is so grown up. Just very neat.

MAYOR

Ya, it represents me nicely. Simple yet difficult to read.

INSIGHT

Ha… ha… but you know what? We're all kind of difficult to read. I never think that those who pretend to be so simple and easy on the outside to read. They're not. Every one of us… I…very multi-dimensional. And very… very unique in our own way. Sometimes the most outgoing people have the most strangest insides ha… ha… he… he… he. I'm very interested. I learn more each day but I'm still only a child of the universe. I don't want to sound too hippy though here. Ya know? I'm not really a hippy. In fact I'm probably s… you know people come to see me or they're regulars and they think I'm going to be this weird person. Well I'm weird, but not like that. I'm quite grounded. I do believe that… you know… I very much believe in the physical world and that which is here. And I think it's very important to focus on what you had before you and to make the best of your life in all circumstances no matter how difficult or how easy.

MAYOR

Of course.

INSIGHT

But… oh that's interesting… it looks like a T… a… l… your… your signature it's kinda cool……… Now I will talk a little bit about the session today, Timothy or… sometimes I might call you Tim. Sometimes I might call you Timothy. I won't pay attention to which way I go. OK?

MAYOR

I go the same way.

INSIGHT

OK, cool.

MAYOR

Depends if I want to feel like I'm young or old.

INSIGHT

Ha… ha… I mean well which one do you think is old… Timothy?

MAYOR

No.

INSIGHT

Tim… you think Tim is old? Oh really?

MAYOR

Yup.

INSIGHT

Ya, that's like Robert and Bob.

MAYOR

All kid's names get abbreviated. Right?

INSIGHT

Ya that's true. My husband you know… I never understood why people went from Robert to Bob. Because Robert is so easy and so… I mean… how… what do you want to shorten here. So I said to my husband… I said I like Bob, but you know I like Robert too. Why did you change it? But here you go… oh you can't see anything here anymore… used to be.

MAYOR

It's easier to fill out paperwork. The less letters you have.

INSIGHT

Now Timothy, what is your middle name?

MAYOR

Michael.

INSIGHT

Michael? M… i… c… h… is it a… e or e… a?

MAYOR

A… e.

INSIGHT

I always do that. OK. Michael. Mayeur. Now just a little bit of information before we begin OK?

MAYOR

Ya.

INSIGHT

How I receive information is in a few different ways it's not ahh… you know like… see… television. I love TV. I love it. But you know how TV is. If you've ever watched Ghost Whisperer. That's a great example of… you know… how people do what I do. Television's version. You know? I mean it's very entertaining. Nonetheless it's very interesting and entertaining for some. You know some people like the show. It's number one. People must be watching it… ha… ha…

MAYOR

It's number one?

INSIGHT

Well, it's up there ya.

MAYOR

In a city?

INSIGHT

In a city… ha… in all of the… in all of the ratings. It's up there. Ya know. Here we go. But it's not my cup of tea. But you know… hey…all the power to it.

MAYOR

Ya.

INSIGHT

And a… but it's not really like that in terms of receiving information at all. Because… that show for example you know when you're reading for somebody then you see everybody perfectly in the room. And so… complete bodies like you are here and I am here. And we just… but you know… they just can hear every single word that that person is saying and they can see them at all times perfectly in the physical world. I mean if it was like that it would be amazing but it would also drive you nuts. I mean literally. But how actually the information is received and at least from the… from my perspective a… the people that I talk to who also do this. And some of which are very well known. For example James Van Praagh I thought he was very well known for many years. He still is actually. Also… I don't know if you've heard of Rosemary Altea. She's huge. She's in the UK. Phenomenal. But a lot of people who do this kind of work and some people are just a little better at it than others……… And of course not to put the others down but really every time I read for somebody, it's like a new chapter. It's like a new experience for me and you know just like the person coming for the reading I'm nervous. Because I question… is this going to be the time I don't receive the information? Is this going to be that time that nothing connects. I always worry that. If you care that is… you worry that he… he… you know if you don't give a shit I'm sure you don't care. So it doesn't matter. But if you do care and I honestly probably my husband would attest I care too much. And that's a problem a little bit. But you know what... I can't change it. I tried... ha... ha... ha... doesn't work. So I just deal with it and I always hope that every reading I do is going to be a good one. Now of course it depends on the person I'm reading for and their judgments. You know? Thankfully ahh... thankfully I would say more often than not... way more often thankfully. I think I could probably count less than five. Probably three times where it didn't go the way I wanted it to go in a perfect world. But you know... there's a lot of reasons for that and I don't take them all on myself. But I do believe if a person does this job and has the ability and comes with an open heart and an open mind and an open spirit and in... shall I say... ahh... with the right intentions. I think like anything else... and you care but I think I... nine times out of ten you'll have a better experience than a bad one. Now of course, everybody's bar is different. You know some people have their bar way too impossibly high. Because it isn't a clear perfect connection. It just isn't. It never will be. Quite honestly because we're in the physical world! OK... ha... ha... so reality check for everybody.

MAYOR

Yup.

INSIGHT

Of course, Spirit is in the spirit world. And because of that our vibrations are on different frequencies. And because of that information isn't a constant thread. And it's not like the timing is exactly perfect. And it's not like a Q and A. You know it's almost like just kinda feel... and see... and we hope and pray... and the intensity and try... see what happens. I do my best to interpret the information. Of course it's not like a type-written... you know. Read it. You know... OK... I'm saying word for word what it said. It's like my own translation. Or my own in... ahh... my own... ahh... belief in terms of what it means. Or kinda like saying to me in some way. I do ask questions to validate the information. So if I ask if you have twelve children, but let's hope not. I'm teasing... otherwise...

MAYOR

Not that I know of.

INSIGHT

We'll start going to you know... the church and start doing our prayers for you and hope that you're going to be OK. But... we really... what I really try to do... I just try to do the best interpretation possible at all times.

MAYOR

OK.

INSIGHT

But it's not perfect. And I think we have to keep that very... very... very much on our mind.

MAYOR

And being a perfectionist that doesn't bother you?

INSIGHT

It's hard… he… he… it's hard. You got it. Now you got it. But I think that's why I do generally pretty OK. Or you know. I'm pretty modest I think. I never want to be Madame Gloat. Madame… you know… oh I'm just so good or I'm so gifted. I love these people I meet and they do what I do and they're going… oh I'm so gifted. You know… they talk like that about themselves. That makes me nauseous. Because I never want to be that person. That doesn't mean that I think badly about myself… you know… I just don't… I don't like hearing people go on about themselves like that. And I think people who try too hard to… to pretend or act like they're so… with it. You know… I think that they have probably you know… they got to work on that a little bit. I think… you know… we can believe in… what we do and follow the path that we believe we're meant to without having to push it on everybody all the time… you know? Just do good work and be proud of yourself. That's my attitude and you know… and if you make a mistake… if you did the best you could it's all you could do. You know? That's all you can do in life. Hello… hello……… OK. So this is going to be a mix of core psychic… mediumship… whatever else is out there in the universe so to speak. That's OK with you?

MAYOR

Yup.

INSIGHT

Don't tell me too much.

MAYOR

Do you like pictures?

INSIGHT

No, don't tell me nothing.

MAYOR

OK.

INSIGHT

Don't tell me nothing at all please. Like… I… I don't read from pictures.

MAYOR

Oh you don't?

INSIGHT

No. I read actually from energy. From mind thought. Ahh… in that way.

MAYOR

Alright.

INSIGHT

Actually physical things can throw me off.

MAYOR

OK.

INSIGHT

It's almost like telephone readings. People go… oh… you know… telephone readings probably aren't as good or whatever. I can imagine thinking that. And years ago I probably would have thought that. But actually… there the same. Because you know… I'm… I'm honest… I say sometimes actually physical readings can be more distracting. So not anymore… hell with it… I'm over it. Ha… ha… ha…

MAYOR

That's good.

INSIGHT

However I received information you know. We'll be here for at least an hour. But probably a little over… like an hour and a half. Anywhere up to an hour and a half. Are you OK with that?

MAYOR

Do you have enough time for that because I was late?

INSIGHT

I do. I have eight… eight… eight fifteen to eight thirty would be probably the latest I could do it.

MAYOR

OK.

INSIGHT

Is that OK with you? But of course we go by what's available. If there's less available than it would be shorter. You see. But I don't like to limit myself in advance.

MAYOR

Yup.

INSIGHT

Is that OK with you?

MAYOR

That's perfect.

INSIGHT

OK good. And… near the end if you have any… areas or whatever… that you want me to look at a little bit more… so that's fine with me. I don't mind at all. And … there's something else… well, it was formed in my memory… I'm telling you… and I'm starting to whoa… wake up there. There's something I wanted to say. Gosh I think I say too many things… maybe that's it… getting away from me. Gosh… where did it go?

MAYOR

Maybe it will show up later.

INSIGHT

Ya, where'd it go? Hello… did you take it? Ha… ha… ha… ha. But… sometimes I get names. Sometimes I don't. Sometimes it's more about experiences or things like that. Occurrences… experiences. But sometimes names do come through. OK? Or if not a name then perhaps the initial. Or something of that nature. OK?

MAYOR

OK.

INSIGHT

But it is almost sometimes moment to moment. It feels like that to me. Sometimes I can get feelings and personalities of people. I'm really big on personalities. I don't… I don't know what it is. I think because I'm like that in life. I'm like that in my own physical world experience. I like… I like personalities and characters in people. You know I don't always take the surface. What people deliver you or show you. I always like to feel things out more. I'm a cancerian. So you know… that's what we do. We're feeling… feeling… everything is feel… feel. You know? They drive us… they drive you crazy. I drive everyone crazy I'm sure with that. But that's how it's kinda like the spirit world as well. I like to feel things out too… a lot.

MAYOR

OK.

INSIGHT

You ready?

MAYOR

Yup. Sure am.

INSIGHT

One more sip God because I won't get another one......... And as strange as this is. If you need to go to the bathroom at any time, just let me know.

MAYOR

I'll hold it in.

INSIGHT

Don't be shy.

MAYOR

No.

INSIGHT

No. OK. OK, Timothy, let's see what we got for you......... Ya, I'm still doing the tape thing. I don't want any files. I don't want any files on anybody. I just want to help not keep anything on anybody........ Today's date is May 27th 2008. I'm here with Timothy Mayeur. This is THE INSIGHT and thank you very much for coming today. For allowing me to read for you today. I appreciate it. And I promise you as I mentioned earlier. I think I did anyway. You never know. In case I didn't I'll do it here. I will do the best reading I can for you based on the information I receive for you. Having said that I know you didn't realize that I'm not God or anything. I'm only mere mortal.

MAYOR

What?!

INSIGHT

I know… eh… it's very scary to find that out! Most people…

MAYOR

Why… what am I doing here then?!

INSIGHT

I know. You're so funny! Ha… ha… ha. You've got a sense of humor too. Ha… ha. But honestly, ya know, I am only mortal. You know… what can you do. But as a mortal I will do what I can in terms of the best reading I can for you based on the information I receive. And the best translation of that information as I can. Please understand… in terms of future events in your own physical world of experience or life… that we co-creating our experiences. This is not a disclaimer, it's just the way the universe works. It is what it is. I am doing the same in my own life. We all are. That being said that our actions… our beliefs… our emotions and whatever else that we put out there really is what we do get back. Sometimes people don't believe that. But some of the nicest people that put a lot of stuff out aren't getting back,, because we still don't believe enough in certain parts of ourselves. That we're… good enough or strong enough or we're able enough. And when we start to deal with those things then we start to see that other things start to reverberate in our direction a little bit. But really we are what we make this life very… very much. We are the creators of our own destiny. But that being said… in terms of any future events I feel for you just be basically… it feels like that your life is aiming more in this direction then say… that direction. OK. So that's all I can do. But I promise you I'll do the best I can with that as well. But we always have choices. And last but not least always and ever follow your own internal guide… your own internal wisdom as best you can. That's all one can do in one's life. If a choice or a direction feels the best… or you think it's the best… or your going over it a little bit. Then trust that it is the best. And trust that those decisions and those choices are the best ones because you think they are. They feel like they are. Or you weighed them and they just look like they are. That doesn't mean that it's a perfect outcome that you're going to get, because it was the right choice. Sometimes right choices equal tragic results. Sometimes they equal better than ever could of imagined results. But no matter what the results or decisions… trust the outcomes as being not a permanent outcome but as the necessary outcome at that time. Good… we know we can. Bad… we always question that. But no matter what… trust we didn't come here as people in the physical world to experience perfection. And we did not. Otherwise we would not be here. We came here for the challenge and experience that life brings and holds. We came here for the rollercoaster ride that is life. No one has a completely perfect existence. No matter what their circumstance is. So just trust that we are here with reason. We are here by grand design. We are part of a larger whole. There are no mistakes. We're meant to be here. We're meant to be part of this co-creative experience. And our physical world life is valuable. It is important. We are not nothing. We are everything. And we are… are… soul experience is… it necessitates this physical world experience. No matter what it presents. We are valuable. We are important and not one person is more valuable than another. Not one. We are all equal value. I'm so passionate about those things and… I get a little carried before the reading. And… everyone has to endure that. Ha… ha… ha… every single person. Let's see what's there for you honey.

MAYOR

OK.

INSIGHT

… OK. We're going to go in a lot of different directions and also mediumship because there are people in the spirit world. Definitely. Excuse me. But I… I… I'm not sure of her category to you or… you know what I mean by category? Like… ahh… the relationship to you at this point. So I just want to leave that alone just for two seconds. First I want to say to you that you're actually a very interesting guy. From the way people may… way… your way you classify yourself may be one thing. I don't know. But you're actually quite interesting. You're quite an interesting idea person. You have… different ideas. You know? You have a lot of different ideas. And they go from here to there from here to there to here. You're very active-minded. Do you understand that? Would you agree with that?

MAYOR

Well, absolutely.

INSIGHT

Ya... Because that's... that's what I'm feeling and uh... also to that travel is really... really good for you. Or that you've done travel. Do you like to travel? Are you big on travel?

MAYOR

Yup.

INSIGHT

OK I'm not sure if you're still doing it now or currently or presently but regardless they do... they just bring up travel with you. And... ahh... liking to do that......... You're actually quite bright. You know. You're actually quite bright. You're actually a quite smart person and I'm not saying it just because you're sitting here. Ahh... I don't say that to everybody.

INSIGHT / MAYOR

Ha... ha... ha...

INSIGHT

Sometimes you can't... ha... ha... ha... ha... ha......... But with you... you actually are quite bright. You actually have some smarts to you and you are a good business thinker. You're very good business thinker. You know. You're still like in the works of your business ideas. Does that make sense to you?......... Even working for yourself. Or attempting to do a business or businesses on your own. Or independently or as part of something somebody else, but nonetheless with your own ideas... your own input... your own thoughts. And your own... running of the business or running of the businesses. Does that make sense to you? It could be premature. It could be premature. Granted. But you do have that... that drive. You don't... you... you don't have to work always for somebody is what I'm saying... it's a choice for you to work for someone. And you're still working through some ideas or you're still working... your kind... ahh... working through to come to more final decision regarding business. Does that make sense to you?

MAYOR

Sure does.

INSIGHT

In some way.

MAYOR

Ya.

INSIGHT

So you haven't really got the target yet. But you're working through to get to a target of an idea... a laser kind of... get to the perfect idea. Does that make sense? You're in the process. So understand that it is a process and... and that's what you're in... but the way your mind works... it sees things from all avenues. It goes all the way around. So it's really going to take a little bit of time to zero in and that's good. That's good. That's how you work. That's how your energy works. Makes sense?......... And I don't know if I told you, but I do ask questions to validate information.

MAYOR

Yes, it makes sense.

INSIGHT

OK. Ha... ha... ha... I didn't mean just there but coming up too ha... ha... ha...

MAYOR

OK.

INSIGHT

OK. Your mom is in the physical world. Isn't she?

MAYOR

Yup.

INSIGHT

Because I get her here. Very sensitive lady. Your mom. Very feeling woman. Would you agree with that? She's very much a loving caring maternal person by nature. And I don't think that is just because another person gives birth doesn't get that automatic right to be this way.

MAYOR

Ya, she is.

INSIGHT

She's very loving. Very caring and very soft inside. Do you know that? She leads by her heart on things first and foremost. She can do things. She's bright too. Don't get me wrong this is not a stupid lady, your mother. No... no... no... no... no. But she leads with her heart in her life. Does that makes sense? And the feeling is that she's a great help to a lot of people. I don't know if you think of her that way.

MAYOR

She is.

INSIGHT

OK. Then thankfully you… you agree with that. OK. Because if she wasn't ,I would be
surprised… because that's how she feels to me. But she's a great help to a lot of people.
And I think she doesn't really… because she's not egotistic your mother. At all. She has no
egotistical nature at all. Do you understand? She's not built on ego. Do you agree with
that?

MAYOR

She needs a little bit.

INSIGHT

She needs a little bit. Exactly. You know… but she… she… she just keeps going. You
know? And… ahh… but she does so much more than she ever realizes. She never really
understands or takes a moment and says… wow I really did a good job or I really did a lot
for a lot of people. And that's kind of very beautiful in… in a… in a way as well. You know?
Because she's just very much a giver. She's a very giving person. And it doesn't stop with
her family. Do you understand that? It's not just her family. It goes beyond the borders of
family. It's almost as she feels as if she could be a teacher. Or work with children in some
way.

MAYOR

Hmm…

INSIGHT

Or maybe even… does she ever work with kids?

MAYOR

Ah yes, and she was a teacher.

INSIGHT

She was a teacher? She ever work with young children? Really young?

MAYOR

Yes.

INSIGHT

Like daycare.

MAYOR

…

INSIGHT

Or just…

MAYOR

Not daycare.

INSIGHT

But young… young… young.

MAYOR

Ya.

INSIGHT

Because that's… like… ehh… ahh… she could work with daycare kids even. She's… she's got… she's got such a way with her. And she's got such a real way with children. You see? Children just feel safe with her. You know? So it's not even just that she can teach well and she loves it… you know? Because she also has… they love her. They feel safe with her. Does that make sense? She just exudes safety……… Your mom has not had an easy life in some respects. So there's been bumps in the road……… Hmm… OK. Hmm… are you one of two children? Are you?

MAYOR

Yup.

INSIGHT

OK remember I'm not seeing because I believe it's true… right? I can be wrong. It's not like it's impossible for me to be wrong… right? It could be you and two others. You know? But they show me two……… Also a little bit something strange with your dad.

MAYOR

What's that?

INSIGHT

I'm not putting him down or anything.

MAYOR

Ha… ha…

INSIGHT

Well I'm not. I've never met him. I don't know him. Ha… ha…

MAYOR

Do your worst.

Do... no I wouldn't. I wouldn't. But it just seems that there were some issues. With... with father. Does that make sense? Is that... is that... is that honest? Is that true? It doesn't mean that they were... they're not going into grand detail because some things are not my business. You know what I mean? But it just feels like there were some issues in the family about dad. Does that make sense?

MAYOR

Somewhat.

INSIGHT

OK it's not like he's the worst person in the world. It's not like he's... ha... ha... Jeffrey Dahmer... or anything. No. But you know what I'm saying? There just is... has been some difficulty around the father figure in this family for me. And... your mom is really kind of where it's at with regard to the family. Does that make sense?

MAYOR

Yes.

INSIGHT

As far as the stronger person in your life. OK? She's a good woman......... Hmm... haa... hmm... I feel as if there's somebody talking about family to me. And... your dad's alive too right? In the physical world is that correct?

MAYOR

Yes he is.

INSIGHT

Because I... I... I feel like it's more female in the spirit world for me. More so than male......... Ahh... hoo... OK. There's someone now putting themself to your side. OK. So this has got to be a close connection. Either friend or a sister or a close cousin or something but I'm not sure yet. I'm actually not sure if I'll be sure but I'll just be coming with... ahh... with what I get... OK? Because...

MAYOR

Was that a question?

INSIGHT

It... no... no... no... it's a statement.

MAYOR

OK.

INSIGHT

OK because I... I think there is......... There's also some other people there... but this... this is prominent. This is the most obvious to me at this time. There... there's somebody who... who's full of energy. And vivaciousness. A lot of energy of... personality... truly big-hearted person. As well this... this... girl... this... this young woman. I'm not sure if it's a girl or a young woman... but very energetic. I... I can't even acknowledge that enough... she does acknowledge you. She does acknowledge your mother. She also acknowledges a dog. Like she had a dog that she really loved a lot. OK... did the dog pass away?

MAYOR

...

INSIGHT

Is there a dog in the spirit world now?

MAYOR

We have two dogs. One of them passed away... ya.

INSIGHT

OK because I get one with her in the physical worl... sorry... in the spirit world... but then now she's acknowledging that dog as well as with her. Who's Dani? Or... or... or... or... Dawny or Dan. Something with a d... n... name. Does this make sense to you?

MAYOR

Dani.

INSIGHT

That's her name? Is that her name?

MAYOR

Yup.

INSIGHT

Dani. Felt it could be either way. You know ha... ha. I wasn't sure if she was acknowledging somebody else or if that would be her name. Would you call her Dani?

MAYOR

... I think my mom would call her Dani.

INSIGHT

So... actually somebody did call her Dani. It's not her whole name is it really?

MAYOR

No.

INSIGHT

OK because... is it... is it... like a short form? Or... like here we were just talking about... Timothy and Tim... and Bob... and Robert... and all of that. OK. Well I just want to say that she's acknowledging family. She's acknowledging the family. I don't... I still don't understand if she's your sister. Is she your sister? OK. She is your sister......... Sometimes it takes a bit. Just stay with me. OK?......... She doesn't want anybody to blame themselves for what happened to her. In some weird way. She doesn't want anyone to feel any guilt for what happened to her. Don't get me wrong I don't feel that anyone hurt her physically like... I don't feel that anyone... you know what I mean. I don't think it was a car accident for example. I'm just using that as an example... somebody hit her and she passed. I don't feel it's like that. But people might be holding still some guilt. Even though they didn't have anything to do with it. Does this make sense to you?

MAYOR

Ya, it does.

INSIGHT

OK... so she does... one of the first things I'm getting is she doesn't want anyone to feel guilt over this. This is not something that anyone did wrong. It's... it's not. I... ahh... and she... it's almost like very adamant in terms of making that point across. Like getting that point across. She doesn't want anyone to think that they had anything to do with this at all. It was like there was no way. It was like a truck spiraling out of control in some weird way. That's just an analogy. OK?

MAYOR

OK.

INSIGHT

It's just an... like a... a... ahh... whatever they call in English. Ask your mother. Ha... ha... ha... I don't know. Ha... ha... ha... ha... ha... you hear me? OK......... But the big thing is that she does not want anyone to feel any sense of guilt about this. There was nothing that could be done. Period......... She's also with somebody who had cancer. Somebody passed from cancer? Somebody had cancer in the family. Somebody passed from cancer? It's a relative. It's not an immediate family person. It's not like it's a sister... or mother... or father. It's... it... it's a... it's a relative. It's... it's like a female relative for me. Did somebody have leukemia?

MAYOR

No.

                              INSIGHT
Or lu something. The only other lu things I can think of are Lou Garrick's or…

                              MAYOR
Lupus?

                              INSIGHT
Lupus. OK, well thank you for that one. I don't know these diseases. But there's something
with a disease with lu in it. Did anyone have that? Anyone that you are aware of who had a
connection to someone who had that. look on your mom's side. Farther back. OK because
there is a connection there. This might be through marriage I don't know. But it is still a
connection to that family on that side……… She is also expressing concern for your mother.
OK. Your mom's a strong… ahh… aa… she's not strong I don't mean strong. We already
talked about how she is. She's loving. She's sweet. She's wonderful… I don't mean like
that. But she… she… she is a pretty keep-going woman. Do you agree? And a lot of what
she's doing keeps her going… but your… your sister wants her to just take good care of
herself. You know? Like to go to the doctor on a regular basis. To take good care of her
physical body. You know. Nothing obsessive. But just to take reasonably good care of her
body. Ahh… I don't think she's in any major problems or major things. But it's just a feeling
that she needs to take good care of herself. OK? There is a connection to that family who
has cancer. Female. Who had cancer. It's not your sister. But it's somebody else………
Does your mom have sisters?

                              MAYOR
Yup.

                              INSIGHT
Am I wrong? I'm right.

                              MAYOR
She has one.

                              INSIGHT
OK, she has one sister. OK because. One sec sweetie… I'm trying to.

                              MAYOR
Oh wait.

                              INSIGHT
What?

                              MAYOR
Ya, there is someone on that side.

                    INSIGHT
Who had cancer?

                    MAYOR
Ya.

                    INSIGHT
But who is…

                    MAYOR
Hmm…

                    INSIGHT
Do you know who it is? Like the connection. The category. Is it like an aunt or is it like…

                    MAYOR
A… wife of an uncle.

                    INSIGHT
Which would be an aunt. Right?

                    MAYOR
Ya.

                    INSIGHT
It's just. Maybe it's through marriage. You see?

                    MAYOR
Ya.

                    INSIGHT
You see we were talking about through marriage. And she… she passed right? She passed?

                    MAYOR
Yup.

                    INSIGHT
She had cancer right? She met up with her. OK, your sister has met up with her. OK, it
doesn't matter how close they were not… you see? It doesn't matter. All the connections in
terms of the family can meet. Especially when you do something like this. Because hey…
everything's open right? Everything's open……… Whose Cara or Corey… c… r…
Catherine.

                              MAYOR
Car'y.

                              INSIGHT
Who is that?

                              MAYOR
That's my mom.

                              INSIGHT
Car'y. That's her name? Car'y.

                              MAYOR
Carolyn.

                              INSIGHT
With a c or a k?

                              MAYOR
C.

                              INSIGHT
OK good. Because that's what I'm getting. A C more than a K. OK, that's it. And like do
they call her Car'y too? Some people.

                              MAYOR
Sometimes. Ya.

                              INSIGHT
Ya?

                              MAYOR
Ya.

                              INSIGHT
That's nice. OK. Well they're acknowledging her. They're acknowledging your mother.
Then… the Spirits are… the spirit world's acknowledging your mom……… Is there anybody
in the family… again… ha… ha… keep an open mind OK. Because it could be any relative.
And it's not perfect hon. Is there an Andy? Or someone that they know. Named Andy or
Andrew? Or Anne. A… n… name.

                              MAYOR
I don't know. I'll have to go back and ask my mom.

INSIGHT

OK......... And also Al... Al... Alex... Alexis maybe? Alexander. Alexis?

MAYOR

Physical or spirit?

INSIGHT

I don't know. It's just a name. I'm sorry I don't know.

MAYOR

...

INSIGHT

But it's being acknowledged. Like... a... a... like a... like a connection.

MAYOR

Alexis.

INSIGHT

It is Alexis?

MAYOR

It was... best friend of my sister.

INSIGHT

OK. She still cares about her. You know she still cares it's... it's not like anything's changed just because she passed away. You know? She still carries the same feelings and the same love for people. It's still with her. All her memories. All her thoughts. All her beliefs. And she continues. You know? So she actually had continued to grow... ahh... you know... think in whatever her way over all the time... that... it... she's been there for some time though. This didn't happen last year. Do you know what I mean? She's been there for some time. She's been there for a long time. For her. Because you're a young guy. You know you're not an old guy yourself right?

MAYOR

Well...

INSIGHT

Unless you've had plastic surgery that I'm not aware of. But you know? So she... what she feels like she's... she's... she's a mature person but she's young. It doesn't feel like it happened last year or so recent. That she's... that's she's a... been there for awhile. That she's gotten settled it. She's got settled in. Basically......... Did your mom have a mammogram lately?

MAYOR

Ya.

INSIGHT

It thought so. Because she's just saying she saw that. Or she saw what she did. You know…
she… she… she… still keeps tabs on you guys you know. It's not like she's gone out of sight
out of mind. Doesn't work like that. She's really watching you guys and watching how
things go on.……… She thinks the world of you. Do you know that? Do you know that?
And she'll always look after you. She'll always look out for you. She wants you to live your
life as fully and completely as you wish. You know what I mean? She wants you to do the
things that make you happy in life. You know? And not be too tainted by the experience
that you had with all this. Do you understand that?

MAYOR

OK.

INSIGHT

Understand that each soul chooses its own path. And nobody else is responsible for it. She
makes me feel that she had a lot of support from the family. You know what I'm saying?
She had a lot of people there for her. This is… this is something that her soul did or… or…
or felt or needed to experience in some weird way. And it doesn't… and… I… a… I don't
mean it doesn't matter. I mean it matters very much. But… it… it… it… almost… it's not
because of anybody. It's not because of you. It's not because of anybody in the family. You
know? Hmm… she doesn't want anybody to feel that their life has been tainted in such a
way that they don't love life and love their own life. And experience their life to the best
fullest capacity that they can. OK? Because believe me she still lives through all of you. She
feels your feelings. She feels your mother's feelings. She feels everyone's feelings and she
feels everything you know… if she chooses to… she can. You know? So when you were
joyful she's joyful. Do you know what I'm saying? She can tap into that. She has a lot of
nice things that she feels for you and about you. Also… who… you're technological? Or
technical in some way? Are you a techie? Ha… ha… ha… ha… in some way?

MAYOR

I pretend to be.

INSIGHT

Well you must be to some degree. Because she makes me feel that that's something that
you… that you like. Or something that you do. Sorry.……… You and your mother are still
very close. Eh? Always will be. You and your mom. She likes that. But also your dad.
Your dad… it's funny… because it seems so much about you three. Does that make sense?
She does acknowledge her dad. It's not like she does not. You know… she doesn't… she
doesn't want him to feel bad either. You know what I mean? She does love him. You know
I don't want to completely exclude him. You know for whatever reason I don't want to.

You know... it's just... it's just... ahh... one second......... I... I don't know... I don't understand that. OK I gotta ask you. I don't really understand. I'm telling her I don't understand...

OK.

This next thing. Is your mom and your dad separated? Or no? They're still together?

They're still together.

Do they... do they have... did they have some real... did they have some stru... a bumpy road there for awhile? Can I say that?

Yup.

OK. Because I'm not sure if it's they were separated or it's almost like they could have been or should have been.

They could have been.

Do you know what I mean? OK. But she does... she does love your dad. You know? Despite everything, she still loves her dad. And your dad isn't terrible. You know?

No he's not.

He's actually quite a nice guy. He as a lot of good sides too him. He's set in his ways.

Absolutely.

You know? He's very set in his ways. And you know... and... and that can sometimes... you know... be difficult for the people... ha... ha... around him. But he's actually somebody that she loves too. You know? She does... she actually is protective now. Now it's coming out. She is protective of him as well. You know that? Believe me she has that too with him......... I don't understand this... her love life didn't work out very well. Is that true? She didn't have a boyfriend or...

MAYOR

She did for a period.

INSIGHT

But it didn't last. Is that true? Because it... it's just... but it's not something that she looks at with negativity. It's just an acknowledgement that her love life didn't always go perfectly when she was here. She makes me feel like she's got a lot of people in the spirit world. So you don't have to worry about her life continuing and meeting new people.

MAYOR

Good.

INSIGHT

She's a good... ya I got to say this... she's a good girl. I... I... I mean that in the most sincere and loving way. She's a good person your sister. She is still a good person. You know she will always be this person. She's not going to change. Hey... we're... you're... our lives are all temporary here. You know what I mean? I'm not trying to make it you know... one or the other. But once we all realize that everybody goes to the same place and that the life continues it's a very reassuring thing also. Not to take away from what happened. You know?... and of course everyone's going to meet her. Regardless. You know? It doesn't matter. It's just going to happen. All the time. But the thing I want to say here is that she does acknowledge that side of her... her... her... she did have a lot of female friends though. Do you agree? Like a lot of people... a... around her. And it's funny because in one way hmm... you know in one way I want to say... mmm... that I don't know how to explain this. In one way it feels like she was and is... ahh... outgoing but in another way she's very shy. Does that make sense to you?

MAYOR

Ya, it does.

INSIGHT

OK. Because there is an extreme outgoing part of her and a part of her for me that's very shy. You know? But I will tell you she's smart too. Your sister. She's got a good sense of humor. Do you know she's got a good sense of humor?

MAYOR

Ya, I know.

INSIGHT

Oh she's got a good sense of humor… and she can say things man… she can… ha… ha… occasionally say things you know… wh… you know… and… it… it's… it's like a zinger. Do you know what I mean? Does that make sense to you?

MAYOR

Ya.

INSIGHT

Like a little bit of a zinger. You know but she gets away with it. You know? In a way. She gets away with it. Because it's not really cruel or mean-hearted. You know? It just comes off as a little bit of a zinger with a question mark. Do… does that make sense?

MAYOR

Ya, you know sometimes it's not what you say ,it's how you say it.

INSIGHT

Ya… ha… ha… she's definitely got that kind of way with her……… She was in the hospital. Ya. She was in the hospital for me. Or she did go to the hospital at some point. Because she's showing me this. And also showing me like intravenous or something. Was she on intravenous? Is that true?

MAYOR

Ya, she did.

INSIGHT

She does… she's not bringing this up to make anybody feel bad. She's just bringing it up to kind of validate that it's her in a way……… Alright… is there someone's birthday in June or July? Or a Summer month? Or August? Does Summer have anything to do with her?

MAYOR

Hmm… hmm…

INSIGHT

There's just something that she's acknowledging. It could be August. Maybe it's August. Of importance. I don't know. In a way it's… it's something to do with her. Something to do directly with her. And just before that she was showing me the intravenous. So I'm not sure maybe she went in the hospital in August. Or June or July.

MAYOR

It's been so long I just don't…

INSIGHT

It's OK. I just... I... I... that's true. OK sorry. Sorry for that. I just keep laughing in here. OK......... Ya she does... July... I'm gunna say June or July. Just go back. Just to go back sorry one more time. OK. But it feels like... that timeframe more so......... OK. Very... very loving girl. But you know what I'm... I'm not kidding you, she's strong too you know that? She's a strong person.

MAYOR

Fighter.

INSIGHT

Oh, for God's sake, ya. Because I thought it was all mush again but then now it's coming in very clearly that she's a very strong person. Believe me. Very... very strong. She... when you say a fighter. Not even just physically. She can actually have a little bit of a fighting personality too. Am I wrong?

MAYOR

Ha... ha... no.

INSIGHT

I'm not.

MAYOR

Not at all.

INSIGHT

I... I'm... I'm not. And yet she's got the heart of... of gold. You know what I'm saying? But boy she can... she can really defend herself. Does that make sense?

MAYOR

Yes.

INSIGHT

If she needs to or thinks she is or even sometimes not so much because she needs to. Do you know what I mean?

MAYOR

Yup.

INSIGHT

Because that... that... that's the feeling I'm getting with her too......... She's very proud of you......... She's also very... very proud of your mom. Wow... in a big way. How your mom has turned whatever this is around in some way. Or is really trying to do good in the world because of it. And you're doing good whatever it is. I don't know what it is. But your both doing very good. Do you see it… does this make sense? God I hope it does. Ha… ha… I can't remember what it feels like.

MAYOR

It makes perfect sense.

INSIGHT

OK. Thanks. It's a very hard thing to transfer that into words because of how it was presented…….. Your dad also has to watch his health a little. Your dad. Is he in his sixties now?

MAYOR

Ya he is.

INSIGHT

I'm… I could be getting this wrong. He's not sixty-seven is he?

MAYOR

Ha… ha… ha… I think you're right on.

INSIGHT

Oh good… ha… ha… you were sort of scaring me. It's just so cute. It's so cute. OK because I just get a little bit with…

MAYOR

I think you're right on.

INSIGHT

Good. Because I get a little bit around his health too. Nothing again… you know… serious… serious. But just a little bit. And again… just affirming for him to take care of himself and do the right things as best as he can. I think he is going to the doctor though isn't he? He's… he's one of these guys who will go to the doctor.

MAYOR

Ha… ha…

INSIGHT

Not very easily though.

MAYOR

Not very easily.

INSIGHT

But he does go. Because you know... I think she's just is kinda saying nothing dire or urgent. It's just that... you know... for him to go you know... maybe more regularly a little bit. And just to take better care of himself in some way... is there anybody that dia... betes? A diabetic connection in this family. Connection? It could be maybe with your dad's family.

MAYOR

I don't know.

INSIGHT

Because I was just right over on your dad's side. A little farther back? OK. Could be? Was there... is there anybody balding? On that side? Or thinning at the top?

MAYOR

Nope. Nope. Nothing.

INSIGHT

Is there somebody like that? Like thinning at the top. Not bald.

MAYOR

Oh, on his side?

INSIGHT

Not bald. Not bald. We'll clarify that. Not bald. Not a cue ball.

MAYOR

Isn't that hereditary?

INSIGHT

Ha... ha... ha... you're so funny. Your hair is all there. Your hair is all there. Don't you worry... I'll tell you it's all on top of your head. But ahh... a little bit of a... because there... she... what I'm thinking is they're trying to show me somebody in the spirit world. Also his dad is passed ya? Obviously. Well I shouldn't say obviously. Because my God...

MAYOR

M-hmm...

INSIGHT

Believe me when it comes through... people are here forever. It's amazing. After... I get clients come here sometimes... when I talk about people a guy whose ninety something years old and he's still here. Good for them. Eh. But the father on your dad's side.

[140]

MAYOR

Yup.

INSIGHT

Your dad's side actually not a bad family. You know? They have their stuff. They have their stuff. And I don't feel like they're always understood. You know? Expression is… can be lacking. The appropriate expression at times. But also his mother's very strong. Your dad's mother. You know that? I'm not saying strong like mean or strong like that. I have to express what strong means to me.

MAYOR

Character.

INSIGHT

 It… it… she… she can do what needs doing. You know? She has some strength to her too. But realize ahh… there's also a November connection. A November birthday? Or an October birthday? It's right around there. But again I think I'm coming from that side of the family. From your dad's side. Someone on the dad's side connection. OK? Can I have… I'm not getting your dad's name. What's your dad's name?

MAYOR

Serge.

INSIGHT

Oh, no wonder!! I was… ha… ha… can you say that again?

MAYOR

Serge.

INSIGHT

Serge.

MAYOR

S… e…

INSIGHT

Now I was trying to hear it. And I was writing H… a… r. Ha… ha… and it's the sound right.

MAYOR

Right.

INSIGHT

And... and... I was hearing this... this... hair. This Serge... I was just getting the hair.

MAYOR

It's like... it's like Sarge.

INSIGHT

They're close. Because they're close. I'm sorry. Serge.

MAYOR

S... e... r... g... e...

INSIGHT

OK. I like when you pronounce it best. Definitely set in his ways. But he's... he's going to be OK too. He keeps a lot of his emotions inside. Your dad. You know that?

MAYOR

He's buried them.

INSIGHT

Ya... he's bury... he's in the physical?

MAYOR

Ya.

INSIGHT

Well don't say that to me... I'm looking at him... ha... ha... like am I wrong? Is he not with you... ha... ha... you buried him. I got to watch you.

MAYOR

Buried his emotions.

INSIGHT

I know. It's really... there really deep inside. But the thing about your dad is...he is feeling them. He is truly feeling them. It's just that he has this belief somewhere deep inside of him even if it's not in his consciousness. It's very deep. That that's what he has to do. That's his responsibility. You know that? That's what his deep-seated beliefs are. And if he cracks, guess what happens. The whole dam breaks. Right? So he has... that's his deep-seated belief. Believe me. That's what he believes. He... he's actually a good man in a lot of ways. You know? It's just that he... you know... it would be nice... you know... if he didn't think so much like that. You see? He does love his daughter very much. It's almost like the pain of going there would be too much for him in some respect. Also he has to watch his cholesterol down the road. You know? Down the road. I'm not sure if it's already but down the road. A little bit of high cholesterol or high blood pressure with your dad.

MAYOR

I keep on bothering him to watch his health.

INSIGHT

Ya. Does he check these things? Has he had those checked?

MAYOR

Sometimes.

INSIGHT

Ya, how have they been showing up?

MAYOR

Fairly decent right now.

INSIGHT

Really good?

MAYOR

Right now.

INSIGHT

Right now? And anything in the past that's happened with that?

MAYOR

No, just a few things that could have been health issues that were checked out and they weren't.

INSIGHT

Good. Glad to hear that. And again nothing serious but I do get a little bit with cholesterol in the future. Possible. Always we can avoid it and a little bit with high blood pressure. Little bit in the future. But then again these aren't huge and horrible......... Also, you have to watch your health. You're not… you're not… you're young. You know you're a young guy. You are… and I'm not saying watch your health. I hate to say that because… ever… when I say watch your health, it like sounds so ominous and it isn't meant to be ominous in any way. Don't become an extremist. I get an extremist tendency with you as well. In some way. Am I wrong? Do you know what I mean by an extremist?

MAYOR

What do you mean by an extremist?

INSIGHT

Like going all the way one way or all the way in another way.

MAYOR

Well, if you're going to do something do it a hundred percent.

INSIGHT

You're so cute ha… ha… ha… you know it's almost like even with your health. You know it… it's almost like if… if… you're going to do it you're going to be like all the way this way. Do you know what I mean? Or… well… who gives a shit. Ha… ha… ha… did I just say this loudly? Ha… ha… do you know what I mean? And it's not so much that it has to go all the way in one direction or all the way in the other. You know what I mean? It's kinda like you know… I shouldn't even be talking because I'm bad at this myself… but oh, well it's coming up here too… so… ha… ha… I got to say it. So it's just a feeling of… of… it's very interesting because… your… your… your sister doesn't want you to go in extremes. In some way. OK? It's almost of a feeling of exercising… exercising… not eating enough food you know… and… or… eating a lot.

MAYOR

M-hmm. OK.

INSIGHT

Does that make sense?

MAYOR

Yes.

INSIGHT

In some way? OK but don't go to extremes. In some way.

MAYOR

Ya , she was pretty concerned about that.

INSIGHT

Did… did you… did… did you do that ever too? Why… why was she concerned about that? Why is she concerned about that now? Because she is very concerned about that. She doesn't want you to go to extremes either in your life.

MAYOR

Yup.

INSIGHT

Don't exercise like a maniac and never ever stop exercising. Like that kind of feeling... you know? Don't Mr. Pump Iron twenty thousand times a day and never say never. You know? And don't be the other way where you say hell with it let's just eat French fries and hot dogs all day and you know? But... but... there's a feeling of... a... but... just to be careful. You know? Do... to... to love your life and live your life and enjoy your life. Without extremes. And that feels... I don't know why... but I... I recognize this feeling. Because... I... in my life had... I don't know if I should be telling you this. I don't know why I'm telling you this. Actually. Maybe it's not even the right time. Maybe I shouldn't even say anything... but in my life I had extreme issues... with stuff. In my life. And... I got over them. Almost too much the other way. You know? And it almost feels like... you know... some of this... is in this reading. In some way. Like two extremes. Too much of one thing and not enough balance... in some way. And I recognize it because of my own history. Very well... and she's warning you not to do that. So I don't know if you've been doing that or if you've had concerns in that area or if there have been concerns in the family in some way. But... you just... you don't do that. Whatever it is.

MAYOR

Ya, she's always been cautious and protective about her family.

INSIGHT

Very much so. Very... she really... is she older than you?

MAYOR

Yes.

INSIGHT

Was she born... of an older sister.

MAYOR

Yup.

INSIGHT

Because she feels like the older sister. You know. Like she really does feel she is protective of you. She loves you a lot. You know? However... again... she doesn't want you not to enjoy your life. She wants you not to think about everything so much. That you taints your experience either. Do you know what I mean? Does that make sense?

MAYOR

It's difficult to do.

INSIGHT

Well think, but don't over-analyze to the point where you don't get as much happiness. Because you're thinking so much that... that you're not allowing yourself any joy. Do you know what I mean?

MAYOR

I know what you mean.

INSIGHT

So allow yourself a lot of joy in life. Of course joy feels good. Not what someone else determines as joy for themselves. Which isn't for you perhaps. But for yourself... so check inside yourself and ask yourself what kinds of things do you individually as a person really truly enjoy. And follow that sometimes. And allow that in your life sometimes......... She thinks you're actually quite... she's actually laughing now. I'm getting like... not in a derogatory manner.

MAYOR

Ha... ha... ha...

INSIGHT

I promise you nothing like that. But she's almost like laughing with me. Kind of give me a feeling that... your really something. Ha... ha... ha... you know what I mean? To her. And this is not a criticism in anyway. It's just like wow... you're really something. The things that you do or the things that you'll try or... you know what I mean? A little bit with you. So it's funny cause how you look or appear is irrelevant really from her perspective about you.

MAYOR

It is.

INSIGHT

Do you know what I mean... because... it feels like... your... you're very a... you will try things. Do you know what I mean? You will try things. You know... if it makes sense to you... you will... who went to Ireland?......... You went to Ireland?

MAYOR

With my dad.

INSIGHT

OK. Because she's talking about that trip... was that after she passed away?

MAYOR

Yup.

INSIGHT

I thought so. I think she's just trying to acknowledge seeing you go there or seeing you...
was that trip special for you? In some weird way. And I know you... you mentioned you
traveled and I don't know where... or wherever you traveled. And I'm sure... you know...
each one of them had their own experience. You know? To some degree. But... you
know... OK... but I don't know Ireland feels kind of... good. You know I'm not sure if you
had the good experience when you were you with your dad...

MAYOR

Ha... ha...

INSIGHT

Or if it will be a different point in time.

MAYOR

Well, good experience in the fact that I went on a trip and I spent time with my dad.

INSIGHT

Oh. So it was good. OK. So he doesn't always accompany you on your trips?

MAYOR

Hardly ever.

INSIGHT

Oh, that's a big deal. That's a big deal. So family wise that would definitely something she
would address. Because that... for me... she's presenting it with good. You know or every
important in some way. Your dad is also... a... a. good thinking man too though when it
comes to... he... he... I won't say he's been in business. I don't know. What I will say is he
does think business. Do... do you know what I mean? Does that make sense? So I don't
know if he's in business or not. But he thinks like that. Does that make sense to you?

MAYOR

Ya.

INSIGHT

Like he thinks like that. He's programmed like that. You know in terms of what's the best
way to go or what's not the best way to go. Do you know what I mean? Smart thinking you
know and he... he... he likes information. Does that make sense to you?

MAYOR

... ya.

INSIGHT

Like he likes feeding his brain. In some way. So like I don't know if he reads certain things or looks up certain things but he seems to want to feed his brain a lot. Does that make sense? Well… that… that's kind of healthy depending on what it is. But it seems like a healthy thing……… Oh I'm sorry… are you comfortable?

MAYOR

Sure am.

INSIGHT

OK good. OK… OK… somebody's making a joke about Antarctica. I think it's a joke. You didn't want to go to Antarctica did you? Where's Antarctica… is it down there?

MAYOR

No. The opposite.

INSIGHT

The opposite? Because I think that she's making a joke. Ha… ha… this is a joke. Do you know that? I think this is a joke. Alaska. It's a joke I think.

MAYOR

OK.

INSIGHT

You know… cause Antarctica's freezing. You know… freezing… freezing cold. You know… so… and… and… there is a feeling of laughter. See they make jokes to everybody. Ha… ha… it's like I have to just go with it. You know? And not always try to make everything literal. Ha… ha… ha… ha… that's OK I'm trying always to make everything literal……… But… cause we're talking about travel or things. And there's also that funny feeling. I… I don't know… OK… OK… thanks……… Ya, I know you're French because you already told me Mayeur. We know. We got it. But because now all of a sudden they were going to go Montreal. But I think… but quite logically. Did you go to Montreal?

MAYOR

I have.

INSIGHT

Ya. Was this for work or for business?

MAYOR

Ya.

INSIGHT

Because it seems like it's attached in some way......... There's also some US connectivity to whatever you're doing. America. Yana. Does that make... ya... I know... scary word. It is.

MAYOR

Question America.

INSIGHT

Especially these days. It's very scary ha... ha... ha... ha... ha... ha... ha... ha. I do feel like they're acknowledging also America or the US of A. So if you're in some connection to that kind of scenario or if you have to travel there. Have you traveled there?

MAYOR

Ya, I've traveled there.

INSIGHT

For work?

MAYOR

Ya... and also...

INSIGHT

And personal?

MAYOR

And for personal.

INSIGHT

OK. Because I do get also travel or connectivity to America for work as well. The funny thing is... you can... you know this is just a general statement really... ahh... here at the moment. A... but you can live anywhere you want to live. You can. If you do it the right way. It's funny because as far as your spirit goes I think you'd like to go elsewhere. Am I wrong? In terms of living. I don't mean visiting. Does that make sense?

MAYOR

Yes, that makes sense.

INSIGHT

OK. And you can. It's free will. Free choice and you can. A lot is about timing. You see? You can't just immediately do everything perfectly exactly right... right now. But the feeling is... is... it is ca... it can be very much part of your future. If you so choose it. If you stay on that mindset. If you stay with that mindset. However it is possible that you might change that mindset.

MAYOR

And end up in Antarctica?

INSIGHT

No... ha... ha... I hope not. Well, anyway it's your choice. If you want to go do that that's fine. But the feeling is... is that... it's still a very real possibility. It's not just hearsay or chat or plot. It can actually happen for you if you so choose. And the funny thing is... you know... you'd be a little open. A... even more than a little open as far as where you would choose to live or go. At that time. Have you been to Australia?

MAYOR

No, I haven't.

INSIGHT

Did you want to go?

MAYOR

Ya.

INSIGHT

Is this big on your agenda? Or has it been big in your mind?

MAYOR

Been big in my mind.

INSIGHT

Because I feel like... you're going to... understand the spirit side hears everything. Our thoughts... our wants or... ha... ha... ha...

MAYOR

I'm in a lot of trouble.

INSIGHT

Ha... ha... trust me honey... nobody's pure. I mean... now... everybody in the world of spirit has had their own thoughts. Believe me. And none of which are always good. OK. We're all people here. But at the same time we're not judged eh... this is very important to also... people don't understand we really are not judged. We're the ones who judged ourselves. You know? So if we don't Judge ourselves so much it'll be a little easier life for our ourselves to... as long as we are real... you know... seriously wrong and right OK. You know what I mean? But as long as you're... you're a half-decent person. You don't have to feel bad... but feeling is... is that Australia would do very well with you and for you. And not only Australia, but even New Zealand. Which is interesting. Now they're very close to each other... well not really. But they're pretty close to each other. Not bad.

MAYOR

Closer than Australia and Canada.

INSIGHT

Well... obviously... ya. With those two... feel very good for you. So I'm not sure if living in Australia and going to New Zealand. You know what I mean? But those two areas feel good for you actually. Australia... I don't know if you'll like it immediately as much as you presume. But I think that you'd like it over time a lot. It's one of those places I feel will grow on you. But it... it's interesting because I don't think instantaneously that you will... ahh... that you will go... whoa! This is the place. You see what I'm saying? But I feel like over time you would start to like it a lot. For some reason, I think you'll like New Zealand. There's some aspects of New Zealand. I don't know if it'll be more of the people or it's the terrain or the environment. I don't know. But I... a... but I feel it's that place you'll like almost closer to immediately. Or very soon after. Strange... though. But I think you will like aspects of Australia. It's hard not to... there's some aspects that are hard for anyone not to like. Right?

MAYOR

Yup.

INSIGHT

But I mean, once you really get into it. It... it'll... it will take a little bit of time you will. You have to be careful you don't isolate......... You know? Does that make sense to you?

MAYOR

It happens.

INSIGHT

It happens to me too. But of course now, I can back off of the whole thing and not worry. But don't isolate yourself too much. OK? It doesn't mean you have to become Mr... a... Party Animal. This is not what this is saying. We don't... we're not looking for you to become Mr. Par-tay. But the bottom-line is to not isolate too much. So don't make it... ahh... ahh... a... ahh... you know... the largest part of your experience. You know what I mean? Because you can do that because of how your mind works too. Because your mind always has something it can focus on. Which is good! It's not bad! It's good! We like that! Don't change it! But at the same time ahh... don't... don't... don't isolate too much. You know... know when enough is enough. And make it... ahh... and effort to kind of... make a... an attempt or a... actually... actually ignite on occasion intentionally. You know a change for short periods to get yourself out of that a... that a thing......... You are actually a person... who does love the idea of love. But you also are OK on your own. You know that? You find things to entertain yourself. You really do. Am I wrong?

MAYOR

No. You aren't wrong.

INSIGHT

You can do that… but don't isolate all the time. OK? Because the thing that's interesting about you is you can do things individually too. You know what I mean? You can go… for example, travel on your own. Am I wrong?

MAYOR

I've done it.

INSIGHT

Well, there you go. Ya know? No problem. You're fine with it. Or you can travel with somebody. That's fine too. But either way seems to be fine with you. You know? But the thing is if you do travel alone, be open to meeting new people. You know… on your travels. It doesn't have to be a whole thing by yourself alone. You see? But it's up to you. I'm not telling you what to do. Just sounds like I'm telling you what to do. Now… in terms of love and romance wow. Sorry sweetie one sec……… Uno secundo……… OK. OK sorry… what age are you now?

MAYOR

Thirty.

INSIGHT

You're thirty years old. Which is really young by the way.

MAYOR

It is?

INSIGHT

Yes it is. Very… very… very young. Like really young. And that's a good thing. It's working for ya. Thirty-three on our current path. And thirty-six. But thirty-three's earlier… ha… seems like very important periods of your life or approximate times of… of good stuff. You're not married? Right? Am I right?……… OK… I… I don't look at rings.

MAYOR

No rings.

INSIGHT

I refuse… but I always look… I stay with the face. You know? But because I don't see marriage here so far. OK… and there's not a girlfriend right now?

MAYOR

Nope.

INSIGHT

Is that fair? Am I right?

MAYOR

Yup.

INSIGHT

OK. You know what's really interesting and I'm not going by what you're saying. Or you would say to me. I'm just going to say it like I think it… OK. You could go with either age higher or lower as far as women. Do you believe me?

MAYOR

Perfect.

INSIGHT

Ha… ha… some people are all about younger women. But believe me, in some respects, I would even say that older women work well for you. In some respects.

MAYOR

Why limit myself?

INSIGHT

Ha… ha… ha ha… ha ha… ha… I like that. OK. Now I'm not telling you how to date or who to date. That's your own choice. Your own decision. But it just feel as that either… either range would actually be OK. Strangely. It really feels that way. And actually… I'm not telling you what to do. I don't know why I keep picking this up. Excuse me. But I even feel that even a much older woman. I'm not talking fifty here. OK, I'm not going… I'm not reading that but I mean ya know… not two or three years. You know? And to be honest with you, it wouldn't be necessarily a bad relationship. It could actually be a good relationship. So I do think that there are two spectrums of… you're not a person who will Judge a woman. Do you know what I mean? You will take a woman as she is to you. Which is good. You know you're not going to pre-judge her because of all her surpassed… or were past or anything like that. You take her as she is. You know… because it depends on the person. And your… you feel that you're very much about the person you meet and how they are to you. And… ahh… it's funny because… I'm just going to say you're going to think I'm absolutely a lunatic, but you're actually pretty open. And I think that actually will work for you. You're open in terms of what kind of woman again as long as they're good to you. And you feel good to them. And you treat each other well. That's really what it is about for you. You're not even concerned if she has a child. Am I wrong?

[153   ]

MAYOR

Not at all.

INSIGHT

That is what makes you kind of ahead of the game. In terms of… you're… you're not judgmental. You are about again how things are between the two of you. And to be honest with you it feels as if there's some… I feel as if you are kind of feeling that you are ready to kind of…be with somebody. You're coming to that point where you're ready to be with somebody or to start the dating process more so. Do you know what I mean?

MAYOR

Ha… start… ha… ha…

INSIGHT

Well, I say start, because it feels like you're not doing a lot of it so far. You're doing some. You know what I mean but not a lot. But you… but you have great initiative.

MAYOR / INSIGHT

Ha… ha… ha… ha… ha…

INSIGHT

You know what I'm saying?

MAYOR

Ha… ha… ha…

INSIGHT

Does that make sense? A little bit.

MAYOR

OK.

INSIGHT

OK. Have you been dating recently, honey?

MAYOR

No not really.

INSIGHT

OK, because it doesn't feel like a lot. Be open to finding women or being with women or getting to know women in different kind of venues. Not in a negative venue. Very positive venues. Don't be locked in. To like…I have to go be at a store and see a woman pushing a cart in a mall or something. You know don't be just like that. You know be open a little bit,

I would suggest. You know that? I would actually say be open a little bit… you're open in so many other ways. You know? So this way is actually the more important one. Because… you know… whether you would be interested in a younger or an older person or a same age person is irrelevant if… if you're not in the places to meet them. Right? In a way……… Now the feeling is too… have you done some online stuff?

MAYOR

Yup.

INSIGHT

Because they're showing me online stuff here. Now I don't know what kind. And they're not showing me specifically. Alright. But the feeling is that… that might not be bad. You know? That might actually be good. Depending on how you do it. Now on-line's a big place. You know? It's… a big world… big world out there. But how you do it is going to be important. Rather than just the fact that you're doing it. OK? So look for kind of… you know… decent places. You know… if you're going to do it online do it in a decent way. You know… in… in… in… in a straight up kind of way. Do you know what I mean?… norm. The normal way. A decent way… in some… I don't know what that means but normal… decent… regular… ha… ha… I don't know what that means. So maybe… maybe it's something… I'm not saying I'm seeing this… something like eHarmony or something. I don't know. But it's something like do the normal way. Ya know… do the… be honest about yourself… you know? Be honest about who you are. Don't try to flash. Don't do the flash. Don't do the flash. I don't know what the flash is but don't do the flash. Because you don't have to do the flash. Do you know understand what that means? I don't know… flash. Ha… ha…

MAYOR

No flashing. Got it.

INSIGHT

Just be you. And that is when you'll get much more… ahh… more… more to the point. More to what you want. Within two years. I think. Maximum three. But I think even within two years with you. And what I'm saying is… like a serious. More serious. Now realize there's somebody that can come in sooner too. You know… mind you, I'm just going by your current path. How you're doing… you know what I mean?

MAYOR

Yup.

INSIGHT

One sec… do you know a Steven?

MAYOR

Yup.

INSIGHT

Who's that?

MAYOR

Old friend.

INSIGHT

OK. A friend of yours in the past?

MAYOR

Yup.

INSIGHT

Did your sister know him?

MAYOR

Yup.

INSIGHT

Thought so. Do you talk to him at all?

MAYOR

No.

INSIGHT

Not anymore? Because I feel her…

MAYOR

Not at all.

INSIGHT

OK. But… did you do that by choice or just by how things kind of went? How things kind of went?

MAYOR

Kind of a little bit of both.

INSIGHT

Ya. Because I think she's just addressing him. He's still in the physical… ya? That you're aware of. Ya? OK……… But anyway, your love life I think will improve. Just don't isolate.

MAYOR

Hallelujah!!.

INSIGHT

Don't isolate. And you know you're a sensitive guy. You're like… I'm a sensitive woman, OK. My husband says that too. But the point I'm trying to make is don't take everything at face… don't take everything personal. Whatever you do. People are all-round shits sometimes. It has nothing to do with you. Don't take it personal. Because there will be times that it isn't going to work. From the get-go. But the point is there is love for you. You see what I'm saying? So don't get caught into a… one experience that didn't work from the get-go. Be glad that you found out from the get-go. And get on with your life. Because don't let it pitch you into the pit. Because it will… it will pass. And believe me like thirty-two thirty-three it feels like those are good time-frames for you. But that does not mean sit on your… you know… on your… on your duff until then. That's not what that meant. It doesn't mean look aggressively and make it your number one priority. That's not what I'm saying. But what I'm saying is don't neglect it completely either. Do you know what I mean? Kind of put some energy towards it but not everything. But put some energy towards it. And do have fun. And do get out with your friends. Because it seems like you're not doing too much friends stuff either. Do you know what I mean? Does that make sense?

MAYOR

Yup.

INSIGHT

So… if you… hey… join something to meet new people for friends. look at meet-up dot com. You ever heard of meet-up dot com? There's a great place. And I think it's… m… e… e… t… u… p… dot com. But for example you look in the area that you live in and all kind of interest groups. It could be interest or just interests and just meeting people in the area and it's so much fun. And there's nothing to do with dating or anything. It's more just to get out. And it's great. I know so many people I've sent to that place and so many people having a good time because of it. To be truthful it… it's just individuals who start a group on their own. You know… so it could be the hiking group. Or the dog-walking group. Or thee… or thee… you know prosperity seminar group. Or you know… the meditation group or the film interest group or the book club group. You know what I mean? But they're all started by individuals. You can even start one. An interest group. The bottom-line is… it's a great place. I'm not a sale person for them…

MAYOR

You're not getting a referral bonus?

INSIGHT

They don't make any off you just visiting either. But it's just that... I still... I still... just to get to open your energy a little bit. Because... you know... a lot has happened in your life you know with what happened to your sister. Do you know that? And... and... it's not your fault that this happened. You understand that? You must expect that as a deep level reality......... Ahh... it is a horrible thing to happen. Whatever this is... is horrible. But at the same time I have to reassure you that she's fine. And she's well and... she's happy. She's in a good place. She's not alone. She's surrounded by love. She's not... in... in a terrible place. She's not. You know what I'm saying? But she... she wants everyone to understand that she's still continuing... her life is still continuing. Do you know what I mean? But she wants everyone also to enjoy their life while they're here because... you know... sometimes grand things have to happen before we really understand things. You know? We... each person is a mortal. That's the bottom-line......... Financially, you're going to do fine. You know? You like to spend money though. Am I wrong? Everybody likes to spend money.

MAYOR

Of course. What else are you going to do with it?

INSIGHT

Oh, you're so funny. Because you... no, you are pretty free with your money. Is that fair to say?

MAYOR

Just recently.

INSIGHT

Ya maybe it is... ha... ha... it's just recently... ha... ha... you're quite funny. You know and nobody's lecturing you about it, cause it's your money and you can do with it whatever you want. It's yours. You earned it. It's yours. However... you have capacity to make good money. You know? You do have that ability. And you know... I'm not... I just... I really do feel you should enjoy your money. However you know... don't let it go forever. Make sure that you're kind of putting a little bit away. You know what I mean? You got to get into that... that... that... thing of life. When you... you can make good money. You really can. You can. You can make pretty good money... you're still incredibly young. You're thirty. You know... I know you don't think it is because it's as old as you've ever been. I know.

MAYOR

That's right.

INSIGHT

I know. But believe me there's a lot to go from here... but you know... now that you're in your thirties, just put a little bit aside. It's always good. Your sister's trying to make sure you take care of yourself. You know what I mean? And also... a... possible purchase of a house. Or a condo. Do you live in a condo?

MAYOR

Townhouse.

INSIGHT

Oh, a townhouse. Do you own it... no right?

MAYOR

Rent.

INSIGHT

That's OK. That's good because... I do get a purchase coming up with you. On your current path. It doesn't feel immediate. It feels I'll say about five... like in your mid... I'm not going to be like that I'm going to say like in... your mid... your mid-thirties. Which is not that far off. So four to six years from now. You know. Maybe even more five... six. It feels like a... a purchase. Or going ahead and doing it. But... so... put your cajoles away. If you got a little extra cajoles put it away. Little bit. You know... give... give yourself some spending money too. No one's stopping you. Put a little bit away ha... ha... ha... ha... don't be giving it to anybody neither. You know?......... Ya... she's just saying to me that there's a lot of love... that's all. Is there anybody with a j name? Like Jennifer?

MAYOR

Ya.

INSIGHT

Who's that?

MAYOR

A friend.

INSIGHT

Of yours or of hers?

MAYOR

... well both really.

INSIGHT

Ya. You both know her? OK. Because she's acknowledging that person too......... Ya. She's basically saying hello to everybody. You know? Believe me. Saying hello to everybody, and again it doesn't matter if the connection continues or if it didn't. It's irrelevant......... Does she have her license? Ya. She drove?

                    MAYOR

Yup.

                    INSIGHT

Did you get a new car? Are you thinking about it?

                    MAYOR

Ya, I am.

                    INSIGHT

Because she's just talking about something with a car with you. Or a new car... see they... they know what's going on. They do. She's kind of funny... she's almost making me feel that... you're going to do whatever you want to do no matter what anyway. Does that make sense?

                    MAYOR

Pretty much.

                    INSIGHT

Ha... ha... you decide and you kind of just do what you do and that's how you do it. Yup. You are a little spontaneous with your decisions but you can think about it. You think about it then you get really suddenly spontaneous. It's very interesting......... Your car right now isn't too bad either right now is it? Some way. It's not in a bad condition. Right?

                    MAYOR

Nope.

                    INSIGHT

It's not that old... and it works well... and... and everything's OK...

                    MAYOR

Yup.

                    INSIGHT

With it... it doesn't feel like any major surgery required... ha... ha......... M-hmm... ya. Ya your life will change bit by bit in your thirties. Little bit by little bit. You know and... and it's all good. It doesn't feel bad. It feels all good. Ya......... How was your mom's mammogram? OK? Ya. Nothing there.

                    MAYOR

No.

INSIGHT

Good. That's what I'm getting. Good. And also too, are you negligent about going to the doctor? Are you... kind of been awhile for you?

MAYOR

Yup.

INSIGHT

Has it been more than three years?

MAYOR

Pretty close.

INSIGHT

About three years? Ya. Because... because it's. it's not like anything's really... really wrong. Don't get me wrong. At all. But you should... you know... hello... once a year it's not going to bend your... out of alignment so much. You know... your universe... you should do it. We should all do it. I don't mean it because there's something wrong here. You just should do it. Ya......... Is there anybody Cathy? Or Katey? Or K... t... y... or c... t... y. That sound. I know your moms Car'y right. You said that?

MAYOR

Ya.

INSIGHT

Because I'm also getting this other name........ Does your mom have a middle name?

MAYOR

Oh God... ha... ha...

INSIGHT

Oh, you're funny. What is it?

MAYOR

I don't know.

INSIGHT

Oh my God, you're funny........ And your last name is the same as hers right?

MAYOR

Ha... ha... ya.

                    INSIGHT
You're so funny. You know I forgot again. May… Mayeur…

                    MAYOR
Mayeur.

                    INSIGHT
That's right……… OK… I keep picking up an e somewhere. Is there anybody with an e?
Who's that?

                    MAYOR
Grandmother.

                    INSIGHT
Is it… is she passed over recently? Your grandmother?

                    MAYOR
Not that I know of.

                    INSIGHT
OK that's OK… that… could be somebody addressing her from the spirit world. It could be
even your sister.

                    MAYOR
OK.

                    INSIGHT
OK? Her… she starts with an e right? Her first name?

                    MAYOR
Ya.

                    INSIGHT
E's are my worst letter. There my impossible letter. E… i… o… u… are hard! I don't know.
What is her name?

                    MAYOR
Elizabeth.

                    INSIGHT
Elizabeth. I couldn't get it. I put Eleanor. Which is an E… l… something. I just thought
ahh… I'm going to ask. Elizabeth. OK. She's addressing… OK… is that your mom's
mother? Can I say?

MAYOR

Ya.

INSIGHT

Yup, she's addressing her as well. Very much so. Who's the s name? Do... do you know an s name like Sandy or Sanny or Sandy.

MAYOR

Sandy is one of my best friends' mothers.

INSIGHT

Ya. You know her. You know her well enough to know that and your sister knows that too. Do you know that? She knows that too. Does your mom know Sandy?

MAYOR

... somewhat.

INSIGHT

Did they meet?

MAYOR

Ya.

INSIGHT

Ya? OK. Because... a... it just feels that ahh... that names also being addressed. And I think it's a way of coming to your best friend but I'm probably having a difficult time with your best friend's name......... OK. Can I have your best friend's name?

MAYOR

Ben.

INSIGHT

Well ya. It's too small too short for me too... Ben. Benji. Ha... ha... I'm teasing... ha... ha...

MAYOR

Benjamin.

INSIGHT

Benjamin! But I will say this that she's addressing that side too. He's a really good guy too, eh. He's also very smart.

MAYOR

He is.

INSIGHT

I think he's very smart. So are you. Very smart. And also there's something about... you don't do business analysis in anyway do you? You're looking at me funny. Maybe it's my interpretation of something.

MAYOR

Business analysis. It's just a broad term.

INSIGHT

Ya, but for me that's a term of special... cause I mean... we never say that to anybody. Do you do anything... with analysis of businesses or business?

MAYOR

Somewhat.

INSIGHT

Is that part of your job?

MAYOR

It's part of my title. Analyst.

INSIGHT

Oh. OK. That works. That works......... OK. I do see travel for you still, you know. And still for whatever it is you're doing for work. You know? It's almost like a feeling. Like you're going to go on... seminars or something. It... it's not really a seminar but it's like going somewhere with a lot of people. And meeting a lot of people from every other place from that company or business. You know... other places.

MAYOR

Hmm...

INSIGHT

I don't know I keep going out west. Is there a connection to Texas? Or to Arizona.

MAYOR

No.

INSIGHT

That's the area I'm getting. I don't know why.

MAYOR

Hmm…

INSIGHT

OK so… well… very close to that and geography was not my favorite but around there.

MAYOR

Arkansas is close to there.

INSIGHT

Yes. Arkansas is very close to there. Is that a connection? Arkansas?

MAYOR

Ya. It is.

INSIGHT

Arizona… Arkansas. I'm going to like on my… my big ball thing there.

MAYOR

Globe.

INSIGHT

Globe. OK because they're acknowledging that as well……… Your… your parents are very good people. They're very set, eh. They're very set people in their own way. And this is not a bad thing. It works for them you know? I get some possible trips. There are possible in the future with your parents too…. of… they have to allow them a little bit. You know? I don't know why I say it like that. But there is also a feeling of going to the south or going to Florida here with your parents. Down the road. Down… down… down the road. Of course, it's only a possibility. Not an absolute… ahh… happening. But…a…you know like something's going to come up. You know? You know. How about we go to Florida? Do you know that? That's going to come up. That's going to be a question. Well, I don't know if we should go to Florida blah… blah… blah. But you know what maybe we should go to Florida. You know? So this could go back and forth a little bit… ha… ha… no we can't do that but then he might… they might go to Florida and they actually might buy something. You know? For some weird reason. This is not right away. This is quite a bit into the future. And it's only a possibility……… Haa… OK. She's very… very proud of you. I can't say that enough. OK? She likes kind of watching how everybody gets on with their lives. You know? And she's a part of all of your lives. That will always be the case. It will never be any different. No matter… it will never be any different. And she wants you to send love to your mom and to your dad and tell them. And especially your mother. But both of them that she's very proud of them. You know? Very proud of the things that they're doing. Did she give your… did she give your mom some jewelry? Did your sister give her something?

MAYOR

It could be.

INSIGHT

It's kind of a strange way to go. Because usually I say the mother gave the child something. And maybe that happened too. I don't know. But I feel as if there's almost like a feeling that there's something she gave her mother.

MAYOR

Possibly. Ya.

INSIGHT

OK, so she gave her mother something. I don't know if they're earrings. Or something. But it just feels like that. You know? And she... and she just is sending love to your... to her mother. She just loves this family so much. Everyone in it......... It's been a rough go for everybody. What does the month of September have to do with anything? Did... did September have something to do? I think it's September. Does that have something to do with her?

MAYOR

I think so.

INSIGHT

Wasn't it the date of her passing or... do you know? If you don't know that's OK. It was.

MAYOR

Think it was.

INSIGHT

You're not sure but you think it was. I don't know... I mean... it feels that September has something to do with relative importance as well......... She just loves everybody. She is starting to fade out. But understand that... that she is close... OK... please. She... she... she's never... she sees you even if she doesn't have always the strength to communicate perfectly you know?

MAYOR

M-hmm...

INSIGHT

Very much so. And also she says watch your eyes. For glasses? Or watch your eyes. Are you wearing glasses?

MAYOR

No, but I probably should be using reading glasses.

INSIGHT

OK. Or watch them or take good care of them. You know what I mean? You're not going to go blind, I promise you. But it's just a feeling that you know… just take care of them or don't be doing something in the dark or… you know… take precaution. That kind of feeling. Ya. Take care of your eyes.

MAYOR

OK.

INSIGHT

You know?……… You know you have a little bit of interest in interesting things too. By the way. You know? I… I… don't know what this is. But are you going to go biking? A… motor biking or…? Something with wheels other than a car.

MAYOR

Hmm…

INSIGHT

Are you going to be doing some kind of like… I don't know. Ha… I don't know… ha… ha… what this is to me… honestly… ha… ha. I don't really know. But it… it's like a little bit of adventure. You know? Outdoors is good for you. I don't know if you're getting enough of it but maybe you should.

MAYOR

I need more.

INSIGHT

Ya, because a little bit of the outdoors is going to do a lot of wonders for you. Really. Ya……… Ya. Do you have any questions? Your future is… it's actually not a bad one. I feel the advice is… take a little care with your money. Doesn't mean you can't spend it to have a good time. Just make sure you put a few pennies away… your work world… I think is going to go very well as long as you're willing and ready and able and participate in what you want. I feel that you will want to do that anyway. You are kind of driven I must say. Inside you. So I think you have the natural drive to do that any… anyway regardless of what… whatever I say. So I feel that… that will be OK and good. Some things will work out better than others. You know that's normal isn't it?

MAYOR

Yup.

But generally you'll… you'll do very well. Just watch the money. Because it doesn't matter how much you make you know. Watch the money a little bit. But I do think you have the ability to watch your money. With regards to love… I feel like you know thirty-two. What are you? Thirty. Thirty-two… thirty-three are good timeframes for love. Building up… the bricks of the house to get to that point. You know what I mean? Building towards it… get yourself… percolate. Get around. Get a little edge. Don't lock yourself… in a closet. You know? Get yourself out a little bit intentionally, even if it's painful sometime. And you really will start meeting people and I do feel there will be some really good luck with love around that age for you. And you may even meet her before that but around that age especially. So good outcome… your mom is divine. You know… you have a good family. You have a lot of love in… the physical world. And you also have a lot of love in spirit world. And they get a lot out of watching all of you do your thing. Ha… ha… ha… ha… they really do. They really do……… And do you have any questions?

MAYOR

No.

INSIGHT

That's great.

MAYOR

You got it all.

INSIGHT

That's really great.

MAYOR

Surprisingly that was the purpose of me coming here.

INSIGHT

Not to ask any questions.

MAYOR

No, this is good.

INSIGHT

Oh… thank God. I… you know… when I started to feel her I knew that it had to be your sister. Because you know… she was so obviously waiting for you. You know. She's been waiting for you… do you… you had another reading before ya? Did you have another reading before?

MAYOR

Ya.

INSIGHT

She's making me feel like you've had another reading. Tried to contact her right?

MAYOR

Yup.

INSIGHT

Is that true? Ya……… She says she tries every time. You know? She does try. Don't blame it on her. She's trying. You know what I mean? She loves you. She wants to be close to you. She is close to you no matter what you get or don't hear. She's close to you. And also, she is trying to give you all signs you know. She is trying. Trying. It isn't easy. You know? It isn't easy. And certain things have to be in play for it to work that way. For example, energy has to be more aligned and resilient. And even though you might think…well, I'm open and I'm receptive and I can you know… blah… blah… blah… blah… sometimes it… it isn't always easy. Because people aren't as aligned as they think they are. You know? And people aren't going to always do things and scare people. Because as well because will question well is it her… is it really her or is it somebody else. Or what's really going on here. So she's really coming the way that she believes she can come… into the scenario. She has had dreams with you. I'm not sure if you can remember them all. But she has been in your dreams.

MAYOR

Hmm…

INSIGHT

At least the way she's projecting to me. She has been in your dreams. You are a heavy sleeper. Is that fair to say? You're fairly heavy?

MAYOR

I used to remember my dreams pretty…

INSIGHT

Ya.

MAYOR

Pretty vividly.

INSIGHT

Do you remember any that you had with her?

MAYOR

No.

INSIGHT

OK. That's honest. That's a very honest statement. She is trying to come into your dreams. So even if you… before you go to sleep… you know… doesn't mean it's going to happen the first time you do it. I bet you it won't. I bet you'll have to do it lots… and lots… and lots… and lots. But it could. It could happen the first time. But before you start to go to sleep. As you're starting to go to sleep. Just ask… you know… for her to come through in your dreams or… if you want her to. You know what I mean? And also ask that you can be open and receptive and also remember her through the dream when you get up. Because I do feel she is trying or she will try to come into your dreams. She says that she's had two dreams with you. Two significant dreams with you. But then when we wake up, sometimes we just forget you know… before we even wake up. So just ask to… to remember them. And also a little bit around electricity. There were a few electrical things…that I feel as though she's been inspiring. Does this make sense at all? To you or your mom?

MAYOR

Electrical things? Ya.

INSIGHT

Electrical things. Like bulbs… lights… or electrical things.

MAYOR

Maybe.

INSIGHT

She has tried to do that. It was… it was probably more now awhile ago then now. But she has tried also that. And also you know… it's… it's just like the energy isn't exactly open to that. Not everyone's on the same page. Do you understand that?

MAYOR

I guess.

INSIGHT

And it's not because they all don't love her. Because they all love her. She really knows it. And it doesn't matter either way. She really is connected, period, anyway. Do you understand? It doesn't matter if she can make a light bulb flicker or she can't. She knows her truth. But… she thinks you're so sweet. She thinks you're so cute. Ha… ha… ha… ha… ha… I can't believe I said that. But she does. She really does. Just keep moving forward and… and follow your own light as much as possible. That'll bring her the greatest joy. OK? And never feel alone. Because there's no such thing. There is absolutely no… ha… such thing. There just isn't. OK? Thank you very… very much. It's Dani right?

MAYOR

That's right.

INSIGHT

Thank you very much, Dani. Thank you. And you can talk to her anytime. She hears you. You know I've had people come here for a reading and they go... tell them this. And I'm like... ha... ha... he can hear you. You don't need me to tell him. You tell him yourself. You know? I can't tell them anything more than you do. In fact they'll listen to you probably a lot better than me. Because they love... they know you more than me. You know?

MAYOR

I'll tell my mom to keep talking to her.

INSIGHT

Oh, ya. She hears everything. She hears everything. It's so important... you know? Gosh it's amazing. You know when my father passed away. And my dad and I are very close. I mean very close. You know how close? I called my dad or he called me every single day and we talked and I'm not joking I know it sounds a little obsessive. But around two to three hours a day. Think about that. That's pretty close. We understood each other. I mean we just did. I don't know what it is. We just understood each other. You know? And we're very accepting of each other. You know? Because we are both not perfect. You know? We're very accepting of each other. We could get really mad at each other. Really mad. But then we'd always... always forgive each other. And like nothing happened. And we'd go right back to square one. We never hold grudges with each other. You know what I'm saying? Shit happens. Oh well. Move along. That kind of attitude. Where everyone else in my life they think ohh... if you do anything it's like they hold it forever. So you have to always edit everything.

MAYOR

M-hmm.

INSIGHT

So anyway. My dad passed away and I tell you it was the hardest thing. Even doing this for a living. It was extraordinarily hard. All of a sudden the calls stopped. You know? Everything just stopped. And... after... I mean... understand my dad knew what I did. You know at first he thought OK I love my daughter but helloo! You know because he... he was a joker. He had such a sense of humor my dad. He still has such a sense a... sense of humor. You know he just joked and would go OKK! We won't get in her way but HELLO! You know? Funny and I laughed too. I said... ahh ya... dad... I know I lost my marbles. You know? Lost them a long time ago. But... but then again... long before he passed away like about the year before he acknowledged my work and he said you know there must be really something to what you're doing because somebody else I knew... it's a long story... so anyway he was very… very supportive actually after that. He was very supportive. He actually said very amazing things to me which… which meant a lot. But to make a long story short. After about one year. Actually once a year. On my dad's birthday. Hmm… this has actually happened. My husband… we were in another place. We were in a townhouse and my husband says honey come here. Come here. Hurry. Come here. This is like two o'clock in the morning or three o'clock in the morning because… I… I was a rather late person sometimes. Not so much anymore. And he goes "come look". Come look. So I come into the bedroom. Rush into the bedroom. We're standing in front of the bed. On both sides we have a lamp. There… it's a touch lamp. You know the one where it's a low light. You just go like this… low…

MAYOR

Oh, you just flick it.

INSIGHT

Medium… high… you know we go them from like a store. And so anyways… so we're sitting there watching the one on my side of the bed. On my dad's birthday. One year after his death. The very next year. The first birthday since his death. We're watching as the light is going in all kinds of intervals you know like all kinds of… the timing is completely crazy. One minute it's fast. One minute slow. Little bit fast. Little bit fast. Little slow. Crazy and we're watching it. As it's just doing this all by itself. And I immediately said I love you dad. I love you! Immediately! Because of what I do you know, I understood it's his birthday logically Hello! It doesn't take… you know… the universe to figure it out. There's a whole lot of days in a year and it was just a coincidental day I'm sure. You know? And the other lamp wasn't doing it at all. Only the one on my side. We watched it do it for, not jokingly, about twelve maybe thirteen… fourteen… fifteen minutes. It just kept doing that. And the amazing thing is… if that wasn't amazing enough… every single morning that I woke up and my husband woke up in the morning… that light was on low. Beside my bed. And this went on… I don't know… maybe six weeks… maybe five weeks… maybe four weeks. But it went on for some time. Not just a full week or a few days. Every single morning, the light went on just like low. But I woke up in the morning and I turned it off, and the next morning it would be on low again. It started after that day. The very first day. After that first day. And it was like my dad was saying honey I'm with you. I'm with you and I love you. I'm still here. And then it stops all together. It didn't do it again for almost over a year… a year and a half. It was a long time. I… I thought he forgot about it. That he would never do it again. And then I woke up after so many months. I'm not kidding you it must have been at least a year. Well, it was on again. And I was so freaking happy. You won't believe it. I was so happy that I left it on all day. And I went in the shower and I was literally washing my hair and remember thinking inside my head… thinking God, I'm silly. This is ridiculous. Turn off the damn light. How could I leave the light on all day. I can't leave the light on for like a week. I have to sleep. You know come on. Don't be silly.

MAYOR

At some point.

INSIGHT

Ya… ya…I got to go out and turn it off when I'm finished the shower. This really happened. So I finished my shower. I came outside the shower. I robed, dried… whatever I could do. And say that's the lamp… and here's the… the bathroom door's here. And I just come out. I've only made the decision in my head so I've told no one that I'm going to turn that off after I come out of bath. So I'm walking… and I swear to you! I screamed! I was walking and I'm about this far and the light goes off by itself. He actually was listening to my whole drama in the bathroom. Ha… ha… ha… ha…

MAYOR

Saved you a few steps.

INSIGHT

Exactly. Ha… ha… but I'm telling you my husband has gotten to the point where he says nothing is impossible. He said man… he goes so many things. When we're open and when we're receptive. But mind you, sometimes we don'…, those kind of signs at all. Because we just know that in here…and also, sometimes, they're subtle. They're very… very subtle. The one person… person! that your sister truly loves is you. She loves you equal value. She loves your mother too so much. She loves her dad too, a lot. She… you know it's funny, it's almost like it's a different energy though. She loves your dad a lot too though. You know… you two are… you know… always going to be very close. Nothing changes that. Nothing. You know that don't you?

MAYOR

I do.

INSIGHT

I love that. And there's no point telling you endlessly the same thing. And now I'm taking… my God the time goes by so fast! What is that? I hope I didn't bore you with that little story too much.

MAYOR

No.

INSIGHT

Is there anything you need before you go? Bathroom?

MAYOR

Ya, I could use the bathroom now. That tea didn't help.

[173   ]

INSIGHT
OK, I'll show you where it is.

EXIT THE INSIGHT AND TIM THE MAYOR

Intermission

05/28/2008

ENTER THE CURTAINS AND TIM THE FOOL

CURTAINS

Alright. So last time you and I had got together… I went to look for you on Facebook. I couldn't find you.

FOOL

No? I'm there.

CURTAINS

Are you there? OK. Alright. I'll have another look.

FOOL

Facebook is a little bit weird. You can't find people if they're in… like… certain networks.

CURTAINS

OK.

FOOL

You're in your own network. And for networking reasons, I choose to put LA California.

CURTAINS

Oh, did you? OK.

FOOL

Ya.

CURTAINS

OK. Alright.

FOOL

That might be it.

CURTAINS

That might be it. OK, so I'll look for you then……… How did you feel when you left here last time? What… any… feelings of… what happened? Anything?

FOOL

Just refreshed.

CURTAINS

Refreshed? Hmm… hmm… hmm……… What about the journey itself? Did any of it stay with you?

FOOL

… pretty much all of it. The interesting thing is that I've been contemplating whether or not if it was actually a past life or if it was some sort of… ahmm… some sort of a way of… guess… not isolating but pushing off some feelings I've had onto another persona. So my mind just getting creative and disassociating with…

CURTAINS

Well, I don't care. You see I really don't care. When… when I'm talking to the media and they say to me how can you be sure that this is real CURTAINS. How can you be… and I say well I don't care. I don't care if it's real or it's a metaphor that the mind makes up. As long as you get the wisdom and the understanding that enables you to make this life better. So it doesn't matter.

FOOL

No, it doesn't.

CURTAINS

So welcome to my world. It really makes no difference what we call it. But the journey that you went on has some meaning and that's the important thing……… So maybe you were creative. Maybe you're not. Maybe you went into a past life. Maybe you didn't. So what?

FOOL

So what?

CURTAINS

So have you been doing your homework?

FOOL

Well…

CURTAINS

Why not?

FOOL

My homework was to increase my interactions with people. And… well that's part of it.

CURTAINS

Ya, it sure was.

FOOL

And ya, I've been doing that.

CURTAINS

How many people a day have you.?.

FOOL

A little bit.

CURTAINS

This much of a little bit or this much of a little bit?

FOOL

A few times a day.

CURTAINS

A few times a day?

FOOL

Ya.

CURTAINS

People you wouldn't normally speak to?

FOOL

… maybe once a day, for people I wouldn't normally speak to. They're just random.

CURTAINS

OK. OK, so you're going to be doing this more OK because it's… it's critically important
and I know it's hard. It's very difficult. That's why you're here. So I'm going to work

subconsciously and you gotta do the work consciously. So we're going to both work on the same thing.

FOOL

OK.

CURTAINS

Alright?

FOOL

Ya.

CURTAINS

Ah, it's like anything you know, if you don't do it you don't learn. We can talk about it forever. Ya know? We can talk about you… I don't know… learning a new computer skill. But if you don't do it you won't learn it. The first time you do it, it's gunna feel awkward. The second time you do it it'll get a little easier. And the third time… hey, you'll wonder what took you so long……… Alright?

FOOL

Ya.

CURTAINS

You're gunna have to do it. Ya……… Do I have to phone you every day and say who… who did you speak to today? Or you're gunna do it yourself?

FOOL

Or you want a list of names?

CURTAINS

Ha… ha… ya. And I will check up on you……… No it's just… because you're too good to waste. And it's a shame if you stay in that corner. You know? You're smart. You're bright. You're cute. It's to… to… to… too much of a shame……… So you're gunna have to push a little bit and get out there.

FOOL

OK.

CURTAINS

OK?

FOOL

Ya.

CURTAINS

Good......... Alright let me just check where we are... so the anger went? It seems. Is that right?

FOOL

Yup.

CURTAINS

Have you... have you been feeling any different? At all?

FOOL

A lot more at ease.

CURTAINS

A lot more at ease?......... So we'll see what we're going to work on this time......... See where we go......... OK. So I'm gunna... I'm gunna... I'm gunna cross anger off......... How's the sadness?......... Still there or it's gone?

FOOL

It's getting better.

CURTAINS

It's getting better? So, say you we're overflowing. Where would it be now?

FOOL

Mid-range.

CURTAINS

OK. So I'll leave it for another week and we'll see where we go there......... So let's work on anxiety this week. Is that good for you?

FOOL

That's fine.

CURTAINS

... anxiety or abandonment or shame... what would you like?

FOOL

Anxiety.

CURTAINS

Ya. OK......... That will help you get out there and chat.

FOOL

That's right.

CURTAINS

Ha... ha... ha... ha... ha...

FOOL

Help me do my homework.

CURTAINS

It really will help you......... Alright, we'll just check......... Alright? Ready? Put your feet up......... Alright... haaaaaaaaah... made you feel good? Yaa... OK. Take a deep breath and just exhale......... And just begin to find your breathing......... And just notice the coolness of your in breath... and the warmth of your out breath......... Just notice how easily and smoothly the cycle of your breath goes......... Coolness in... and warmth out......... Now I count from one to twenty and as I do just allow you with just your mind... body and your spirit to relax......... Follow your breath......... One... two... three... four... five. Follow your breath. The coolness of your in breath. The warmth of your out breath......... Six... seven... eight... nine. Relaxing all the way down......... Ten... eleven. Feeling safe and secure and very... very good......... Twelve... thirteen. The deeper you go. The better you feel......... Fourteen. That's right... letting go now. Fifteen......... Sixteen... seventeen... eighteen... nineteen... twenty......... Relaxing all the way down. Finding yourself in your safe place......... Wonderful space......... You feel so good......... You're little place. And a magic place. Inside or out. It's your safe place......... And find some way to sit in this wonderful and beautiful place. And allow yourself to drift deeper... and deeper... and deeper......... Now imagine your timeline stretching all the way back into the past. Way... way... way back. Into a sort of misty cloud. Way... way... way back......... And all the way out into this future. A very clear bright future......... Put right where we are today. Put a big flag......... So that you know... we're here today......... When you have that in your mind. Whether you see it or think it or hear it. Just let me know by moving your yes finger......... Good. Thank you......... Now in your mind, just lift yourself above that line. Way up above. So you get an eagle eye view... of your life and lifetimes......... Looking down. And begin to float back. Begin to float back. Over the days... the weeks... the months... and the years. And maybe even generations. All the way back to the very first time that anxiety came into your body. The very first time you felt that anxiousness come into your body......... Feeling... being unsafe. Anxiousness. Being judged. Whatever caused the anxiety. All the way back to the very first time. The point of entry of that feeling of anxiety......... So floating back now over the months... the years... the years... and years and come on down on the timeline into the womb of your mother. Into that dark and warm place. The sound of the heartbeat. Just imagine yourself there. Feel it. Feel the rhythm of the heart......... The sound is all around you. And while you're here in the womb just notice if there's any anxiety with you... in the womb. If there is, your yes finger responds. If there isn't, your no finger responds. Just notice......... There is. Good. And just notice, does this anxiety come from your mother?......... If it does, your yes finger responds. If it doesn't, your no finger responds......... Good........ Then begin the journey back... beyond the womb. Through the blue mist of life between lives. Following that feeling of anxiety all the way back. All the way back to another time and another place. With the count of three find yourself there. One... two... three........ And notice where you are. And what is happening........ Notice whether you're inside or outside........ Whether it's daytime or nighttime. Whether you're young or old. Just notice. Become aware what's happening. And bring moisture to your mouth and tell me where you are. And what is happening. Become aware of what's causing the anxiety. And tell me. Don't let your voice disturb you. Tell me what's happening. What you perceive. Are you male or female?......... Allow yourself to speak even if you're very young. Allow it to come through. And tell me where you are and what you perceive.

FOOL

I'm not anywhere.

CURTAINS

OK......... In the... womb of your mother you felt the anxiety but it didn't come from her. Is that correct?

FOOL

No.

CURTAINS

It's not correct?

FOOL

No, it didn't come from her.

CURTAINS

OK, good........ Then let's go back. Beyond the womb into the blue mist. And see if it came from the time of choosing to come into this life. You're looking for the point of entry of that feeling of anxiety. As you ready yourself to come into this lifetime with you are guides or others who travel with you to help you make decisions. As you get ready to choose to come into this lifetime, just notice if that gives you the feeling of anxiety. Or if it was before. Just notice. And let me know when you have the answer.

FOOL

It was before this life.

CURTAINS

OK, good. And allow yourself to move through the blue mist. Asking your guides and those who travel with you in this lifetime or other lifetimes to be with you as we go to that lifetime.

That brought in the anxiety into your body. And as you go through the blue mist the mist begins to dissolve. And you come down... down... down onto the planet earth. In a different place in a different time. And you set foot on the ground. Just look down. look around you. And tell me what you perceive. Where you are. Whether you're inside or outside. Daytime or nighttime.

                              FOOL
There's no place.

                              CURTAINS
What do you perceive?

                              FOOL
Almost looks like a face.

                              CURTAINS
A face? Uh huh.

                              FOOL
Almost. It's not clear.

                              CURTAINS
OK......... Ask that face to take you where you need to go.

                              FOOL
The face won't show me.

                              CURTAINS
Is it something that has to be hidden? Secret.

                              FOOL
Doesn't want me to see. It wants to watch.

                              CURTAINS
Ahh... OK......... Can this face that is watching you help us to understand the anxiety?......... Whose face or what face is this? Who does it belong to?

                              FOOL
Can't make it out.

                              CURTAINS
OK. Ask.

FOOL

It just shows me my own.

CURTAINS

Ah. I'm going to talk to that face directly. And ask... Face... whatever your name is. To take us to the time you had your own body. Because right now you're attached to Tim's body in this lifetime. Take us to that place when you had your own body. Tell me what's happening.

FOOL

He won't. They're just impatient.

CURTAINS

Say what?

FOOL

Impatient.

CURTAINS

Impatient? He's impatient? The Face is impatient or we're impatient?

FOOL

Face.

CURTAINS

OK. Well, what does the Face want from us? What does it want us to do?......... What does it want us to do?

FOOL

Game.

CURTAINS

This is a game? Uh huh.

FOOL

I see a chess board.

CURTAINS

Well, we're not playing a game... this... Face... is an energy that doesn't belong to Tim. I'm going to call on the Arch Angel Michael and Gabriel. To come along with the guides that travel with Tim. And take this energy. This Face that is preventing Tim from moving forward. Take it into the light. I'm going to call, with humility and respect, the Archangel Michael and Gabriel to come down. Tim's guides. We're going to let that Face go into the light. And go home. And leave Tim alone......... Surrounding Tim with one-hundred percent pure light... and anything other than that leaves......... As the light expands. The pure white light... expands. The energy. And anything but that... is let go. Has no place around Tim. This is a planet of free will. And nothing can force itself on you that doesn't belong to you......... And let me know if he's gone or it's gone. Or where it is? Or what's happening?

FOOL

It's gone.

CURTAINS

Good......... Now let's find that anxiety. Let's go back into the womb. That dark warm place......... The sound of the heartbeat. You can feel the heartbeat......... You feel those around you. Connected......... Sound. All full sound. The rhythm of the heartbeat......... And just notice why you're here. The gentle movement. All full sounds......... And just notice if there's any feelings of anxiety in the womb......... No. Good. And while you're in the womb just notice how good you feel here. But also check to see if you carry any other feelings with you that don't belong to you. Any feelings of... abandonment... or shame... any feelings of shame in the womb?......... No. Good......... You feel yourself growing and growing... towards birthing......... And as you come into the world a brand-new baby. Make your way forward. From a new born to two... to three... four... and along the way just see if shame comes into your body. Along the way. Carrying shame at age four... or five... or six. Six years old just see if there's any sense of feelings of shame within. There is, your yes finger responds. There isn't, your no finger responds......... Any shame at age six?......... Good. Seven?......... Eight? You just keep going forward until that feeling of shame connects with you......... When it does your yes finger responds......... Nine... ten......... Eleven... twelve......... Sense or feeling of shame......... All the way into the current day. Thirteen... fourteen... fifteen. And just move your finger. Your yes finger when shame comes into your life. Fifteen... sixteen. All the way to now just journeying along the timeline. And if you make it to the end of the timeline and there is no shame just move your no finger......... Good......... And let's journey back along the timeline. Back and back and back......... Through the womb of your mother into the blue mist of life between lives. And while you're here in this... in this mist... ask those that travel with you to take you to another time and another place. That will give you an understanding and insight about your current life. Ask if it's appropriate that you take this journey. And if it is, your yes finger responds. If it isn't, your no finger responds......... No. OK......... And go inside your mother's womb. And back along the timeline to your safe place......... And while you're in your safe place, go deep inside yourself and find that part of you who is the little boy. And hold him and keep him warm. Maybe four or five. Wrap your arms around him and tell him that you love him......... Tell him what a great kid he is. So cute to look at. So smart and bright......... Just hold him close to your heart. He needs to feel safe. He needs to feel loved......... As you hold him... ask him if he'd like for you to do this on a regular basis. And he would make that promise to him. But also tell him that you're going to listen to him. Because he needs to be heard. This child needs to be heard. He needs to be loved unconditionally. He needs to be heard.

FOOL

It's not important to him.

CURTAINS

To be heard?......... Is it important for him to be loved? Curious.

FOOL

No.

CURTAINS

Is it important for him to be feeling trust and safety?......... He needs to feel safe.

FOOL

It's important for him to grow up.

CURTAINS

OK. As he grows, up he trusts. Because if he doesn't trust and love, then part of him will always stay a frightened child......... Important for him to learn how to nurture and love and be nurtured. And important for him to feel safe. And also, he'll not be able to interact with anyone else without trust. There'll always be a part of him that will be a frightened child who doesn't learn to trust... and love. Does that make sense to him?

FOOL

Ya. He doesn't have time.

CURTAINS

He has all the time in the world. He's a little boy. He's four or five or six. And he can learn. He has twenty... thirty years to learn. He can learn. There's nothing else to do but to learn to trust and love... and be loved. That's his job......... What else does he have to do?......... Hmm?......... What else does he have to do?......... Except to grow up... as a warm and loving kind good baby......... Tell me what's happening.

FOOL

It's not the right time. He needs to grow up.

CURTAINS

He needs to grow up?......... When you plant a seed and the seed begins to sprout...unless that seed has guidance, it doesn't stand tall and strong. Sometimes it just flops over and becomes weak and can't reach the sun. What we're doing now is giving him the opportunity to be attached to a stake that will help him grow tall and strong. And grow up.

[185]

Absolutely. Grow slowly and appropriately because it wasn't done right the first time.........
And who is this that's making judgment about how he should be and what he should be?
Who's judging him?......... Who is it that's telling him that he has to grow up? To have no
time to do anything else. Who's telling him that?

FOOL

Sense another person but they're not there anymore.

CURTAINS

Right. Right. So maybe it's the part of you that is the Judge. Because we're all many
parts......... I'm going to ask that part that is the Judge... to stand aside and let that child
grow up with joy and trust. We don't need you anymore. We might have needed you
when the boy was young. Because you thought you were doing a good job about keeping
him on the straight and narrow. But we really don't need you right now. We may need you
in the future but right now we don't need you......... So I'm going to ask that part of you
that is the Judge to step aside. And let the boy grow up strong... true... healthy... loved and
loving person.

FOOL

He won't.

CURTAINS

Who said?......... The Judge won't stand aside or the boy won't grow up?

FOOL

The Judge.

CURTAINS

Won't stand aside? OK. OK.

FOOL

He's not done yet.

CURTAINS

So when will he be done?......... When will his job be over?

FOOL

Soon.

CURTAINS

What does that mean? A day... two days... a week... twenty-four hours. What does that
mean?......... I want a commitment from the Judge. What does soon mean?

FOOL

He's not gunna make a commitment. He's getting angry.

CURTAINS

Good. Good. Ya, very good. The interesting thing about judging… Judges… is that they are
very judgmental of others but the minute they're questioned or judged, they get put into a
corner and they get angry. It's really quite interesting. So we know that people… and
Judges usually have very low self-esteems. Because they can't stand in the light. Because
you're putting other people in the light. Shining a spotlight on others and judging them.
The minute they're judged, they get angry. So it's all to do with that low self-esteem
because… so tell the Judge to get over it. Get over it. You said soon. I just want to know
what you mean by soon. It doesn't have to be to the hour. Give me an approximation of
what soon means.

FOOL

Two years.

CURTAINS

Soon is… that's not soon, that's later. What's going to happen between now and two
years?……… What's going to happen between now and two years? Why two years?………
Hmm?……… Is it a benchmark time or what is… what's… what's the two years?……… It's
pretty specific. I mean there must be a reason why?

FOOL

Some sort of purpose is going to be fulfilled.

CURTAINS

Oh. Like what?

FOOL

He's not saying.

CURTAINS

Hmm… hmm… hmm… OK.……… Alright, Judge, we're going to let you be for now. But
I'm going to get back to you later. We're going to bring in the other archetypes because
you're not the only archetype that's contained. There's many others around you right now.
You're probably the loudest and most stubborn. But there are others we can work with. So
right now, Judge, we're going to let you go and we're going to ask Tim to recognize that
that's somebody that's trying to get in the way of his little boy. But the interesting thing is
what you discovered ,what it is, and who it is ,then you can deal with it. It is what's
undiscovered that is a problem, but now we know. So as an archetype of Judge, I'm going
to ask Tim to consider who in his family was very judgmental.……… When you were
growing up Tim. When you were very young who was very judgmental of you. A teacher?

A parent? A caregiver? Who was it that was judgmental of you when you were young?........ Your mother? Who was it?........ You're having a hard time finding your Judge?

FOOL

It's no one.

CURTAINS

No one? OK........ We may be aware that we're all made up of everything. We are kind and we're all stupid. We're all smart. We're all unkind........ We're all everything. And the archetypes are part of us all. And the ones that we choose to use help us through rough times in our lives. But we can choose different ones. So I'm giving warning to the Judge. That his time with us is limited. And it's certainly less than two years. Because it's too interfering in the way of Tim's growth and flourishing in this lifetime........ I'd like right now for Tim to emerge and moving forward on his timeline........ Moving forward a year. A year in which he's been working and doing his homework and working with me. And become stronger inside........ More sure of himself. Seeing himself as he truly is. Letting go of the judgment. Letting go of the fear. Moving forward in confidence. Meeting people. Dating. Having fun. Living his life's purpose........ Having fun. Joy. Love. Laughter. All the things he's been denied up to now. He's moving into that time in his life. And as you see yourself moving into that time... notice the light around you. Imagine that light around you. The bright white light. Helping you feel safe and protected. Confident. Loving. Loveable. Loved........ And when you can imagine that. When you see that. When you feel the possibility of that. Just let me know by moving your yes finger........ How good it's going to look and feel........ Good. Now take a picture of that. And place a copy of that picture on your computer screen. And a copy of that picture by the side of your bed. So when you go to bed at night and when you wake up in the morning, it's the last thing and the first thing you see. A picture of your future. And put a copy on your fridge. Anywhere else you want........ You have a picture of your future right there before you. When you have done that just take yourself back to a place of safety........ And I'm going to count from ten to one as I do just slowly bring yourself back to the here and now. Coming back now. Ten... nine... eight... seven... six... five... coming up to full awareness... four... three... moving your hands and feet... two... moving your hands... and one. And bring yourself back. Come on back to the here and now. Come on back........ Welcome back. That was interesting........ Do you know about archetypes?

FOOL

No.

CURTAINS

OK. Have some homework for you.

FOOL

More homework?

CURTAINS

More homework.

FOOL

Is there a test at the end?

CURTAINS

Ha... ha... ha... yes. You're the test......... You can get these all online or you can get Caroline Myss' book on archetypes......... Research archetypes. We'll see where you fall. We'll see where you are. We all have the Judge in us. Frankly we all have every piece in us. The archetype. Whether it be the God or the Goddess or the Prince... King... the Emperor. We all have these pieces of us... simpleton. But we need to know which piece is playing on us at each... which times so we can recognize it and say... get rid of my Judge right now. I'm not being judged or whatever it is. And the Judge quite often is the strongest. But we have to recognize it and just move it aside. It stops us from moving forward. Because nobody likes being wrong all the time. And when you got a huge Judge sort of sitting there. It makes us wrong with everything we do. We don't do anything. Right?

FOOL

Or we keep on doing it and keep on doing it wrong.

CURTAINS

He... he... he... or being told we're doing it wrong. By ourselves, which isn't necessarily the case. So tell me what happened with that... that Face. It went away obviously......... It blocked you. I wonder if it was an energy of something or someone. You get a sense of what it was or who it was.

FOOL

Actually, I thought it was kind of alien.

CURTAINS

OK. May well have been. May well have been. Yup. This Judge may well be too. I don't know we'll have to see if we can get rid of it. If we can't, we'll have to do something else.

FOOL

I think it was the same thing.

CURTAINS

It's the same thing?

FOOL

Ya.

CURTAINS

OK, so the Judge is the same thing. OK, so we got somebody monitoring you. But we'll just have to make sure… but check on the archetypes. Let me make a note about that……… So the anxiety went away with it though? You said it's gone. When that Face left, the anxiety left. Because you went back into the womb, it wasn't there……… Do you remember anything when you were young about any visitations or anything at all?

FOOL

No.

CURTAINS

No? OK……… Because some people do. I don't know if you did. OK. Alright. So when you scan your body that anxiety's gone. It's all gone?

FOOL

Well, we'll see when I leave here.

CURTAINS

Well, ya. There's no shame? It's gone. You seem confused when I asked you about shame. But you told me last week…

FOOL

I took care of it.

CURTAINS

Did you take care of it?

FOOL

Ya.

CURTAINS

OK. How did you do that?

FOOL

I had a good psychic reading with a Medium who got in touch with my sister.

CURTAINS

Oh, great. And that's gone? Ya?

                              FOOL

A lot of that shame and guilt is gone.

                            CURTAINS

Terrific. So let me look at see what we got left to work on. Let me find it. M-hmm. Alright anger's gone. We knew that. So anxiety. You have any in your body now?

                              FOOL

It's probably still there.

                            CURTAINS

Well, you don't know that. When you go and chat with people we'll find out how much is still there. OK?

                              FOOL

Yup.

                            CURTAINS

Abandonment? Nope?

                              FOOL

No.

                            CURTAINS

Because you had ninety last time. OK. Grief?

                              FOOL

No, I think I've taken care of all that.

                            CURTAINS

Good. Sadness?

                              FOOL

Little bit.

                            CURTAINS

Still there? Ya… shame seems gone. Feelings of not good enough that was in there. Fear? Still some?

                              FOOL

Still there. Think it was coupled with the anxiety.

CURTAINS

OK… alright……… So if you've taken care of that we don't need to work on things like forgiveness. Because you've looked after it. So tell me about your psychic reading. What happened?

FOOL

Actually pretty accurate. I didn't reveal any information upfront and she was able to pull things about my sister having passed away and her name and I guess some of the circumstances around it. A lot of what she was saying did sound like it would be her communicating it.

CURTAINS

And how did you find this person?

FOOL

Hmm… online.

CURTAINS

Oh really. So you did it all online? You didn't speak to her or anything… it was all online?

FOOL

Oh no, I found her online.

CURTAINS

OK. Then you went to see her.

FOOL

Went to see.

CURTAINS

So she could feel your energy. Some people I know can do it over the phone. What's her name?

FOOL

THE INSIGHT.

CURTAINS

Oh, I heard of her. Ya. M-hmm. And she's good huh?

FOOL

Ya.

CURTAINS

I'm going to take a note because I always get people asking.

FOOL

So I had a tape of that and my mom is listening to it right now.

CURTAINS

Ahh.

FOOL

Because she had some concerns about... she felt that she would get communications or support from my sister and she felt that went away, so it's a little encouraging for her to hear this.

CURTAINS

That's very kind of you. Nice thought........ So in fact a lot of what we were... what we were planning to work on has shifted. Because what you did in the psychic reading. So what we really have to focus on now is your social anxiety.

FOOL

Ya.

CURTAINS

OK. That's what we'll do. That's what we'll focus on from now on. Because all the other stuff has gone by the wayside. That's good news. Social anxiety. OK. And that's been with you since pretty much for as long as you can remember. When you're a kid almost.

FOOL

Since the start.

CURTAINS

Since the start? Hmm... ya... OK. Alright so... let's see what the time is... we don't have time to do anything right now. No let's do that next time and I'll just charge you for it... because we only got ten minutes. Fifteen minutes left. So I'll just charge you for the hour today.

EXIT THE CURTAINS AND TIM THE FOOL

ACT V

SCENE I

05/28/2008

ENTER THE HOLY GHOST AND TIM THE MAYOR

HOLY GHOST

Turn the… turn the news on… turn the news on?… turn the sound on… is it work… is it on?

MAYOR

Yup.

HOLY GHOST

OK. Where would you like to start?……… There's something about August. I get my mom here… I get August… August… August. So I'll go say… Spirit thank you… my mom is saying… like if you feel right now like…hmm you know err… err… err… I'm being pulled this way… I'm being pulled that way. I just get my mom saying… August… I'll give you August the 8th. I don't know what day that is of the week but August 8th I feel like… Spirit… mom… my mom is saying everything's going to come right on time. Right on time.

MAYOR

OK.

HOLY GHOST

And I'll just go into your diet. And I'm not telling you what to eat. But I just get Spirit showing me turkey. So I don't know if turkey has protein or whatever turkey… means.

But… so say… I'll just say if you eat ribs or whatever or beef or whatever. Nothing against the cattle raisers… cattle farmers out there. But Spirit is saying… I feel it… OK two things. You're gunna eating turkey but you're gunna be talking turkey. OK so this is symbolic. So these powers in the universe or powers that be… you'll be talking turkey. And I get my mom saying you're going to be signing deals right on time. Right on time. Do you… now I'm not trying to be a smart alec… do you send your clothes out to the dry cleaners or something? You will. Cause I feel… I feel you moving. But when you do… I just get my mom saying you're going to be so busy that you're gunna drop it off at the corner. You know like there's a lot of little places around here. So wherever you're living… just like… just like mine are laying over there. It's not dry-cleaned. It was just in the laundry and I gotta hang it up. But my mom is saying you'll be busy. That…

MAYOR

That's good.

HOLY GHOST

And I'll tell you… she… I know she gave us August 8th but there's also something about August 16th. So I'll say… I don't know if you're looking for an apartment or a place to live. You find it August 8th and you sign whatever this… lease or what not… August 16th. So you're set to go.

MAYOR

Great.

HOLY GHOST

But… whatever you want to think about or talk about. Pick out any seven cards and we'll see what shows up……… You're also going to know a Kevin. So if you don't know a Kevin…

MAYOR

I do.

HOLY GHOST

Is he in Toronto?

MAYOR

No.

HOLY GHOST

You're going to know a Kevin in Toronto. Nothing against the Kevin that you know. But there's another one. I feel that… in downtown Toronto.

MAYOR

OK.

HOLY GHOST

Hang onto that.

MAYOR

My question is… ahh… last time I was here you mentioned that I had three guardians.

HOLY GHOST

M-hmm.

MAYOR

So I want to get an understanding of who those guardians are.

HOLY GHOST

OK.

MAYOR

Already have seven cards…

HOLY GHOST

Well then. you were meant to have that extra card.

MAYOR

Ahh I…

HOLY GHOST

Whichever one it is or whichever one it was. You were meant to have it because something drew it to you……… OK, one moment and I'll tell you what happened here. There's one… two… three… four… oh there's five six seven. OK… OK. First of all… you do have… I do feel your sister with you. But she's going to guide you with work. And even if… maybe she didn't have interest in… what the heck is my brother doing? I feel she's one of them. I feel another one is an older… I get… an older man. But I don't feel the family vibration. But I get an older gentleman that would be in his late fifties. That… he ran a company. I feel he was in Toronto. And he's saying… thank you Spirit… he's saying when you… cause I feel you coming to Toronto. I don't know if you want to or if you like Toronto. But I just get him saying the reins will be placed in your hands. Like… he ran a business… you will too. And I get… I hear his name as Martin. Marty. I feel that was his first name not his… I know it could be a last name. But I hear him saying… thank you, Spirit… I hear him saying his name was Martin but they called him Marty but… what was I going to say. He ran the business and he's saying… oh, I thank you… you'll trump other… not just… not in your company but say the company's competition. Where with your ideas… that you come up with Tim…

you'll trump... you have the trump card or you think of Donald Trump or you'll trump this and you do it one up. And one up-man-ship. And you'll be in the right place at the right time. I get my mom coming in... and symbolically she's showing me at the Kentucky Derby... the horse that wins... he gets a horseshoe of roses. And symbolically I get your guardian angel putting this... horseshoe of roses around your neck. And he's saying you'll be in the winner's circle. You are... you are gunna move. You definitely are moving. But you're gunna have a contract to sign. You will. Does somebody watch the TV show Law and Order with you? With you? Cause...

MAYOR

Sometimes I watch it with my mom.

HOLY GHOST

Because Spirit... Spirit... well I get... I feel your sister's there watching it too. Not to scare you or not to upset you or hurt your mother. But I get her talking about Law and Order. I wa... I see it once in a while. But she's saying... she's there... she's in the mix or like in the middle. She's there. She's also... Spirit thank you... she's also talking about an interview you're gunna have. And she's saying you'll be spot on. That's a very British acce... British accent? British term. Where you're spot on. Dead on. You're right on the money. And she's saying you're spot on. You're just... thank you Spirit... you're just who they're looking for and just who they need. OK?

MAYOR

Well I just a... a second interview yesterday.

HOLY GHOST

I feel she's around you a lot to give you... your sisters with you to give you encouragement......... There's something about the number eight with you. Now... I have the number eight at my door. The number eight on my computer. I know what that means to me. It's a number of prosperity. Where you turn eight on its side...

MAYOR

Infinity.

HOLY GHOST

It looks like the DNA strand. But I get your sister saying... you're gunna be... thank you Spirit... you're gunna be moving. There's something about... number eight. The 8th of the month is going to be important to you. So whether it's my deadline time or my meeting time... or we have meetings... the 8th of the month or every eight days my boss wants my opinion. Your sisters there saying she's coming along. She's not far away......... This represents you. Where you've been and where you're going. And that your plans will come to fruition. You're gunna be extremely... this is... this represents... this guy needs a rest. Because I get my mom saying over the next six months you're gunna need a break. Cause I

[197   ]

feel if we went from June... July... August... September... October... November... December... into Christmas time. That November... December... you're ready for like... a mini-vacation. Like I did... where I get... your sister saying you'll... to compare... and not that you have to compete. But you'll get done... you'll get more done in six months when some... what somebody else would get done in like nine or ten months. Cause I feel... your sister is here talking... thank you... you're gunna do... you're gunna come up with... ideas... not just to save money but to save time. When I say cut corners... she's... like... where I have this corner here... I'm gunna cut this corner... like this table off. She's saying but you'll cut corners to get results faster. Is there at that company a guy by the name of Vincent? And if there isn't... OK... hang onto that name. Hang onto that name. You're gunna make a smooth transition into a new home. It'll be... your sister's saying... it'll be like seamless... like when you stitch up your pants... there's a seam in my pants. But it's seamless means... it's just... effortless. It's effortless. But I love this. This card represents... when you want something... the person I'm reading... has the mental ability to focus on it and to attract it like a magnet into your life. Because ... I get s... again I'm seeing this number eight. And I don... and I'll say... I don't know if there's eight managers... or eight people on a board of directors at the company you interview with. Something about number eight. And I just get your sister saying... where... when you're there you'll manage your time very wisely. Not onl... cause I feel that... not just like whatever's written on the resume, but it's what you do when you think on your feet. Because your sister's talking about when you think on your feet... boom... you'll spring into action. But you'll come up with solutions that the company's looking for. And I do get you up a little later at night. So say like now... say today whatever you do... say you're about to... say I go to bed at ten o'clock or whatever so I can get up early in the morning. But I feel that you're going to be staying up a little bit later like to eleven or to midnight. But I get your sister saying you'll have more energy. You know? But I just feel...

MAYOR

That's good.

HOLY GHOST

Ya, they're cleaning the windows. Anybody without a balcony... they're cleaning... the windows. So... ya... I get from Spirit you'll make a smooth transition. You'll make it very effort... well, not effortlessly... least... like sometimes when we try to do something or change or make a move... change a career... we have problems after problems after raa... roadblock. But I don't get that... I get the total opposite with that. Somebody's going to make... I get this with you... it's very strange but different... organic lemonade. All natural lemonade. Where it's not sugar... it's not... it's all organic and natural. So Spirit is saying when you do... when you have your move... and it's a life change. And it's... it's... a little stepping stone in life. It's going to be not... natural... it's not gunna be stressful... it's not gunna be... you know... keeping me up at night and worrying. You're gunna know... Spirit thank you... you're gunna know a guy in the... in the... name of... in the name of Toronto?

MAYOR

In the name of Toronto?

HOLY GHOST

Gosh... no. Spirit is saying you're going to know somebody named Paul... who's gunna to be like a brother to you. I think I know who that person is. We haven't met them yet... I'll say we haven't met them yet. But I get Spirit saying... you'll be two peas in a pod. Like-minded and... when you... when you... not when you need something but when you want something. Trying to reach a specific goal. You and this guy Paul... you're both on the same track. You're both on the same page. But there's a reason why you'll meet them......... What else would you like to ask about? Or focus on?

MAYOR

Well, I have a feeling that something... not someone... is pushing me towards some end goal. Whether it be like a life purpose...

HOLY GHOST

Oh you have a purpose. You definitely do.

MAYOR

Something that someone or something else wants me to achieve.

HOLY GHOST

Oh I believe that. It's no accident... that uhh... that we're here. Some days we'll ask why we're still here. As long as we're here there is a purpose for us to be here. Think about that and pick out any seven cards......... I had some... a girl here yesterday. And I know she's come to see me before and... but I forgot she was... she was born in Asia and dumped in a garbage... in a dumpster. In a basket... her mother put her in a basket. And she just said I'm the dumpster baby. I just wanted to cry. And I said... well you know what... there... I'm glad you're not in Asia. Cause that's... stressful over there. But there's a reason why she's in Toronto. So she's supposed to be... and she's young... But she's gotta get that mindset of I'm a dumpster baby... no she's a beautiful, wonderful person. .... Well, first of all, I have to say any disappointments are in the past. Or anything... I'll say... that you might have questioned. Can you place a relationship that... I'll say... you were in a relationship but it ended?......... Cause I'll tell you something... I'll... well I'll say I don't know if you ever knew but I feel somebody... I'll just say... had their eye on you but they're gunna come back. I just hear Spirit saying there's a surprise around the corner that... you know when somebody has like a secret cru... well a secret crush on you but they never got the words out. Or they never articulate it. Well I feel this way about you. But hang onto that. Because I feel this year... like I'm in 2008 where this is gunna come to the surface... again I'll say through your work... it's a... I get from... I get your sister here saying it's not just gunna be work. It's just not gunna be a job. But there's a higher purpose with this work. It's not... I'll say... Spirit thank you... I'll say... your sister's saying... to other

[199]

people… other people might give you a label and say Tim is the… I'll say… manager of department x at department zee or zed company. That's what they would think of you. But your sister's saying here… thank you… this is going to lead you to your true purpose in life. You're not alone. That this career move is going to set you on your life path. And she's saying and she's saying you don't have to hurry because everything is going to come naturally……… This card represents that you have a lot of intuition yourself. You may dream of your sister. You may not have ever dreamed of her but I feel her coming around to visit you. In your… in your dream. I have to say you're gunna have an incredible amount of wealth at your disposal. OK? But that's fine. Somebody else may go to Las Vegas and lose it all in a weekend. But no… I get your sister saying… you'll contribute. You won't use it friver… frivor… frivolously. OK? But you're gunna have… I'll say it this way… this is a card not only of new doors opening but as I touch that… and as we sit here… I get… and I don't know if said this to you… in a way it seems familiar. Think maybe I did in the last time I saw you. But I feel there's three things for you to do. One is… your career's going to open the door, but then there's two other avenues that are gunna… thank you Spirit… gunna place you in a role of prominence. OK? Where you're not in the back pages of… like say… say if it was something… say… I… we were from a small town where… like oh I'm going to the back page and the next to last page and there's your name. But I get your sister saying no… you'll be on front and centre……… Cause I do get you in the media. And I… and I don't say that to make you feel like a big deal or I'm the big cheese or I'm a… really important guy. Or I'm a V… I… P. But your sisters saying you'll hold your own. You will be in a prominent role. Like… I'll say… I'll say… name recognition. Or you know how we say like M&Ms. Everybody knows that brand.

MAYOR

M-hmm.

HOLY GHOST

But I get your sister saying… this is a test you're gunna go through. People will know your name. Your name will be your brand. Your name will be out there. And if… and Spirit thank you dear. It'll be in the media. But you won't be an ar… and I'll say… an arrogant son of a bitch. I'm not conceited. She's saying… you'll have the vibration of a giver not a taker. We get choices we can either be greedy. You know like the pig… he's always me… me… me… me… me you know I need everything. But she's saying no… you'll scatter the wealth. You won't… you won't… mismanage it. But with the amounts of money that you do… you will… you won't even be tempted to steal any of it. Like I'll just give an example. The Catholic school board of somewhere in Toronto. You're not supposed to be taking other people's money. You're not supposed to be wasting my tax money, but they have and they should be held accountable. But your sister's saying you wouldn't even be tempted to even… skim off the top like some people on Wall Street have done and Bay Street and blah… blah… blah. But she's saying… you'll be… you'll be held accountable but your books… your books will balance. OK?……… But I… as we sit here… I get you knowing somebody at the Canon Theatre in Toronto. I'll tell you where the Canon Theatre… is on

Yonge… this is where I'm seeing the east side. Cause I saw the east side of Yonge. If you're at Yonge and Dundas. The Eaton Centre's here and the Canon Theatre is across the street. Is across the road from the Eaton's Centre. And… and actually Garth Dabrinksy and Cineplex used to own that theatre, but now it's the Canon Theatre I think. Or maybe it changed names again. Used to be the Pantages Theatre, but anyway I feel you'll know… the… if… what's the… the owners… the bosses… the management at that theatre for some reason. I also get the name Roger with you. But as I say that name Roger… I feel like I'm talking about Rogers Media company there's Rogers… Rogers has…

MAYOR

Rogers Video.

HOLY GHOST

Astral Media. They owned… they own a truckload of radio stations.

MAYOR

Sky Dome.

HOLY GHOST

Astral… ya… well didn't he… and he turned seventy-five yesterday. Happy birthday to Ted Rogers. But I feel… I hear this name with you. So there's some connection through whatever you do… and… ya because your sister's saying the delivery service. But Rogers delivers media. They have SUN TV… they have TV… I guess across Canada. I don't know everything but I know that… there's some connection. There's some reason. She's saying it's not gunna go to your head. Like other people would get goofy you know… like some child stars… or that… you know and then they blow their inheritance or they waste their money or their residuals. But she's saying…no you'll be balanced. You'll be balanced professionally… emotionally… financially. You'll be… she's saying… thank you Spirit… you'll be in the driver's seat. I have to say… were you thinking of a different car when you get situated? Because I feel there's going to be a change in… I don't know if you go buy a hybrid car… or you don't need a car or something… something.

MAYOR

I was thinking about that.

HOLY GHOST

I feel there's gunna be… cause I get as your sister speaks to us… she's saying there's gunna be a change in transportation. You may even get a company car. Let them pay for the insurance… no… I'm joking but I'm not joking. Let them pay for it… you know? Down the road. So it may not happen tonight. It may not happen this week or it may not happen August the 8th. But I feel somewhere down the road… where… people in Toronto are going nuts with the gas prices. And she's saying… and that's not gunna affect you. And that's just gunna go… phmm… no big deal. I'm OK. I'm taken care of.

MAYOR

Great.

HOLY GHOST

What else would you like to? You know what… you're gunna know… it's not me… you're gunna know somebody that writes something for TV about a spy show. So I think when you're here in Toronto, you'll meet writers for television. But I'm seeing… and I don't know if this is the guy… Paul or whatever name I said. But they write some kind of a spy series… spy… spy… something to do with spies or something. Hang onto that. And I feel CTV with you. Now CTV is not Teddy Rogers… that's Bell Canada. That's Bell Global. Bell Global Media. But I feel… Spirit… your sister is saying… when you are here in Toronto you're gunna feel different. And I mean emotionally. I don't mean that you're miserable now. But your sister's saying when you come to Toronto… it's where… it's a whole new ball game. You'll embrace the emotions because I just feel… nothing wrong with your emotionally life now. But I just get where your… I just get where she's saying you're gunna be on an emotional high. Not drugs. Not alcohol. Not that you can't have a glass of wine. That you're gunna be on an emotional high. I get where… and I'll go fifteen months and that will be into 2009. So fifteen months would be June… July… August… into August of 2009. Where she's saying… it's where… it's a complete turnaround. Nothing wrong with your life now. But she's saying when you look back fifteen months from now you'll say… wow… how… how did that happen? But you'll look back and say that was supposed to be. That was no accident. That was no coincidence. Like my show tonight is all about coincidences, but I don't believe in them. I get your sister saying… this is not a coincidence. You know?……… What she's saying about the guy is that he'll feel like your brother. He'll feel like your brother. That… you're… this close… that you have so much in common. But that's no accident either. That's no coincidence……… Anything else that you can think about? Or ask about? Or ponder about?

MAYOR

Think those were the main points.

HOLY GHOST

Well, you're on the right path. Whoops!!. You know what? I have to say… now these were gunna fall out. So again you are going to have a lot of responsibility to do with money. And I don't mean that you have to be… you're not gunna be the control… the Controller of that… of a… of a company. But you'll be in that vibration. Where… and I'll say it this way… money won't be an issue. Or some people say ttt… OK… do I fill up my gas tank or do I pay my rent? Or do I fill up my gas tank or do I buy groceries. But that's not gunna be an issue. But you're here for a reason. But you know… you're gunna have a… you're gunna have a lot of people around you. Cause just as I was gunna say that… I was hearing… there's an expression… legions of angels which means many… many… many… many… thousands of angels. But your sister's talking about legions of people around you. Where you're gunna influence a lot of people. So she… she knows you'll do the right thing.

You won't be a goofball. You won't act like a self-centered idiot or goof. And she's saying you're gunna have a lot when you come to Toronto. You're going to have a lot... extreme amount of people around you. A lot... a lot. You know you how... I'll just say... a rock band has fans. Like the Rolling Stones or Howard Stern or the Beatles had fans. And they did influence people. I hope for the better. And she's saying... your gunna have your followers to. But all for the right reasons. All for the right reasons. It's not to make your ego... you know... puffed out and it's all about me. But she's saying... your purpose. Your gunna enlighten other people. Your gunna... enlighten other people. And also empower them. Cause I feel... just like... remember... I was telling you about that girl that was here yesterday. And I guess she doesn't think much of herself being dumped in a garbage can by her mother. But I get your sister saying you'll... thank you Spi... thank you... you'll make people like that feel better about themselves. You know? But she's using that girl that was here yesterday as an example of... I don't feel too good about myself but she's saying... you'll make other... you'll make others that have that low self-esteem... or that low opinion... come higher. Come higher. You'll heal a lot of people. You may not... you may not be Doctor Tim.

MAYOR

Amazing.

HOLY GHOST

But... you're not... may not have... Spirit thank you... she... your sister's saying... you may not have MD after your name. She's saying you don't need it. Because you'll heal... thank you... heal people on a completely different level. But you'll still heal. Just as much as if... you were a surgeon in an operating room. Which leads me to say... you do have one of your guides... was a doctor. Was a doctor. And he's saying... thank you Spirit... you're gunna lead a group. You're gunna lead the... the group. I do... and he's talking about August. August... August... August... I get you so tremendously busy. And he's saying... but you'll do it... you'll do it. And I get your sister saying this is gunna be you. When you do one event or one project. And so you go... oh... and she's saying... and this is you. Where you won't rest on your laurels. You won't say OK... I did that and now I'm done. No she's saying you'll have that... I feel as if... there are three things at once but you get one thing done. One thing completed and then you take a deep breath... and then you're on to the second project. Cause she's saying it's not gunna break you... like... it's not going to overwhelm you. You'll welcome it with open arms. But you'll be... you'll be blessed in ways you can't even dream of. Ya but I just get her saying there's gunna be a circle of people around you. But you're going to influence... a multitude of people. Absolutely you will......... Who has... whose looking for furniture? I don't know if this is you or somebody else but hang onto that. I just get that around you. So I'll just say... you'll know when that happens... it's not me... but you'll just hear of that. And that's a little sign along the way from your sister that you are going in the right direction. You definitely are. You definitely are......... Well, I'll say thank you so much. How was... how was your day... what else are you up to today? It's none of my damn business.

[203   ]

MAYOR

… nothing… this is it.

HOLY GHOST

Oh well. I had a day yesterday that was so nuts. I could not get anything done… it was like my phone all of a sudden did not stop ringing. And it was like… I was trying to say some prayers… healing prayers I say every day. But anyway. Every time I started the phone would ring. Then I changed my sheets. And I had my sheets and all. I did like three loads of laundry. And last night I'm looking in this bag for my sheets. They're not there… they're gone. I know I did my… I know… I can remember putting the sheets in the dryer. So at nine o'clock last night I'm going they're still down in the dryer. It's like…

MAYOR

Oh no.

HOLY GHOST

It's like I'm losing my mind. You know? It's like ahh. Today I'm like you…

MAYOR

Just taking it easy. So you need a break.

HOLY GHOST

I had like nine… eight or nine people call and they all wanted to come over like right now! And these women must think I don't do anything. They must think I'm like in bonbons or something… watching TV or I'm not… I'm actually doing work. They might not think of it as work, but I'm doing work. And I learned my lesson. So I don't know if I'm older and wiser today. I'm certainly a day… a day older. I don't know if I'm wiser.

MAYOR

Always. Always getting wiser.

HOLY GHOST

Indeed. Indeed I wonder. I'm thinking where were those sheets last night. I know. And this girl…

EXIT THE HOLY GHOST AND TIM THE MAYOR

ACT VI

SCENE I

06/04/2008

ENTER THE CARDS AND TIM THE MAYOR

                                    CARDS
Everything been good?

                                    MAYOR
Everything been good?

                                    CARDS
Ya.

                                    MAYOR
Ya.

                                    CARDS
What's been new since we last met?

                                    MAYOR
Quite a bit actually.

                                    CARDS
Ya.

MAYOR

Ya. So I started to go through kind of the process of change and getting ready for it. And involving my friends and family in it. And ah… it's very contagious.

CARDS

Yes.

MAYOR

So… uh… one of my friends… started to look at his situations. He's working at Tim Hortons… in his thirties so… still going to school, unsure of what he wants to be and what he wants to do. But he uh… has a couple… he has a second job now. He has another offer coming. And hopefully he'll be making some more money so he can start focusing on uhh…

CARDS

Woow…

MAYOR

… some of the ideas he has……… And another friend she started her… she started going back to work again. And she's enjoying it and she started to do her… her writing and focus on her writing.

CARDS

Woow… so you're having this kind of rippling effect across everybody you know?

MAYOR

Yup. Uhh… my mom. She's the toughest one. Uhh… she had half completed a book and uhh… she wasn't sure if she should go through with it. Hopefully… hopefully that will change and she'll… and she'll finish it off.

CARDS

Ya.

MAYOR

Cause it's going to be something that's pretty powerful.

CARDS

Woow… is this a personal story?

MAYOR

Ya… ya it is.

CARDS

Ya.

MAYOR

And… had a… a few job interviews for one company that I'd like to work for. It's a… a
pretty high up position.

CARDS

Ohh… congratulations.

MAYOR

But uhh… I had my own little conundrum. As was foretold in the cards, I guess.

CARDS

M-hmm.

MAYOR

… I had an appointment with a psychic medium.

CARDS

Yes.

MAYOR

And… I was asked last second to come in for a 2nd and 3rd interview right before that
appointment and in another city. So the 1st interview went well…

CARDS

Ahh… huh…

MAYOR

The 2nd one, I guess I was a little bit rushed so I didn't convey my… my desire to work there.

CARDS

Ahh…

MAYOR

I ended up forty minutes late to the… the appointment but I knew my sister was waiting to
communicate through this woman so…

CARDS

Ohh… how wonderful. And so she came through?

MAYOR

Yup.

CARDS

Yeah. Wonderful.

MAYOR

Stuck in traffic I was calling the… calling the lady saying I'm on my way… I'm on my way…

CARDS

Ha… ha… ha…

MAYOR

And I was telling my sister to wait too.

CARDS

How… good… well of course she would. Of course she would wait.

MAYOR

Yup.

CARDS

Was it a good message?

MAYOR

Ya. Very positive.

CARDS

Good.

MAYOR

So I know I needed to go through that anyways.

CARDS

Yeah.

MAYOR

It was part of this process. So… even if the interview did go well and I ended up getting that job, I don't feel that I would have been ready… spiritually… or emotionally to… to really do it head-on.

CARDS

And sometimes it's that way. Sometimes timing is not… it's not right. And it… even though… we can think we can really want something… hmm… timing isn't right.

MAYOR

Well, I'm not giving up.

CARDS

Oh good. So you got back to them and said… did you explain to them…

MAYOR

Ya.

CARDS

… about what happened?

MAYOR

Ya, I offered to… to get on the phone or to meet again to help convey that message and…
I've been trying to communicate or continue to communicate with the hiring manager.

CARDS

Good. Good.

MAYOR

Be a little hard to explain… hard to explain why I felt rushed so… ha… ha…

CARDS

Ha… ha… he… he… he… well, the… the hiring manager is a woman?

MAYOR

No, uhh… the person above… above him is.

CARDS

Is?

MAYOR

Ya.

CARDS

Cause I can see a woman would… she would understand that actually. Or think that's really
wonderful. So… if you could get at her ear… then she would understand.

MAYOR

Perhaps.

CARDS

Ya.

MAYOR

Perhaps.

CARDS

So what are we doing? What are we looking at today?

MAYOR

I don't know.

CARDS

What is on your mind?

MAYOR

What's next?

CARDS

Ha... ha... ha...

MAYOR

I'm so close to this period of change.

CARDS

Yeah. So you want to see what signs are coming next?

MAYOR

Ya. Am I still on track? Did I make the right decision... well, either way, I know I made the right decision.

CARDS

Uh huh... ya... it feels that way to me. And I always... whenever I'm going through an experience like the one you're having. I... I always have to remind myself there's no mistakes in the universe. There's no mistakes. It's all OK. It's all right. We have a few cards and... which ones do you like?

MAYOR

I'll go with that one. Just one second. I got to check if this is working, because I think I have the wrong button on.

CARDS

OK......... OK, the Queen of Swords comes up in what needs protection. And when you described your mom doing writing... this would fit perfectly because... the Sword is a pen of course. And... she... this writing piece... the oracle is saying that this is a... it's important in that it's conveying... something about your mother's journey to independence. Like independence of mind. The way it… the Queen of Swords would be. And it would… hmm… it would… it… hmm… contain some really good advice for other people. And so she would be writing it not just for herself. In fact very little for herself. And my sense about that writing piece for your mother is that she feels as though she has moved so much further past it. That… when it was started and worked on… it's… it symbolizes for her a certain time in her life. And a certain kind of headspace that she was in at that time and she's zoomed so far beyond that. That feels like… it's almost like going back to where you used to live or going back where you were. So it doesn't call to her the same way. And that's why it's really hard for her to m-mm… reclaim the motivation that started it in the first place. But oracle is saying it's in need of protection. And so your support… along those lines will be really helpful. And to point out to your mother that she writes it not for herself but for someone else. That Spirit wants someone else to read this story… and she may be able to get help with that… help with… like a… student… writing student. Somebody that would be very interested in the story as well. Writing women's stories. She might be able to actually get some help with it… So they can… get… finally… finally done and get out there……… the Princess of Cups comes up in what needs patience. Which is you being of service. And that's a Fall card. So when we see you shifting into… like really shifting into a new position… this Princess of Cups is you going to do something which you have been interested in doing before but left behind. And now are… in this Fall are going to take it to a higher level … and this is in some way of being of service. So it doesn't mean necessarily a job. It could mean helping people… it could be… hmm… passing messages along. That's another thing the Princess of Cups does… hmm… passing messages along. Have you been having… really strong dreams?

MAYOR

I started to have a few dreams recently. Not that I can remember them minutes after waking up. But at least I… I know that they're there now.

CARDS

And so when you wake up you have that kind of sense that you've had a dream, but you can't grasp the details.

MAYOR

Well, it's in the few moments when you just wake up you can… you're still in the dream.

CARDS

Yup.

MAYOR

And you can control it a little bit. But then when you finally wake up… a couple minutes later you forget exactly…

CARDS

It's gone.

MAYOR

Ya, it's gone.

CARDS

Ya. Are you putting this trusty little thing by your bedside?

MAYOR

No.

CARDS

Ha… ha… you need to do that. Put this by your bedside. So as soon as you… as soon as you're awakening and you're in that kind of twilight ahh… frame of mind… get that going and just whatever is in your mind. Even if you're kind of half asleep, it's even better. And just what you're seeing… what you're feeling… what your sensations are… get that into the little recorder. And each morning that you do that, it will stimulate and help you to reclaim uhh… clearer and clearer messages from your dreams. Because I have this feeling that you are… when… it… it's just when occurred to me about messages… messages from your dream world. You know that's when the veil is very thin right?

MAYOR

Yes.

CARDS

So messages are coming through. But you're just… when you're sort of pulling yourself into ego state. Which is what you're doing as you wake up. It's leaving a sort of… messages of that unconscious or self behind. But your recording device and leaving it by… right by your bedside should help……… the Four of Swords comes up in what needs acceptance. Which is you are relaxing your mind. Your mind is finally coming to a nice even keel. So stress has reached… has pitched. It's now finally under control. In fact, I would say it's even in decline. So in other words, you've moved forward to embracing this coming transition and change. And the more you have done that the more ease of mind you're experiencing. Your mind is much better shape……… Now what needs release comes up the Fool card. Which is releasing that taking a risk. This is the time to do it. And the 21st of June is the end of Fool time. So this contacting people… sending out missives… resumes. All that… that you're doing. This is a very good time for you to be doing that. So keeping doing it… if anything escalate your efforts between now and the 21st of June.

MAYOR

Hmm…

CARDS

Which is about seventeen days. About two and half weeks. So in the next two and half
weeks, really put the push on to do that.........the insight card comes up the Star. Which
is... you're feeling there's a lot of hope. So the actions that you've done over the last couple
of weeks have generated a lot of hope. And you see that in the people around you sort of
saying... ya... transition... that's... I want... I want some of that too and sort of picking up
the fire from you. So you're instilling hope in the hearts of other people. Which is of course
a gift that comes back to you as well.........the Princess of Swords in the new perspective
card is about... studying. She's ahh... the student of the deck and... it's a good time for you
to think about what you want to learn next. So that would be another important piece of
your coming change. What course you want to take... how you want to expand your
learning. And you're moving into a good... probably because your mind is coming to
more... even balance and less stress... it's a good time for you to think about that. You were
a good student. You were a good student, weren't you?

MAYOR

Yes.

CARDS

Ya. And is... ahh... because the Princess of Swords is a wonderful student. Does her...
her... assignments on time. Always attentive. Hard-working. Uses her head all the time.
Doesn't have any patience for moodiness. Ha... ha...

MAYOR

Ha... ha...

CARDS

... from other people. Ha... ha... and ahh... is very good at blending old and new. So
it's... ahh... in new perspective it's saying that's something... start... that to become of your
planning. Where you're going next in study. And that doesn't necessarily have to be work-
related by the way. It could be completely not related to your work actually. Just... like
philosophy... is the first thing that popped into my head is to take a course in philosophy.
Even if it's... correspondence through one of the universities or whatever... you... just
something part-time. Philosophy course. Ya, that's perfect. Just for the heck of it. Stimulate
your mind... to expand your reasoning and... have you ever done any... study of Thomas
Paine's work?

MAYOR

No, I haven't.

CARDS

Have you ever heard of Thomas Paine? Thomas Paine was really ahh... the true father of
Confederation for the States. And he was a Quaker in 1789. And... he had a vision really.

I mean… I think he was a spiritualist. I'm pretty sure he was a spiritualist. He might not have called himself that, but I think he was a spiritualist. He had a vision of a republic. Which was a… a country that was run by the people… owned by the people… and organized by the people. A republic as such. And he was really the father of Confederation. And when… and he wrote… he helped out George Washington. George Washington got all the credit of course. But… this… sort of real philosophical rigor that went behind the thought process. I mean they eventually jailed Thomas Paine and they burned all his writings. I mean he… he was a fascinating read. Actually Thomas Paine's… wa…s a brilliant man. An angel really. I think.

MAYOR

Well, we're heading into time where corporations are run by consumers.

CARDS

Oh, that's interesting.

MAYOR

With ahh… social media. People can go and rate products or give their reviews and add their feedback to inspire other people to buy. They're the ones companies are going to be relying on to do the selling for them. So there's going to be a huge shift to people running corporations and of course, corporations are what run politics. So people will have their say.

CARDS

That's interesting. Actually I find that amusing. Cause I would always said that where your real vote is… is in what you buy. I always said that because it's true…

MAYOR

Yes.

CARDS

As consumers we have tremendous power. Much more power than the average consumer really realizes. Now with internet, of course, they really are… that power…

MAYOR

They're in charge.

CARDS

That power is getting very manifest. Ya. That's true. So ahh… Thomas Paine's… ahh… kind of philosophy is unfolding. Of course it does. Great wisdom does eventually…

MAYOR

Takes it's time.

CARDS

Lead to unfoldment. Ya.

MAYOR

Ya.

CARDS

So my sense is that ahh… Thomas Paine popped into my head and I think… one of his books is called the Age of Reason. And you would find that very interesting. But philosophy in general… it feels like it will add the comer and dimension to what you do. But it… it's like shooting off in a different direction. But… and you go off… I can see you going off in this direction. But when you come back to where you are… of course you move along this way as well. But as you come back… all of that study… ahh… greatly supports your movement at that time. It's like… you move along like this and you do the study of philosophy and when it comes back to here… that's how I see it… that it's like ohh… wooww… and I get to this point in my life and I have this wonderful pot of gold. And that pot of gold is great philosophical… ohh… hmmm… what do I want to say… a… a… philosophical grounding. Rich… it… it's rich. Ya. So that's what the Princess of Swords… when I think about you taking a course… a… that's what it feels like to me. A really good rigorous course in philosophy. And I think that… you'd really enjoy it. And it would hmm… foster an interest that might surprise you……… What needs healing comes up the Chariot… in mundane terms, is that your car? Is your car in need of repair… replacement or…

MAYOR

That's interesting. I've heard that a few times now. And it's not in need of repair or replacement. It's just I feel that it's time to…

CARDS

Get rid of it.

MAYOR

Start looking at getting a new one.

CARDS

Hmm. And it's true. For some reason, it's true. The oracle is supporting that. There's something wrong with your car.

MAYOR

Maybe I don't realize it yet. Ha… ha…

CARDS

Ya, maybe it's not manifesting. Ha… ha…

MAYOR

Ha... ha... Maybe I just know it's supposed to... something's going to happen.

CARDS

Maybe it's imminent. And maybe when it's so big... you'll be faced with a kind of awkward choice of putting out a great deal of money to repair it or fix it or get rid of it. But take a hit in some way on it. But if you do it now,... it's before it... we're at the cusp of when it could happen.

MAYOR

Hmm...

CARDS

That's ahh... what the Chariot... it's about traveling and it's usually how we travel. And it... ahh... the only... in a symbolic reference it would be to ego. Because ego is how we travel through life. That sense of I. But it doesn't feel to me, quite honestly, that there's anything about your ego that is suffering or damaged. It feels very intact to me. For... like solid... so it feels like this has got something to do with your car. How you travel around. Is it a very big car? No.

MAYOR

No.

CARDS

Small car. How old is it?

MAYOR

Ahh it's a... it's a 98.

CARDS

OK.

MAYOR

So it's...

CARDS

Ya.

MAYOR

It's got some years on it.

CARDS

Ya. So you might think about that. Put your name in for one of those Hybrids. Ha... ha......... The Six of Coins comes up in recommended. Hmm... this is... the Six of Coins is about you dividing your time... I think this came up for you in the last reading. This is about dividing your time between two sources that require your attention or your resources in some way. And trying to be fair in giving equally to both. So you're still coming up as the one with all the resources. And being fair and generous in how you... ahh... give those out or distribute them. The oracle is highly recommending it. Share your gifts. That's ahh... the recommended card......... And then the outcome shows you heading into smoother water. So within the next two and a half weeks, because this is a Spring card again. Within the next two and half weeks, we see you heading across the water into much smoother ground. And you're feeling much calmer. But in that calm frame of mind knowing that your... the water is smoothening out it's time for the release of Fool. Because this is the perfect time for you to take a risk and start sending all that stuff out there because that's... the Fool card's Spring as well. So while your mind is calmer... you know you're getting into smoother water. Change is imminent. Lots of reason to be very hopeful and optimistic. And start pheww... sending those missives out there about where you want to go. Where you want to be. So... it looks like Spring to me. It looks really good. I think your reading did last time, didn't it?

MAYOR

I did.

CARDS

Ya. It was very good.

MAYOR

Interesting. Hmm...

CARDS

Do you have any questions about that?

MAYOR

So, the Fool...

CARDS

The Fool is the main character in the Tarot story. The Fool... see the Tarot is actually a prescriptive story of enlightenment. And the Fool is the character. That's why it has a zero. The Fool... so the Fool is sort of us... symbolizes us coming into physical form from spirit. And then ahh... when we get here on... on the earth plane, then we have these series of tests... and difficulties and challenges to reach enlightenment. Which is at the Universe card or number twenty-one. So the Fool is the protagonist of... of the Fool... the archetypal Fool story. And you're... when the Fool... whenever the Fool comes up in a reading, it means that you are the main character of your story now. You really are inhabiting that. It's time to launch that risky journey. And go now. Like this is… next two and half weeks is the very best ideal time for you to take the chance. Take the risk. Do whatever you can imagine. And do it fast. Ya.

                              MAYOR
Hmm… hmm… would it be possible to do a reading for a couple of other people that are on my mind?

                              CARDS
Sure. OK. Who are we doing?

                              MAYOR
Hmm?

                              CARDS
Who are we doing?

                              MAYOR
They're just a couple of friends that I helped get in the door at my company.

                              CARDS
OK.

                              MAYOR
And I still feel that where they are… they could do a lot better.

                              CARDS
Ohh… OK. So you're feeling responsible for them, because you helped get them in. Is that?… ha… ha…

                              MAYOR
A little bit.

                              CARDS
Ha… ha… ha… ha… and you feel they could do better elsewhere? And they're kind of stuck there. Is that what you're feeling?

                              MAYOR
… well, one of them is doing… I think they're doing what they want now.

                              CARDS
Good.

MAYOR

The other one isn't.

CARDS

Ohh... OK. So you would like to... what are you really wondering? Are you wondering what... what's going to happen to them? Or you're wondering how you can help? Or... what are you wondering really?

MAYOR

How can I help?

CARDS

OK. OK. What I want you to do... think of one. We'll do one at a time. Think of one and you're going to... ahh... pick three cards. For one and then we'll pick three cards for the other. We'll deal with one at a time.

MAYOR

OK.

CARDS

OK. So you know who this is? You have them in your mind?

MAYOR

Yup.

CARDS

OK. OK this is their story. A... at present they're coming up the beginning of fire. This is the Ace of Wands. This is the start of fire... at present they are on the cusp of a new identity. That... that would be the best way to describe it. The Ace of Wands is like the first time that humanity could make fire. It was like wooww... be warm... we can cook. It's... it... but it's a symbolic of an inner experience. So this person is heading into a wonderful Summer is what I would say. Whatever will transpire this Summer... it's new... it's exciting... it's passionate... it's like... yess. It's very good. So they have a wonderful Summer ahead......... Now what got them to be where they are today has come up sort of the Fate card. Because... here she is... they show perched a... spinning her wool. So how they got to be where they are today is because they expressed a passion to you and you, as fate would have it... ahh... between them telling you where they were at and what they wanted... and you... you know... having just the right place to convey that information resulted in them working there. But it was a combination of your perception about what they wanted and fate. So there's... so there's very much a fate thing that they are there......... Now what comes in the future has come up the Moon card for them. Meaning that... and that's where your dreams come in. Moon comes out... we dream. So you're going to dream about this person. This will be one of your dreams. Ahh... so you'll want to… especially watch your dreams for this. But the Moon card also has a… I would say… sort of a shadow aspect to it. And it means that… I would say there's rumors… ahh… this is about rumors too. Sort of the unfoldment of rumors. So almost like hmm… what they fear the most. That's going on at work. Or about to transpire… is true. So it is a… going to happen. What, are they afraid that they're going to get fired? No.

MAYOR

No.

CARDS

They're afraid the company's going to close? They're going to lose their department? Or… nothing like that eh?

MAYOR

Nope.

CARDS

So what… is… uhh… have they heard rumors or do you know anything about that? No. The Moon card. When it comes up… is like… hmm… it's like some kind of suspicion or intuition… that feeling that they had. And it… it's Fall. Will manifest actually in the Fall. So they have a great Summer and as we look into the Fall we see… little bit of trouble I would say… what you would hear them say is… I was afraid of that and then it happened. So whatever that is. That's… so I would say to them… what's your worst fear that could happen? And see what they say. Because the oracle is suggesting that there is some… it's like they're having… suspicions or intuitions about something or maybe even they've had a dream about something unfolding. And it does happen. Which can be looked at like a confirmation from the oracle to be listening very carefully to their intuition and… and does… maybe… you know… Spirit is just getting them to make changes too. So that's what I suspect.

MAYOR

And maybe it's a wake-up call.

CARDS

Ya.

MAYOR

OK.

CARDS

Ya. But tell them too. The other thing to tell them about is… this can some… the Ace of Wands can sometimes point to opportunity. And if they hear about an opportunity this Summer. Between the 21st of June and the 21st of September. If they hear of a great business opportunity or work opportunity. Like other job. They should do it. They should take it because my feeling is by the Fall… they are having a feeling about what's going on at work. And rumors… and things like that. There's sort of a darkness about this card predicted for the Fall. That's what I would say.

MAYOR

OK.

CARDS

Then this is the other person........ Hmm… very different. Hmm… the Conflict card. Thee Conflict card is what you picked out in the middle here. It means that they have some… they're… m-mm… threatened by a conflict. It doesn't mean that… actually… stuck right in it right now. But it suggests is that they're in the middle of a situation that has tremendous… ahh… potential for war. And this is about somebody in a situation… it's either them or the other person wants change and the other one doesn't. There's also a feeling of betrayal and deception that has come up in this… car… this card. But it suggests there… they're right in the middle of what could erupt into… a… war. And they'd be wise not to. Because they can't win. That's what the oracle means by this card........ Friendship comes up in the past. Very good friend. This person values their friendships and their relationships highly. And they have a… good friends. And ahh… so that would mean to me that… alike… if you're seeing the Three of Cups and then the Five of Swords. This would be really awful for this person. Because they do like harmony and peace and getting along with people and you know… that's really import… their relationships are really important to them. So to find themselves in the middle of what could be a terrible conflict… would be very painful for them. So… I would say they're going through rough time........ Now what comes is interesting. Because the corresponding card to the Moon card which came up in the last person's future is the High Priestess. Which comes up in this person's future. Meaning that they have a very similar experience. And meaning that their intuitions and feelings and dreams and what they hear as rumors and gut feelings. They're right on. And that all comes to light by the Fall. So there's something… I would… and they both work there?

MAYOR

Yes.

CARDS

There's something going on in that workplace. For two people's readings to show… one show the Moon and the other to show the High Priestess. Means there's some kind… there's something unfolding in that place… that they have feelings about. And when they both get past the Fall, it's like they both say… I had a feeling about that. And they were right.

MAYOR

Hmm.

                              CARDS
I don't know what that is. Any chance it would close?

                              MAYOR
No. Restructure maybe.

                              CARDS
Ya, maybe restructure. Ya. New departments or letting go of old departments? Or… are
they in the same department? No. Hmm. Hmm.

                              MAYOR
Interesting.

                              CARDS
Do they know each other?

                              MAYOR
Yup.

                              CARDS
Are they friends?

                              MAYOR
Yes.

                              CARDS
Because there's one with friends here. Maybe it has to… maybe it's not their workplace
then. Maybe it ahh… has to do with another part of their life.

                              MAYOR
Perhaps.

                              CARDS
Cause then their lives cross outside of work too then?

                              MAYOR
Yup.

                              CARDS
Hmm. They're not in a relationship? Just a friendship.

                              MAYOR
Friendship.

CARDS

Friendship? Hmm. I wonder if it has to do with... Friends. It... it doesn't feel likely. They... do like their families know each other?

MAYOR

Ya. I mean they are both married and they all get along with each other.

CARDS

So they would ahh... get together and visit each other and that kind of thing?

MAYOR

Ya.

CARDS

It could be a family. It could be a family matter. That's interesting they both... like the High Priestess and the Moon... they correspond and very similar meanings. You know... dreams and intuitions... and feelings. You know... having ahh... having to face the truths and the darker side of the truth. To acknowledge it. Not lie to yourself. Be really honest. That's what both cards would say to both those people. So that's what... it... it's somewhere where I... feels like their lives are connecting... crossing. Hmm.

MAYOR

Guess we'll see.

CARDS

Fall. It's a Fall thing. So really... I guess... what I would say to them is how are you both having the same feelings about work. And what's that about and how is this going to unfold. Ya. Is it a union company? No. Hmm. So employees wouldn't necessarily talk about their respective positions. They wouldn't necessarily talk to each other about the jobs that they do?

MAYOR

They might.

CARDS

OK. Hmm. And one likes it and one doesn't? One likes the job and one doesn't. Ya. That's interesting. And they're both happy people? Would you describe them as happy?

MAYOR

In general.

CARDS

OK... OK... and both married?

                              MAYOR

Yup.

                              CARDS

And happily married?

                              MAYOR

As far as I know.

                              CARDS

Ha… ha… ha… OK. Well, something comes to light. Something that is now just a feeling…
an impression… like rumors. But something like that… it feel like they should… like they
know about together. And that comes to fruition.

                              MAYOR

OK.

                              CARDS

And I don't see either one of them though… it's not revealing that either one of them will be
leaving that workplace imminently. Certainly not before next year anyway……… You'll be
leaving. They must be very envious. Certainly the one.

                              MAYOR

Ya, he would be if I got it.

                              CARDS

Ya.

                              MAYOR

Alright. I don't think I have any more questions.

                              CARDS

So you just needed a half-hour meeting today?

                              MAYOR

I guess so.

                              CARDS

OK. I'm glad everything's unfolding as well as you went to see the Medium. I'm very
excited. How did you find her?

MAYOR

… pretty good. The most impressive part was the fact that she was adamant about not… of me not revealing any information… at all.

CARDS

Ohh… OK.

MAYOR

So if I started to talk she would be like… no… no… don't tell me.

CARDS

 Ya, because that can… be a… a greatly distracting in a mediumship. Because they have to know… they have to listen and they have to know that the information is really coming from the spirit world. Otherwise when… when you're talking or when you're telling her things… it can be a huge distraction and her… get confused about where the information is coming from. So she wants it… I can understand that. She'd like it pure. Which is… ya. That makes a lot of sense actually……… Hmm… so your sister's very happy in the spirit world?

MAYOR

Ya, she's keeping busy.

CARDS

Good. What's she doing? Did she say?

MAYOR

Keeping tabs on me right now.

CARDS

Ya… ya… she's helping. That's wonderful. So she's been busy?

MAYOR

Ya, I've been keeping her busy.

CARDS

Good… ha… ha… ha… good. Do you feel better? Having made that connection with her.

MAYOR

Absolutely.

CARDS

Good. Good.

EXIT THE CARDS AND TIM THE MAYOR

Curtains

06/10/2008

ENTER TIM THE FOOL AND THE CURTAINS

> CURTAINS

Welcome back.

> FOOL

Your foot's getting better?

> CURTAINS

A little better yahh! A little better. I still wear my cast when I'm outside, because I don't want to get it kicked or banged or anything… you know… so?

> FOOL

Ya.

> CURTAINS

But I can limp around the house. So it's good. Your phone's off?

> FOOL

Yup.

> CURTAINS

Turning it off right now. So what's been happening with you since I last saw you?

> FOOL

Just been thinking.

CURTAINS

Oh. Tell me what you've been thinking. Sounds profound.

FOOL

Well, not necessarily profound. At our last meeting… you mentioned that understanding was the important part.

CURTAINS

Yes.

FOOL

So I did some extra homework and came up with a list of understandings.

CURTAINS

Ohh… like what?

FOOL

Ahh… just looking at all the influences in my life.

CURTAINS

Great.

FOOL

So…

CURTAINS

Good for you.

FOOL

I'll read you it, I guess.

CURTAINS

Yes.

FOOL

I understand that I care very deeply about my friends and family but I need to start taking risks in order to become the person I'm supposed to be. To become the person I'd be happiest being.

CURTAINS

M-hmm.

                              FOOL
They've taken me so far and the rest of the journey is up to me.

                            CURTAINS
M-hmm.

                              FOOL
I understand that surrounding…

                            CURTAINS
Slow down.

                              FOOL
Sorry.

                            CURTAINS
The rest of the journey is up to me… ya.

                              FOOL
I understand that surrounding myself with friends that haven't been able to find their own drive, their own passion provided me the opportunity to try to help them. Now I will… I will really focus on my own drive and passion.

                            CURTAINS
Shake my hand. That's profound.

                              FOOL
… oh there's more.

                            CURTAINS
Go ahead.

                              FOOL
I ahh… I understand that setting up my male friends with girls I originally had interest in…

                            CURTAINS
Ha… ha… ha…

                              FOOL
Is because I knew they were better suited for each other.

                            CURTAINS
Right.

FOOL

I understand that… my parents staying together because of their kids. Sleeping in separate bedrooms without passion is a type of marriage that I do not wish for myself.

CURTAINS

It must have been sad for you to realize that. Yes.

FOOL

There's another one that's sad too. The next one.

CURTAINS

OK.

FOOL

I understand that my mother provided me with a lot of security. That her strength and guidance provided me an excuse that I took not to develop or not to go out and live up to my full potential. It was ahh… a safety blanket. Though she did provide me with a great foundation. I'm sure she would be happy if I lived at home with her and my dad… for the rest of… their lives… or my life……… I understand that working at the same company for seven years is also about security and I will pursue what I'm passionate about……… I understand that I needed to finally come to terms with the loss of my sister……… I understand that until now I've been going through life observing it instead of living it.

CURTAINS

Hallelujah!!!.

FOOL

I understand that security is what I needed in the past, or at least what I thought I needed - so I chose it. But now I know there are forces guiding me to move forward……… I understand that I have no social anxiety when I'm doing something for someone else or when I have focus, passion and direction. And I will going forward have no anxiety doing things for myself……… And most of all I understand that I choose right now, to change.

CURTAINS

Bless your superb heart!……… That's superb. Wuhh! You must be very proud of yourself.

FOOL

To a degree. There's still some work to do.

CURTAINS

Well, there's work to do… but… but you can't un-know that. I mean that the point is that some people take three years or five years of therapy to get there……… You can't un-know that. And no one… I can lead you. But people can show you, but you have to come up with that. And you did it! Can't un-know that......... I'm going to make a copy of that and put it in your file. I'll give it back to you but I'm going to make a copy of it. That's phenomenal. Phenomenal! Fabulous!

                              FOOL
So, there's another note on there too. So I was thinking about some of the things that have made me hesitant… in talking.

                              CURTAINS
M-hmm.

                              FOOL
… well, there's a couple factors. One, being raised in a family of teachers where education is important and the educational system is based on asking kids questions…

                              CURTAINS
Ha… ha…

                              FOOL
And only having them talk if it's important…

                              CURTAINS
Or right.

                              FOOL
Or right. It isn't really ahh…

                              CURTAINS
Cond… con… con…

                              FOOL
Ya.

                              CURTAINS
Conversation. There was no discussion.

                              FOOL
That's right.

                              CURTAINS
Everything was either right or wrong. But that's not real education. You know that right?

                                        FOOL
No.

                                        CURTAINS
Discussion is education.

                                        FOOL
It's not… it's not social interaction.

                                        CURTAINS
No.

                                        FOOL
It's not development.

                                        CURTAINS
No.

                                        FOOL
And… also that when I was younger. Through elementary school through to high school, I
was made fun of for my voice. And so… yaa… so I guess I was a little late in developing.

                                        CURTAINS
M-hmm.

                                        FOOL
And so that made me a little hesitant in talking unless it was…

                                        CURTAINS
M-hmm.

                                        FOOL
Vital.

                                        CURTAINS
M-hmm……… You've done a lot of work.

                                        FOOL
Ya……… Hmm… a lot of work.

                                        CURTAINS
Superb. I'm going to ask you to stretch yourself.

FOOL

Stretch myself?

CURTAINS

Yess. There is a course at the Conservatory of Music… called Singing from Scratch. And there are two people that run it. One is called Linda… Amen… Linda… Amen and she is a little thing… like this. Bubbly and warm and kind and she makes a safe place for everybody and nobody… but nobody can sing. Except people who think they can and they find out they can't. You're going to join.

FOOL

I am?

CURTAINS

Yes.

FOOL

Alright.

CURTAINS

Alright. So you get all sorts of people, all ages and all sizes… ha… ha… when I was there because I took it… because I wouldn't really refer anyone to anything unless you know… I've tried it. There was one guy who showed up who was convinced that he was a rock singer and he brought his guitar. And she said OK… and he kept saying I'm just here for the breathing, I'm not here because I know how to sing… I mean I know. And she said… fine. And when he sang all one note… I mean he only had one note and even I could hear that. And then she just said OK terrific… I mean that's your note. Ha… ha… and he kept saying it's not a note it's my song! OK. So I mean… and… so there's between eight and fifteen people in the class.

FOOL

OK.

CURTAINS

Once a week. Usually on a Monday and at six.

FOOL

It's downtown Toronto?

CURTAINS

M-hmm.

                              FOOL
OK.

                              CURTAINS
OK? It's fun. Terrifying the first two weeks, but after that it's fun. Good… this…

                              FOOL
I was thinking of actually…

                              CURTAINS
Improv?

                              FOOL
No. Not improv ha… ha…

                              CURTAINS
Ha… ha…

                              FOOL
Ahh… voice acting.

                              CURTAINS
Voice?

                              FOOL
Voice acting.

                              CURTAINS
Voice acting? Like voice-overs or things like that?

                              FOOL
Ya, it's more like video games or cartoons.

                              CURTAINS
Yahh. Ya, so you need to make some demos and get it to an agent… and go from there.

                              FOOL
Guess so.

                              CURTAINS
Yaa… a friend of mine is with a voice agent, so when you're ready I'll just give you the
name. When you've got all your demos and everything.

                    FOOL

OK.

                    CURTAINS

Alright?

                    FOOL

Yup.

                    CURTAINS

Good. But it's still singular in a booth. Ha... ha... ha...

                    FOOL

It's true.

                    CURTAINS

OK? But that's OK. So improv wouldn't hurt either?

                    FOOL

Alright.

                    CURTAINS

One step at a time though. Let's get you one step at a time. That is amazing! OK. OK.

                    FOOL

And I've also been thinking because I was very aware of what was going on when I was being hypnotized.

                    CURTAINS

M-hmm.

                    FOOL

And... for one thing that kinda got me was... what was my safe place.

                    CURTAINS

M-hmm.

                    FOOL

It was in meadows at night time and... there was... ahh... there was a body of water. Calm water. I was swimming in it making my own little ripples.

                    CURTAINS

M-mm.

FOOL

… but when I was looking at the timeline. The timeline was a shooting star and it just kept going forward and the trail was dissipating behind it. And that might be why I have a little bit of an issue going and trying to latch onto a spec… specific time that something happened in the past. I'm not… I'm not really logging things in mind based chronologically. I'm not attaching dates or years to them. I know that some events have happened but I can't say it was this year on this day and this time.

CURTAINS

No. Doesn't matter. All… all we're looking for is the source of the feeling.

FOOL

Ya.

CURTAINS

And when the feeling came in. We don't need a date.

FOOL

OK.

CURTAINS

Ya.

FOOL

Well maybe, even the order in which it came in is a little…

CURTAINS

Cause. Ya. Doesn't matter.

FOOL

OK.

CURTAINS

As long as we get the first time.

FOOL

OK.

CURTAINS

Ya. As long as we get the first time……… No, I totally understand that. Ahh… and it's a very creative mind. It's a very holistic mind. You know? And just ahh… it's lovely that you got a shooting star for… moving forward though. Which means that when you… when you get on track. When you're on traction… ffcheeww…

FOOL

I'm off to the races.

CURTAINS

You're going to wonder what took you so long. OK......... So as you were writing, this how did you feel? Was it like a a-ha one evening or did you sit down and work it?

FOOL

It was… ahh… two nights ago.

CURTAINS

M-hmm.

FOOL

And it was not really an a-ha. Some of those were things that I've known and never actually said.

CURTAINS

M-hmm.

FOOL

Or some of those are things that I've known and didn't want to say.

CURTAINS

M-mm. M-mm. M-mm. M-mm. Courage. Ya. We… we need a lot of courage to live our truth......... I was teaching last weekend ahh… a group of… hypnotherapists who've been in the business awhile, because it's a master level course. And I was quite shocked at the bullshit that… of themselves. That they carried with them and I called them on it. Because what happens is if you get good at what you do… some people… they begin to think that they're God or close to… or they think they're powerful or whatever. They don't understand that it's not about who we are… it's about the work right? So, well I called them on it… and they… made them go through something very similar to this. Because it's the paradigm of the fish in water. You don't know your own stuff until you're taken out of it. And a lot of people can't do that and you did that. You took yourself out of it and said OK, what's really going on here? What's my truth that isn't true anymore?

FOOL

Ya.

CURTAINS

Ya and ahh… ya… so I'm… I'm proud of you. You could have taught them how to do it. I mean… it's really… it's really great. It's terrific......... So now we have to… find a way. So that's a commitment right? You're going to go to that? You still have to go just because you put it away… ha… ha…

CENTER
FOOL

Ha… ha… ha. It's in my pocket… that means I'll pull it out later.

CURTAINS

Ha… ha… ha… and?

FOOL

Yes.

CURTAINS

And… OK. So… and make sure you get her. Because she's… she's quite wonderful.

FOOL

OK.

CURTAINS

The other one's probably OK too but… but I know this one. She's just… lovely. And you can say I sent you. That'd be great. So the work you're going to do on a day-to-day basis… about chatting. Are you going… really… are you serious about looking for another job?

FOOL

Yup.

CURTAINS

OK……… What are you going to do about it? And you want it in the IT business obviously? That's what you do right?

FOOL

Yup. I have a 4th interview in two days.

CURTAINS

With?

FOOL

Cineplex.

CURTAINS

Ha… ha… ha… ha… doing what?

                              FOOL
Ahh… Director of Web Operations.

                            CURTAINS
Well, that will improve your people skills. How many people will be working for you?

                              FOOL
I imagine six internal.

                            CURTAINS
How are you feeling about that?

                              FOOL
Good.

                            CURTAINS
Really?

                              FOOL
Yes!!

                            CURTAINS
Good. Good. And you're the like… final two or three their interviewing or? You don't
know. When will they let you know?

                              FOOL
… good question. It's already been a month and a half

                            CURTAINS
M-hmm.

                              FOOL
Of discussion so…

                            CURTAINS
M-mm……… So that's a big organization. Are they international… or Canadian only?

                              FOOL
It's just Canadian.

                            CURTAINS
Is it? I wasn't sure. I don't know if they were a part of something else. Wasn't sure. Wow!!

FOOL

Better be just Canadian… they only have a hundred and thirty some odd theatres. Can't be… you know… US.

CURTAINS

Right. Ya. I didn't know if it was part of something else. Ya. But I guess not. OK. But that was started by Garth Dabrinsky wasn't it? Cineplex. Did you know that? You did?

FOOL

Yup.

CURTAINS

Ya. OK. Course you probably did your research. Knowing you. So alright… so… how are you going to be ready for this 4th interview? What are you going to do?

FOOL

Ha… ha… work on my anxiety.

CURTAINS

Ha… ha… ha… hmm.

FOOL

Good question.

CURTAINS

Who's interviewing you?

FOOL

… older… female.

CURTAINS

What's her… what's her role.

FOOL

… Chief Customer Strategist.

CURTAINS

Ohh… OK … Chief Customer Strategist? So… and I'm just trying to give some ideas, because I'm an old marketer from way back. So if you took in a disk or you gave her a website she could log into as you took… as you gave her your laptop to take her on… on a web that you had prepared on customer service through the internet or something like that. So while she's talking to you she could look and see how your mind thinks. That might be… give you an edge.

                                    FOOL
Perhaps.

                                  CURTAINS
What does that mean?

                                    FOOL
The website I have to offer-up isn't too impressive.

                                  CURTAINS
You've got two days to do something about it. Ha… ha… ha…

                                    FOOL
Alright.

                                  CURTAINS
Think about it though. Think about something different that allows her to see you as
innovative, but understanding of what they need.

                                    FOOL
OK.

                                  CURTAINS
So not only… not only is she buying your expertise and how smart you are and your track
record… and all that. She's also seeing futures in you. She can see futures. That it may not
be… exactly what they need, but at least you put yourself out there to think about what's
next. Go that extra mile.

                                    FOOL
OK.

                                  CURTAINS
OK?

                                    FOOL
Yes.

                                  CURTAINS
Because that's what they're looking for. OK. And they know they're looking for a nerd and
they know that they're looking for someone whose really ahh… technologically good. They
also… if they can get someone whose got a little bit of market awareness or something.
That… they… they'll… they'll be thrilled. Making sense?

                                  [240]

                              FOOL

Yup.

                            CURTAINS

OK. Right. So what are you going to do to improve your verbal skills?

                              FOOL

More interaction. Practice makes perfect.

                            CURTAINS

Ya. How are you doing with that?

                              FOOL

Alright.

                            CURTAINS

What does that mean?

                              FOOL

It means I'm doing alright.

                            CURTAINS

OK. So who are you practicing with?

                              FOOL

Ahh… some strangers.

                            CURTAINS

Really?!

                              FOOL

Ya.

                            CURTAINS

Bless your heart! How… where?

                              FOOL

Just random.

                            CURTAINS

OK?

FOOL

I always hold doors open for people… whatever… so… have a quick conversation and then spending more time opening up to people that I thought I was close to ,to begin with ,but haven't really been talking too much with.

CURTAINS

OK. Good. So you're playing safe… in a safe area and also reaching out a little more. Alright ya. So… you're going to start talking more to people in stores. OK? I don't care if it's Future Shop or Loblaws. The people that serve you. You're going to chat.

FOOL

OK.

CURTAINS

OK? I know this works. I have proven records that it works. So as you're going through the Loblaws line-up, and the woman behind the counter who's there taking your cash… you just say oh boy you… when did you come on duty or what's your shift?… are you tired?… you know what's it like working by the door?… is it noisy or… whatever? Start a conversation. It gets easier the more you do it… like anything……… Can you do that do you think?

FOOL

I will.

CURTAINS

Good. Good. Alright and what are we going to work on today? Hmm… I'm blown away by the work you've done this week……… OK. So we worked on shame and anxiety. And… ahh……… How about Judgment. Sadness. Where are you on sadness now? How do you feel?

FOOL

Alright.

CURTAINS

So it's… so not… so it's not there anymore? Doesn't feel like it's there anymore?

FOOL

No.

CURTAINS

OK. We'll just let that go then. That's alright. Alright……… OK. This is where you don't go into hypnosis right?

FOOL

That's right.

CURTAINS

Ha… ha…

FOOL

I'll take my shoes off this time.

CURTAINS

OK. If you can just turn a little that ways, so when I turn to face you, I can reach out and just touch your hand……… When's your birth day?

FOOL

January 26th, 78.

CURTAINS

You'll be twenty-eight?

FOOL

Thirty?

CURTAINS

You'll be thirty?

FOOL

I am thirty.

CURTAINS

You are thirty? So why did you say January twenty-eight?

FOOL

January twenty-six.

CURTAINS

Oh, January twenty-six.

FOOL

That's right.

CURTAINS

I'm just thinking to make sure that you really celebrate your next birthday. So that gives us… six months. Ohh… way before that I think……… Alright, so take a deep breath and

[243   ]

close your eyes and do whatever you need to do to make yourself comfortable......... And just connect with your breath......... I'm going to count from one to twenty and just follow your breath. Noticing the coolness of the in breath... and the warmth of the out breath......... Counting down now. One... two... three... four. Relaxing all the way down......... Five... six... seven... eight... nine... ten. The deeper you go...the better you feel......... Eleven... twelve... thirteen... fourteen... fifteen. Relaxing down... down......... Sixteen... seventeen... eighteen... nineteen... and twenty......... You find yourself in your beautiful wonderful safe place......... A place where you feel really... really good......... Where nothing bothers you. Nothing... disturbs you......... And take a moment now and go deep... deep inside yourself. Deep inside to that part of you where there is peace......... A big quiet centre that is you. The quietest part of the being......... And as you go deep inside you become aware that there is a spot of light deep within you. This spark can be... just that... or it can be like a candle flame or a ball of light. However you perceive that light. It's there......... This is your soul light. And whether you see it or imagine it or think it... it makes no difference. This is the light that's been with you since time began. It will stay with you as long as you have breath on this planet. Until you return to the stars. This light connects you to all there is in time and space......... It's your soul light. But from time to time the soul can be fractured... trauma... trauma of spiritually or emotionally or physically. And today we're going to make it whole. We're going to retrieve all of those splinters and fractures that have happened through time and space. In this lifetime or other lifetimes. So look very carefully at that light and you may see some silver threads that come from that light. And these silver threads are attached to splinters or fractures that you saw. And some can be as tiny as grains of sand or as large as a limb of your body. And these fractures or splinters can be attached to other times or other places or even... other people. Trauma. Causes the soul to splinter and fracture. So today we're going to retrieve all of those pieces, one by one. And as you follow each silver thread... you'll find it... bless it... heal it and bring it home to your centre. And as you bring it home, you'll place it deep within you with the light... the source of your light. Your light will burn just a little brighter each time. And stronger. So begin to follow the threads one by one......... Through time and space......... Rescuing each peace from another place... another time... another person. Heal it and bring it home......... Each and every time. Bring it home. That's right......... One after another. After another. Taking all the time you need......... And when you bring them all home, just let me know by moving your finger. But in the meantime, take all the time you need. One after the other. After the other......... Through time and space. Collecting each piece and bringing it home......... Bringing it back to your light. Your centre. One after the other. After the other......... Each time you do, your light burns a little brighter. And stronger......... There. Good. Now look at that light within you. That strong light that connects you to all there is. This is your internal self. And as you recognize that light in yourself, so you'll recognize it in others. This is truly who you are......... Now go deep into that part of you that understands. Where the child is. Little boy. Little Tim. Maybe five or six years old......... And wrap your arms around him. Stroke his hair and his cheek and tell him what a great kid he is. Smart and bright and as cute as a button......... And tell him how much you love him......... Unconditional love......... And tell him that you're always there for him. And that nothing and no one will ever hurt him again. Because you're going to take care of him. You're there for him......... And hold him close. He needs to feel your heartbeat. He needs to feel loved. He needs to feel trust. He needs to feel acceptance......... And while you're holding him ask him if he'd like you to do this on a regular basis. And if he would make that promise to him that every night you'll hold him like this. Just before you go to sleep. So he can feel safe......... Also tell him that you're going to listen to him. Because he needs to be heard......... He needs to be listened to. So this gift that you can give him... is your love... unconditional love and listen to him......... And while you're holding him, wrap him a beautiful blanket. Something soft and fluffy that makes him feel cozy and place him back in your heart right next to that light. So he can see and feel the light. The light of unconditional love and acceptance. Your soul light. Where as a child of God, he uses the light and just is......... And ask him if there's anything he would like you to do with him... to play. Just to have some fun. Maybe... I don't know... go to zoo or go to Harbourfront or just hang out and have some fun. Do some kids stuff. If he would remember, you'll listen to him. Whatever he wants. You'll listen to him......... That's right. Now as you wrap him in a blanket and place him in your heart, just tell him that you're going to see him soon......... Now we're going to move forward... in time. Maybe two months... three months... I don't know... doesn't matter... and just surround yourself with people that you care about. People who care about you and maybe some people you've not met yet. And just notice how easily you laugh and interact.

VOICE FROM ANOTHER ROOM

Ha... ha... ha... ha... hmm.

CURTAINS

And how you make people laugh......... And how with those beautiful eyes of yours... you charm people and make them feel good about themselves......... Just notice how easily it comes. All it takes is practice. Because you got what it takes! You got the smarts. You got the knowledge. Interested in a lot of things. Can talk about a lot of things. All it takes is practice. The more you like and honor and respect yourself the more people will feel that in you and respect that too. It feels good. It feels very good. .... Practice of all else the realness of free interaction. It makes this so much easier. And as you look at yourself and feel yourself... become easier and easier... interacting. With people you don't necessarily know. Men and women. Just becomes easier......... And as you come back now to your safe place. Bringing that future planning with you. Coming back... into full awareness. As I count from ten to one just bring yourself back into this room. Coming back now... ten... nine... eight... seven... six... five... four... three moving your hands and feet. Come on back. Two and one. Take a deep breath and bring yourself back......... Welcome back.

FOOL

It's good to be back.

CURTAINS

Ha… ha… good to be back… that's good…….. How did it feel holding that kid? That little boy.

FOOL

Well, he didn't object this time.

CURTAINS

He didn't? We won't… the more you do it the easier it becomes……… Listen. All children love to be held. They may fight it, but they love to be held. Especially if it's unconditional……… You don't seem as though you're too trusting in that.

FOOL

Sure I am. I'm not a kid.

CURTAINS

… well, there's a part of you.

FOOL

Ya.

CURTAINS

Ya. Part of us always……… How was the soul retrieval?

FOOL

Good.

CURTAINS

What did you discover there… anything? There's lots of pieces coming back?

FOOL

Yup.

CURTAINS

Do you know where they come from? Did you see them come from… anyplace… or wha… wha… what happened? What was it like for you?

FOOL

Oh, I was just collecting up some things that had to do with… well most of my points really.

CURTAINS

Had to do… what… with all of your points? Oh.

FOOL

Pretty much.

CURTAINS

Ya. OK. Ya. But all from this life nothing from b... previously?

FOOL

No.

CURTAINS

OK. Good. You got them all back... and schh... you're whole again.

FOOL

Ya.

CURTAINS

Good. OK. Does it feel different inside yet or you don't know yet?

FOOL

Don't know yet.

CURTAINS

OK. Alright. Ha... ha... see what you come up with this week.

FOOL

I'm a little slow. It'll take me a day to sink in.

CURTAINS

OK. OK. You just process differently. Ya. You're not Wi-Fi yet. Ha...

FOOL

That's right.

CURTAINS

Ha... ha... still dial-up?

FOOL

Ya.

CURTAINS

Ya. OK. So what happened when you... experienced those? Do you see them or do you feel them... or what happens? Or do you think them?

FOOL

Well I don't really... it's... I don't know. I only see... see in terms of black and different color shades. So I do see them...

CURTAINS

M-hmm.

FOOL

Sometimes it's difficult to make out.

CURTAINS

What they are?

FOOL

But I just know what they are.

CURTAINS

OK... that's good. So... so you know? Right so it's not a question of visualizing; it's a question of just knowing. Which is fine. Because as long as it... ya... that's good. OK. That's great......... Oh ya... when you came in... where's my notes?... you did. We did a measurement form. Do you remember? Because I wanted to know... about progress. If I can find the measurement form. I need a system for this. I... remember when we measured your anxiety?

FOOL

Yup.

CURTAINS

Anger. Sadness. And ahh... I can't find it... it's here somewhere. No... no... no... OK here it is. OK so let's go through them now and see where you are.

FOOL

I feel that most of them are in check.

CURTAINS

I'm not sure what that means.

FOOL

Meaning that you can't go throughout life without having any anger, but at least when you demonstrate anger it's warranted. It's not that it's just there for some unknown reason.

CURTAINS

Right.

FOOL

Just being moody.

CURTAINS

Right.

FOOL

And …

CURTAINS

So that all the stuff you've been carrying is pretty well gone do you think?

FOOL

Ya. But I feel that anxiety was the only big piece that was still out there.

CURTAINS

M-hmm. OK. On a scale of one to ten how much is it? That's still there.

FOOL

Think I'm still in the seventy range…

CURTAINS

OK.

FOOL

And it was about ninety or a hundred before.

CURTAINS

Ya. OK seventy. OK. Good.

FOOL

So at least now I'm realizing where some of those sources of anxiety are coming from.

CURTAINS

M-hmm. Are you going to do anything this week at Luminato? Are you getting together with any friends or anything and going down to some of this entertainment stuff that's happening in the city?

FOOL

Luminato?

CURTAINS

Ya, you don't know about it?

                                    FOOL

No.

                                  CURTAINS

Oh my goodness! Oh my goodness!

                                    FOOL

What's Luminato?

                                  CURTAINS

Luminato. OK, get on-line. I wish I had the brochure but it isn't here. It's happening…
ahh… all last week and this week and this weekend. And it's literally music, dance, theatre
happenings… sculpture in the city. Everywhere. Dundas Square for instance has music
every night. And they have dance class first and then you… they have big bands and they
have swing lessons for everybody and then… then… everybody listens to music. It's
happening down at the Harbourfront. Most of its free. Some of it you pay five dollars some
of it… everything you can imagine.

                                    FOOL

And that's all weekend long?

                                  CURTAINS

All week and weekend.

                                    FOOL

Hmm.

                                  CURTAINS

Everywhere throughout the city. It's called Luminato. So all types of music. From Indian to
jazz to classical to African chant to everything. Everywhere. All throughout the city. Ahh…
walk into some of the public buildings they got big sculptures hanging from the ceilings…
there could be light shows and water shows. Down at Harbourfront. There's going to be
everything. And it's on all the time.

                                    FOOL

OK. Well, I better get out then.

                                  CURTAINS

You have to get out. So get a group of… of people from… the office or something and just
go. You know. Go for a couple of nights or go during the day. Just wander down to the
Harbourfront. Or see what's happening all around the city. It's uhh… quite magical this
week and last weekend. So… you know… it's a happening place.

FOOL

OK.

CURTAINS

Alright?

FOOL

Yup, I'll ask a few people.

CURTAINS

Ya… but… and the brochures are everywhere. So if you enter a store you'll see them laying around. About Luminato. Ya.

FOOL

Ya, I didn't hear about it in the burbs.

CURTAINS

Ha… ha… where's Cineplex situated?

FOOL

Oh, it's Toronto.

CURTAINS

Ya. Ya, so are you going to move here or are you going to commute?

FOOL

I'd have to move here.

CURTAINS

Ahh… be still my heart. How are you going to manage that?

FOOL

I just will.

CURTAINS

Yes… ha… ha. Good.

FOOL

I'd probably commute for the first couple of months then get sick of taking the 407.

CURTAINS

Oh, ya. Especially in the Winter. Ooff. Ya. OK, good. So you're getting out this weekend. OK? So, homework. What are you going to do this week?

[251   ]

FOOL

Luminato.

CURTAINS

Luminato and what else? Ha… ha… ha…

FOOL

Harass people in shops.

CURTAINS

Ha… ha… ha… OK. Harass everybody. Alright. I'm writing that down. Harass people in shops.

FOOL

And you want me to say sign up for singing lessons. Ha… ha…

CURTAINS

No I don't want you to say it. I want you to do it.

FOOL

Ha… alright.

CURTAINS

I want you to do it. I don't know when it starts. So where are we now… no… you might have lucked out. It might not happen now until September. Doesn't mean that you can't do it……… Oh my God, that's my mobile. No it's not… is that yours?

FOOL

No.

CURTAINS

Can you hear that buzzing? Hmm… OK.

FOOL

I don't know.

CURTAINS

OK … how… how do you normally spend your weekends and evenings? Do you spend them socially or do you normally spend them by yourself?

FOOL

Hmm… family and friends.

CURTAINS

And you…

FOOL

Like I'm going out the movies as soon as I'm done here.

CURTAINS

OK. And what do…

FOOL

Hmm talk… go out…

CURTAINS

What about meeting new people? How do you… how do you guys do that? You don't?

FOOL

Not really. I do on-line.

CURTAINS

Mmm. And do you actually date on-line or just chat on-line.

FOOL

Both.

CURTAINS

And how has it been when you dated?

FOOL

Ha… not too good.

CURTAINS

No. Because?

FOOL

Because it's not real.

CURTAINS

What do you mean it's not real?

FOOL

People either get caught up in their emotions…

CURTAINS

M-mm.

FOOL

Or they pretend to be something they're not.

CURTAINS

And that's…

FOOL

So I guess it is real!

CURTAINS

That's right. So when you meet someone face to face you mean they've been pretending on-line about something they're not or…? Is that what you mean? Or what did you mean?

FOOL

The way people type out or interact that way is a lot different from the way they talk face to face.

CURTAINS

Mmm. Do they feel more free to you think on-line then they…

FOOL

Ya.

CURTAINS

OK. And that includes you right?

FOOL

Yup. I can type a lot faster than I can talk. So it's a… it's a much… I don't know… it's a much more established connection to the brain.

CURTAINS

M-hmm.

FOOL

Connect to my fingertips than to my mouth.

CURTAINS

Except when you're talking to someone, that's not the way you communicate right… you communicate with the heart not the brain.

FOOL

Ya.

CURTAINS

So when you date on-line, what do you do it through? Do you do it through Yahoo or…
what… how do you reach people?

FOOL

MSN.

CURTAINS

MSN? OK. So you don't go through a dating process. A dating service type thing?

FOOL

I have. Not very effective.

CURTAINS

No? OK.

FOOL

The men outweigh the women on those sites.

CURTAINS

Oh, do they?

FOOL

The ratio is pretty extreme.

CURTAINS

Oh, is it?

FOOL

Guys might get a couple of messages and girls might get a couple thousand messages to go
through.

CURTAINS

Oh. OK so you have to find another way of meeting women. To meet people. M-hmm. I
mean… because I get so many women in here looking for guys you know… so many guys
looking for women and I sit here thinking I'm going to start a business. Ya. And everybody's
hungry… you know. They want to meet someone who matters. Hmm. Do you go to clubs
or anything like that?

FOOL

No. That novelty wore off.

CURTAINS

M-hmm. It's hard to talk as well you know unless you…

FOOL

Over the loud music.

CURTAINS

Ya.

FOOL

Ya.

CURTAINS

Ya. Oh well, a lot of people I know pick up people in strange places like Supermarkets and ahh… Canadian Tire and places like that. You know. They just start chatting. So… a… chatter. Become a good chatter. OK……… I'm going to make a copy of this. So when you look at your friends, are any of them… ahh… achievers? No. These people you went to school with?

FOOL

Yup.

CURTAINS

Ya. OK. Alright. So maybe you need to start… doing something where you mix with people who are achievers. Either when you move back to Toronto or before maybe you start taking night classes at U of T of something that interests you that's nothing to do with business. Whether it be music or whatever it is. Literature. So you meet people who are… ahh… as brainy as you are. Who want to get there to learn something different.

FOOL

Ya.

CURTAINS

… or you might even take a part-time MBA course. Who knows… but… but you got to get out there and… and… and meet people that way to learn Because there is smart people. Does that make any sense?

FOOL

It does.

CURTAINS

Ya. Even the ROM… the ROM Museum has singles evenings. They have lectures. They have lectures and… on all sorts of things from why the star moves that way to is the dinosaur really that old? You know that sort of type of lecture and cocktail party. I think they're fifteen bucks or twenty bucks an evening. And people go and just chat. So there's a lot happening in the city for you to plug into. But if you want to plug into people who are thinkers, you know, you might consider taking some courses. You know?

FOOL

Philosophy.

CURTAINS

Philosophy? Sure. And tell me about your sister. What's your feelings about your sister. Still grieving? Still feeling usurped or you just put it in its place?

FOOL

No, I'm feeling good about it.

CURTAINS

Good. You put it… you put it where it belongs.

FOOL

Ya.

CURTAINS

OK. You've done good, boy. I'm just going to go and get this copied. I'll be right back……… That's yours. There. Alright. So let me know about Luminato.

FOOL

OK. I'll go.

CURTAINS

Hmm?

FOOL

I'll go!

CURTAINS

I know you will. You're doing really good now. Because there's so much going on, there's got to be something there you'll enjoy. See and touch and feel new stuff.

FOOL

Yup, anything to do with the arts.

CURTAINS

Oh really! Then you're going to love it!

EXIT TIM THE FOOL AND THE CURTAINS

Take a Bow

Special Thanks To

KALE

BEN SMITH

CAROLYN MAYEUR

SERGE MAYEUR

DANIELLE MAYEUR

THE FOOL

Final Curtains

06/17/2008

ENTER TIM THE FOOL AND THE CURTAINS

CURTAINS

Is your phone off?

FOOL

Yup, my phone's off.

CURTAINS

You're recording everything.

FOOL

That's right.

CURTAINS

Tell me how you're doing. What's happening with you?

FOOL

Doing good.

CURTAINS

Feeling good?

FOOL

Ya.

CURTAINS

What happened about the job?

                    FOOL

… the interview hasn't happened yet.

                    CURTAINS

OK.

                    FOOL

… so I went ahh… and created ahh… a social networking site, unofficially, on behalf of Cineplex and sent them over the link.

                    CURTAINS

Good on ya. Did you feel good about that?

                    FOOL

Ya, took a little bit of time it's ahh… it's a GPS user kind of social network.

                    CURTAINS

M-hmm.

                    FOOL

So I went in and I posted all their locations and their coordinates. People have been downloading it… so…

                    CURTAINS

They have?

                    FOOL

Ya.

                    CURTAINS

Ha… ha… ha… ha…

                    FOOL

It's the new rave.

                    CURTAINS

Ha… ha…

                    FOOL

GPS users.

CURTAINS

So did you hear from them? Did you follow-up and say what did you think? And by the way… it's working.

FOOL

I will.

CURTAINS

When? When did you send it?

FOOL

When?

CURTAINS

M-hmm.

FOOL

Late last week.

CURTAINS

Did you? OK. Great……… Good……… So, I guess, you're going to give them until Thursday or Friday?

FOOL

Yup.

CURTAINS

Great. It's a neat thing to do. For you it's a shrug on the shoulder, but for someone who doesn't know… it's a neat thing to do. Good thing to do. And what else?

FOOL

And ahh… I went out to Luminato.

CURTAINS

Good.

FOOL

Well, I couldn't find anyone to go with, so I just went by myself.

CURTAINS

Good. And what did you see?

                              FOOL
Well, I saw the commercial on Sunday.

                              CURTAINS
Yah.

                              FOOL
So I looked what was available on Sunday and I just went to the Canon Theatre for the all…
all-Indian version of A Midsummer's Night Dream.

                              CURTAINS
What did you think of that?

                              FOOL
Well, I'm familiar with the… the play.

                              CURTAINS
Yah.

                              FOOL
I got it. But for someone who's never seen it before or never read the script…you can still
pick up the concept.

                              CURTAINS
I thought it was brilliant actually. I saw it and thought it was absolutely brilliant. Did you
love it or did you not like it?

                              FOOL
I loved it.

                              CURTAINS
OK. With the drumming and the music and the dancing. And the whole interplay of
language.

                              FOOL
The acrobatics…

                              CURTAINS
Acrobatics.

                              FOOL
Were pretty good too.

CURTAINS

Ya. Didn't you love that backdrop that was all white and then suddenly…

FOOL

And they tore it apart.

CURTAINS

Ya.

FOOL

Ya. They were flipping between ahh… the bars.

CURTAINS

Ya. I thought it was pretty brilliant. And she fell asleep in that silk little nest that she made and ya… ahh… I… I'm glad you saw that. Good. Did you catch any music or anything else?

FOOL

There was some music going on but, once again, ahh… started to rain again.

CURTAINS

Right.

FOOL

So it didn't last too long before people started to clear out.

CURTAINS

Right. Then you got the Jazz Festival coming up soon and… there's a lot happening in this city.

FOOL

Well there's… on the weekend there was the Sound of Music too in Burlington.

CURTAINS

Oh right. Yah. You getting out and chatting? Have you?

FOOL

Wyaa.

CURTAINS

Wyaa… that's a little squeaky yes. What does that mean?

                                    FOOL
It means yes.

                                  CURTAINS
OK. To people you don't know?

                                    FOOL
Ya, to a few people I don't know.

                                  CURTAINS
Good. Good……… Good……… So you feeling a little stronger… a little better or… about
the same or… ? How are you feeling about yourself?

                                    FOOL
Stronger.

                                  CURTAINS
And what are you doing about every day? How are you making that strength manifest in
you every day?

                                    FOOL
Just through my regular interactions with people.

                                  CURTAINS
OK. Are your friends noticing any difference? Or not? Ya. They are?

                                    FOOL
They should.

                                  CURTAINS
They should? Ha… ha… ha…

                                    FOOL
If not… they're not very observant.

                                  CURTAINS
OK. Has anybody said anything?

                                    FOOL
Not yet.

CURTAINS

Not yet? OK……… Yah. Good. That's great……… Alright. So when do you expect to hear from Cineplex?……… Did they tell you?……… You know if you're recording this you have to talk. Otherwise you're going to get a silent tape. Unless it's visual as well.

FOOL

No it's… they're just a bit slow.

CURTAINS

Ya, they are slow. Ya.

FOOL

So I'm… I'm following up but if I'm not hearing back then I wait a little bit and I follow-up again.

CURTAINS

Yah. Yah.

FOOL

But I can't say for certain that something's going to be happening on…

CURTAINS

No.

FOOL

A set date. I'm not getting answers…

CURTAINS

No.

FOOL

About that.

CURTAINS

No. No. No……… Remind me again how you found that opening?

FOOL

… a business partner of theirs referred me.

CURTAINS

OK. So that's a good one……… It wasn't a head hunter or anything so… this is… so this is good……… Today we're going to do some work around you visioning… imagining

interacting with women......... Meeting... saying hello. Chatting. Getting comfortable.
That good?

                                CURTAINS

FOOL

Sure. Alright.

                                CURTAINS

Ha... ha... ha... ha... ha...

                                FOOL

I still subscribe to the philosophy that the right one will find me.

                                CURTAINS

You can be alone a long time. What...

                                FOOL

Well I have.

                                CURTAINS

Do you want to continue that way? Of course, it's more fun when you meet more people.
And you get to meet different types of people. You know... this is not like one bee finding
the jar of honey this is like... you want lots of bees. So you get to choose and have fun and
date and get out there. OK. Understand what you want and what you don't want.

                                FOOL

OK.

                                CURTAINS

Because otherwise it's a little bit... cowardly. What was that? Was that the program from
Luminato?

                                FOOL

That's proof of me going. It's the receipt or my ticket.

                                CURTAINS

I believe you.

                                FOOL

Just in case you didn't.

                                CURTAINS

I believe you. Why wouldn't I believe you? This is the ticket. I went Wednesday night
ya......... I believe you totally. You have no reason to lie to me.

FOOL

That's right.

CURTAINS

You're kidding me, ha......... Ya, so consider the idea of ahh... dating two or three women at once. Doesn't have to be intense. Just having fun. Movies... dinner... a walk. Museum... the zoo... the art gallery... coffee... whatever. Just hang out.

FOOL

OK.

CURTAINS

OK? OK......... Alright. Let's put some music on......... Mm... kay. I'm just going to count from one to twenty and as I do just allow your mind, body and spirit to relax......... Counting down now. One... two... three... four. Relaxing all the way down......... Five... six... seven... eight... nine... ten. Nothing bothers you. Nothing disturbs you......... Eleven... twelve... thirteen... fourteen... fifteen... sixteen. The deeper you go. The better you feel......... Seventeen... eighteen... nineteen... and twenty......... And you find yourself in your safe place. The place where you feel the most good......... You find somewhere to sit and as you sit just allow yourself to drift down... down deeper... and deeper. All the way down. Feeling safe and secure. And feeling very... very good. And as you relax down. All the way down. Just imagine that timeline. That line that stretches all the way to past. Way back when. Blue light misty cloud. And all the way into the future as far as your eye can see. Big bright and clear future......... And right where we are today. Put a big flag......... So now lift yourself up above that line. And look at it below you......... Just look at all the memories past, present and future in this great distance......... And we're going to journey back now through time and space. To the very first time that feeling of anxiety... about mixing socially came into your life. That anxiety about being social. Open to meeting new people. The very first time you felt that way. And it could be before you were born. In another time or place. Could have felt that way in your mother's womb. Could have come into you shortly after you were born and you were very young......... And when you're there, your yes finger responds. As you journey back and back and back and back and back to the very first time that anxiety becomes a part of you. And fear of being with others. New people. Meeting new people. Being open and maybe vulnerable to new people. Al the way back and back and back and back. And your conscious mind doesn't know where it is but your body knows. It's a shyness. It's a fear. All the way back. And just move your yes finger when you're there. This finger's yes. As you go back and back and back. And back in time and space......... And come on down on the timeline. And about the time you're two-years old in this current lifetime. Little boy of two years old. And if you're like other two-year olds you're full of curiosity. Just a little toddler wandering around. Exploring. Everything's new. Everything's the first time......... But just notice if, at age two, you carry that feeling of anxiety. If you do just let me know by moving your yes finger. If you don't move the finger in your other hand. Just notice at age two if you carry that anxiety in you. You do. OK......... And move back. Lift yourself up above again over timeline. And move back. All the way back. All the way back. At the count of three, find yourself in that time and space when anxiety came into your body. One... two... three... snap. And just let me know when you're there. And let me know by moving your finger. When you are at the beginning of that feeling of anxiety......... Maybe it came from your mother. I don't know. So let's... let's go in... drop down on the timeline into the womb of your mother. Into this dark warm place. The sound of the heartbeat. Where you can feel the heartbeat. Take in all that's around you. The sound. Feeling. The rhythm of the heart......... And when you can imagine yourself there just let me know by moving your finger. As you imagine yourself there in that place. Dark warm place. And just notice is the feeling of anxiety there with you......... If there is, move the finger on your right hand. If there isn't, move the finger on your left hand. There is. Just notice if that feeling of anxiety comes from your mother. Or if it comes from somewhere else. If it comes from your mother, just move that finger. If it doesn't, move the finger on your left hand......... Good. Then journey back from the womb. Going back and back and back and back. Back and back. Through the blue mist of time. Back beyond. Back and back and back. All the way back to the source of that feeling. The source of that anxiety. All the way back. Whatever it is just let it unfold. And when you are there, your yes finger responds. Whether you feel it or see it like a movie or... just know that that's the source. Not knowing exactly what it is. And when you're there your yes... that finger responds. Move your hand. As you go back and back and back. The source of that anxiety......... All the way back. And as you're there just look and see what is happening to cause that anxiety......... And where you are. And who else is involved. And just let the story tell itself. And whether you see it or feel it or just know... it makes no difference......... And you allow the story to tell itself so allow the understanding about the source of the anxiety come forward......... And move now to the end of that particular time. And let the curtain drop on that time. Let it fade as you leave behind the anxiety associated with that time. Where it belongs. Just leave it behind......... You come forward finding yourself once more in the blue mist. A gentle time. Peace. And just ask while you're there if there's another place we need to go to release that anxiety that you carry with you in your current life. If there's another place and time that we need to go. If there is your right hand finger responds. If there isn't your left hand finger responds......... Good. So come forward now along the timeline. Moving through the time of that dark warm place. Come forward to the time of being very young. Two... and three... and four. Letting go of that old anxiety because it doesn't belong in this time. Just letting it go. Through your early teens... eighteens... twenties... just letting it go like leafs on the trees in Fall. Letting the old... release... allowing space for new ones......... And move out now along the timeline into the future. And see a whole new place. A new way of being......... And as you are now in a state of appreciation and gratitude of what's good in your life. And you begin to release the thoughts and physical control that you have over any anxiety to meet new people meet... date women. This abundance has been waiting for you. And you allow yourself now to arrive at this... this future. Future of freedom of thought and emotion. Freedom from fear and anxiety. Knowing that you are on a healthy and positive path. And so much more fun is generated in creative ways as your subconscious mind finds ways to express truly who you are as you meet new and interesting people. You stay healthy and responsible. And you enjoy sharing yourself. Your knowledge, your humor. Your intellect. And you create more joy. A benefit for yourself and for other people. As you grow and flourish. And take a moment now and just imagine standing at the edge of the universe. Your universe. Safe but happy and free. Your heart and mind are open. You allow abundance to flow into your life. Abundance of love and laughter and caring. You feel so good to be free of this anxiety. And you begin to attract like-minded people. You begin to attract those who also enjoy life. Have a zest for life. And feel good about who they are. Emotionally. Physically. Spiritually. And as you see yourself and hear yourself in your future free from anxiety and fear. Just laughing and having fun. Experiencing new forms of relationships. New ways of being with yourself and with others. Understanding that this is your choice. This is how you choose to be......... And while you're there, just look around you. Hear yourself surrounded by those you love and those that love you. Hear the laughter and the chatter......... And feel it... feel how good it feels in your life. And the other thing to notice is as you feel better about yourself you begin to take more care of yourself. More care of what and how you eat. How you exercise. You begin to honor and respect who you are......... Good. Now using your very powerful mind scan your body. See if there's any part of your body holding onto that old... old anxiety. If there is, your yes finger responds. If there isn't, your no finger responds......... Good. Now check your mind and see if there's any part of your mind... conscious or sub-conscious holding onto that old... old anxiety. There is, your yes finger responds. There isn't your no finger responds......... Good. Good. Now while you're doing this, just check to see what are the next steps you need to take. To plan toward the feeling of strength and good strong self-esteem. Moving forward without anxiety. And just notice if it's something you may want to do. Maybe meet new people or might join a Toast Masters or go to a gym. Doing some volunteer work. I don't know. But just make some choices about the next steps......... And when you've done that...just let me know by moving your yes finger......... Just think about some of the things that you could do. That are your next steps to moving forward to the change that you really want to make......... OK. Great. Now just go safe deep inside. Safely inside yourself and find that part of you that is that little boy......... And just give him a hug......... And tell him you love him. And tell him what a great kid he is. And how much fun the both of you are going to have together from now on......... And while you're there with him with your arm wrapped around him, just become aware that over to one side is the higher self of your mother. And she's standing there with her arms open asking you to forgive her. And you move into her arms and you wrap your arms around her and forgive her. Remembering she behaved the only way she knew how. And you realize that behind her is her mother. Asking for forgiveness from her daughter. And behind her... her mother. And so it's going around and around until you feel behind you movement and you turn around and it's your inner child. Little boy. That's right. Who is forgiving you for not listening to him. The circle of forgiveness allows love and peace to flow where there was pain before......... And the same with your father. The part of him that is his higher self that knows better asks for forgiveness. As his father in turn also asks for forgiveness......... Good. All the way around to meet that child within you. For there's a time to feel safe and loved.

Unconditionally loved and whole……… And take that little boy now and place him back in your heart. Make him feel safe. And as long as he feels safe you can be adventurous and expand. And try. Experiment. And get out there in your own safety blanket. Because as long as he feels safe, there's freedom to move……… Good boy. You make your way back to your safe place……… At the count of ten to one. And as I do just bring yourself back to the surface. Coming back now. Ten… nine… eight… seven… six…

                        FOOL
I'll come back to you here.

                        CURTAINS
Huh?

                        FOOL
I'll come back to you here.

                        CURTAINS
OK. Good. You're back……… So what did you learn, oh wise one? Going to try to shock us? What did you learn?

                        FOOL
I'm going to jump on a plane.

                        CURTAINS
You're going to jump on a plane?

                        FOOL
Apparently.

                        CURTAINS
Good. And you're going to go somewhere?

                        FOOL
Ya, I was feeling a little turbulence on takeoff.

                        CURTAINS
Same thing. Living life. Eh. So when you went back to that anxiety did… where did you go? Anywhere in particular? No.

                        FOOL
No.

CURTAINS

OK. It was with you at two which is interesting.

FOOL

Ya, I saw the same Face again.

CURTAINS

Mmm.

FOOL

I think its self-imposed.

CURTAINS

Ya. OK.

FOOL

Self-imposed since before birth.

CURTAINS

Just before birth because? Why? Well, if you did…

FOOL

It was always there.

CURTAINS

Hmm?

FOOL

Just always there.

CURTAINS

Well it can't always be there. You self-imposed it for a reason. Usually people want to be safe for a reason. So they will move away from pain so… why would you put that anxiety on yourself to prevent what happening? What if you did know…?

FOOL

A matter of control.

CURTAINS

Control? M-hmm. It's a control thing because…?

FOOL

I don't know yet.

OK. Alright. So… so part of it is if… you know… if you control the environment, then nothing can go wrong. That nothing can happen.

FOOL

M-hmm.

CURTAINS

Which is great for a kid, but an adult it's like being in a cage. So where are you flying to?

FOOL

Australia or New Zealand.

CURTAINS

Great. On business or pleasure?

FOOL

Pleasure.

CURTAINS

M-hmm.

FOOL

At first.

CURTAINS

Why those two? Just because?

FOOL

Just always felt it.

CURTAINS

OK. There's something about New Zealand… that… that's very appealing. For me anyways… so. Ya. I'm not sure what it is. If it's the beauty of the place or the fact that it's not very populated. They say there's more sheep than people. Very friendly. It's a great place to start something.

FOOL

It is.

CURTAINS

M-hmm……… Right. So when you do that sort of exercise and I ask you to imagine yourself in a situation, how does it work for you? Can you do it?

                              FOOL

To a degree.

                            CURTAINS

Because I see changes in your face. See I watch very carefully and you get flush sometimes.
Go back to regular sometimes. So obviously something's going on physiologically.

                              FOOL

I was just getting in touch with those feelings.

                            CURTAINS

M-hmm. Sometimes for the first time?

                              FOOL

No, not necessarily.

                            CURTAINS

No?

                              FOOL

Sometimes I go through a little mixture of emotions happening at the same time. So this
allows me to focus on just one.

                            CURTAINS

You're right. OK......... So what's your plan? Your goal after this week.

                              FOOL

Take on the world.

                            CURTAINS

Ha... ha... ha... good... Ha... ha... let's be more specific.

                              FOOL

Continue to grow. Continue to interact.

                            CURTAINS

M-hmm. Would you go to a gym? It's one way of meeting women.

                              FOOL

No, but I'll go get a bike.

CURTAINS

But that's singular again, unless you join a cycling club. It's just not… unless you join a cycling club……… Would you join Toast Masters? No. Because? Because you don't know what it is?

FOOL

No. I know how to meet people. The best way I know how.

CURTAINS

Which is?

FOOL

Internet, but as friends.

CURTAINS

You're not talking to people on the internet.

FOOL

No! No… No! Just to get in contact in order to meet them.

CURTAINS

OK. The reason I'm suggesting Toast Masters is that one of the things you had as a child was people making fun of your voice. And if you learn to speak on your feet, it'll give you more confidence. Do you know how it works? Toast Masters? Do you have any idea?

FOOL

No.

CURTAINS

OK, it's a group of business people. Of all levels… who get together and there's thousands of them… Toast Masters during lunch-times or after hours. And it's usually around an hour or an hour and a half at a time. And there's maybe fifteen to twenty people in the group and they take turns doing ninety minute… ninety second presentations. Two minute presentations. And it's all volunteer. And you just learn to think fast on your feet and speak on your feet. You evaluate each other and it's all very friendly and collegial. So you get people from… like sales people who've been promoted to sales managers who need to… well… make presentations. Or you get people who are… ahh… come from another country and English is difficult for them. Or you get people who are getting married in six months time and never given a speech in their life. Or you get people from work who just know they have to start speaking up at meetings and they don't know how. So… so it's a whole mix of people. All ages. All levels. And it's very friendly.

                              FOOL

OK.

                            CURTAINS

Look it up. Toast Masters. Because I'm sure there's at least five or six where you are. At
different days and different times.

                              FOOL

OK.

                            CURTAINS

One of the guys here went and really made some friends through it. Because sometimes
they go for a drink afterward. Sometimes… you know… just different people. Check it out?
Ya.

                              FOOL

Ya. OK.

                            CURTAINS

Good. And that's your homework this week. The thing about being stuck on the internet. I
know you're going to make the introduction. But I'm trying to get you out of the cage. So
the internet is one way but there are many… many others. Like you went to Luminato even
though you went by yourself. It was a new experience. But this… will be a new experience.
And the more experiences you have the more comfortable you'll be. That's why I'm
pushing you a little.

                              FOOL

OK.

                            CURTAINS

OK?

                              FOOL

Ya.

                            CURTAINS

It's not done just to be nasty.

                              FOOL

Fair enough.

                            CURTAINS

OK. I know you think it is but it's not. Ha… ha… Alright.

FOOL

And ahh… change my viewpoint of humanity too. Was just having lunch with friend from work and he got into a car accident a couple years ago. A drunk driver with no insurance ran into him and nearly killed him. And he just got notice that the passenger of the drunk driver's vehicle is suing him.

CURTAINS

Suing him?

FOOL

Ya.

CURTAINS

About what?

FOOL

Because he can't sue his buddy because his buddy has no insurance.

CURTAINS

What's he suing him for?

FOOL

To try to recoup costs. I don't know.

CURTAINS

Ya, but he's got to have at least…

FOOL

He's probably hoping for some sort of out-of-court settlement.

CURTAINS

Nah… he… he doesn't have a leg to stand on.

FOOL

No.

CURTAINS

No.

FOOL

So still… to do something like that.

CURTAINS

Well, that's not humanity. That's one person. One person who should consider themselves lucky they're alive.

FOOL

Yup.

CURTAINS

In order to… or something. M-hmm. That doesn't even begin to make sense.

FOOL

No.

CURTAINS

There's a police report on it and everything… so… so what's your friend going to do? Ignore it?

FOOL

Well, his insurance will probably take care of it.

CURTAINS

And that means his premium will go up.

FOOL

Ya. Well, his premium, I don't think was affected to begin with. Because the other guy was charged and went to jail.

CURTAINS

Oh, OK.

FOOL

For drunk driving.

CURTAINS

OK. So the insurance will just say no, go away… probably.

FOOL

Hopefully.

CURTAINS

Ya. OK. Well, but that's not humanity. That's one person. That's one idiot. You know? We need idiots to make the rest of us look good. Ha… ha…

FOOL

That's right. We need balance.

CURTAINS

We need balance. That's right. Where there's up there's down. And dark and white. And left and right. Idiots and splendid people like us......... OK. So my dear. I think you're cooked. How are you doing on your list here?

FOOL

Doing good.

CURTAINS

Your understandings? Hmm?

FOOL

Looking great!

CURTAINS

Looking great? OK. Are you pleased with your progress?

FOOL

Yup.

CURTAINS

You should be. I know you really want this, so you're making it work for you. Good.

FOOL

In my own way.

CURTAINS

Well, who else's way is going to do it?

FOOL

Exactly.

CURTAINS

Ya. And I'm going to push you beyond your boundaries......... The other thing you can think about doing. Not right now but in the future. Because you like the arts so much is to volunteer with one of the arts. Either volunteer in the theatre. Or volunteer in... You know... a musical group or an art gallery of some sort. You meet people of like-minded... something to think about in the future.

[279]

                    FOOL
I will. I'll make myself part of the arts.

                    CURTAINS
Ya. Great.

                    FOOL
OK?

                    CURTAINS
OK. Are you staying here for lunch or do you go back?

                    FOOL
I have to go back and I have to book my car for an oil change. All the driving around last
couple of months.

                    CURTAINS
Ha… ha…

                    FOOL
Just realized I'm over two thousand klicks past due for an oil change.

                    CURTAINS
Whoops.

                    FOOL
Yup. So no problems yet.

                    CURTAINS
Ha… ha… ha… ha… Ha…

                    FOOL
We'll see how the drive home goes.

                    CURTAINS
But your car's probably happy that it's got some mileage. I mean… the engine likes that
though.

                    FOOL
Ya, it likes being stressed a little bit?

                    CURTAINS
Ha… ha… don't we all? Ha… Ha… ha…

FOOL

Ya.

CURTAINS

A little bit. Ya. OK. I'll see you soon.

EXIT TIM THE FOOL AND THE CURTAINS

La Fin